Music and Mayhem

Music & MAYHEM

PASSION, ADDICTION and REDEMPTION in the Golden Age of IRISH MUSIC

Keith DONALD

THE LILLIPUT PRESS
DUBLIN

First published 2025 by
THE LILLIPUT PRESS

62–63 Sitric Road,
Arbour Hill,
Dublin 7,
Ireland
www.lilliputpress.ie

10 9 8 7 6 5 4 3 2 1

Cover photo from the author's personal archive. Every effort has been made to source the original photographer, and we welcome information on this photograph's provenance.

A CIP record for this title is available from The British Library.

Paperback ISBN 978 1 84351 918 8
eBook ISBN 978 1 84351 937 9

Set in 12 pt on 16 pt Adobe Garamond Pro by Compuscript
Printed and bound in Ireland by Sprint Books

To Alex

1

JANUARY 2023

My days are numbered. Sure, you might say everyone's days are numbered, but my numbers are a tad more predictable because I have cancer. The wonderful doctors in St James' Hospital here in Dublin can't be definitive but the fact that treatment hasn't started yet (I got the cancer diagnosis in April 2020) and they see me at three-month intervals gives me some hope that my number of days has at least three digits. Whatever the number, I'd better complete the memoir I've fumbled with for years. Why'd I never finish it before? Because the act of remembering shit stuff (that I've done, that others have done, that just happened) has a shit effect on me. So why write it? If some reader gets something helpful or hopeful from it, it'll be worthwhile. If not, finishing it just might be good for me.

This book is about music. Music and drink, not always in that order, and sometimes one without the other. As soon as I found music, or it found me, it took me over. Ditto drink. So that you'll understand my need for them, I'll start from the beginning. I'll be truthful. I'll race through the mundanities and slow down for the hard stuff (pun intended).

I was born in the Mary Rankin Maternity Home in Coleraine on 8 February 1945 to Denise and Raymond Donald who lived in Portstewart, County Derry with my brother, Philip, who had just turned eight. They had moved from Belfast when many homes on the Antrim Road were bombed by the Luftwaffe. Reports say that the Germans had either mistaken a reservoir for Belfast Lough and thought they were bombing the nearby shipyards, or were trying and failing to bomb Belfast's water supply. Either way, German efficiency had taken a holiday.

My parents came home one day to find they were in danger of not having one, so they moved in for a year with my aunts and their families in rural County Down before my father got a job in Portrush, on the north Antrim coast.

Dad, a tall, bulky, genial man, quite loud too, worked in an office by day and played golf at the weekends with American GIs on the links courses in Portstewart and Portrush. Mum, who was quiet and calm, played bridge. Philip learned to swim and play golf almost as soon as he could walk. We lived in several rented houses. The last two were on O'Hara Drive, where the little houses were separated from the North Atlantic by a patch of grass, a lane and rocks. When there was a storm, huge seething waves would crash onto the rocks and their foam would clothe the houses and gardens. Sometimes it looked like snow in summer. It must have been idyllic but my memory hadn't begun yet so I've pieced all the foregoing together.

My memory kicked in at the end of 1949 and went straight from zero to overdrive. So many things happened in quick succession, few would have coped. I didn't.

We moved to the city. No more seaside, no more sea sounds, no more salt in the air. We were no sooner settled in a rented bungalow in East Belfast when my father's father, Thompson Donald, a former MP in Westminster and in the first Northern Ireland parliament, came to live with us. Before he had unpacked, he and Mum had a row, which I overheard but didn't understand. Listening outside the door, I became confused and unhappy, angry at the stranger who was upsetting her, wanting to defend her but not knowing how. When he took on the chore of walking me to the torture they called school, I summoned all the dislike I was capable of and focused it on him. I was rude to him when nobody else was around and it made me feel guilty, unsettled.

I just used the word 'torture'. I meant it. Even now, seventy-three years on, I get a shiver when I have to think about it. For a five-year-old, school should encourage curiosity and creativity and be a gentle introduction to learning. If you ask me what was the dominant feeling in St Hilda's, I'd have to say fear, with a capital F. Soon after I started there, the headmistress, Miss Hucker, a plump, scary, unsmiling, middle-aged woman, began putting her hand up the leg of my short trousers. It unnerved me so much that I was in a state of terror every moment I was in the same room as her. Fear consumed me. It became a barrier to learning. She would punish me for my lack of comprehension by making me stand in a corner of the classroom, where I couldn't see anyone but they could all see my disgrace. I'd stand for up to an hour, feeling twenty pairs of eyes boring into my back, sweating with shyness and embarrassment, a country mouse freaked out by the city. When that failed to improve my learning skills, she'd grab me by the ear and haul me to the back corridor where she'd open a trapdoor and push me down wooden steps into a coal cellar. She'd slam the trapdoor and I'd hear her strut away ranting while I stood crying. The smell of coal dust, the silence, the complete absence of light disoriented me, terrified me.

I had to escape.

Grandpa would leave me off each morning at the school gates. I soon found an alternative route and ran home before he got back. I hid under the bed until my mother's panic-struck face peered at me hours later. She made me promise not to do it again. In desperation, I tried another escape: as soon as Grandpa turned to walk home, I'd hide behind bushes before walking miles around East Belfast. Grandpa began handing me over personally to Miss Hucker, like he was transferring a troublesome prisoner.

Miss Hucker's abuse removed all my confidence and left me in a state of constant tension. But, and it's a big *but*, she was unwittingly the major factor that determined the course of my life because my third escape route was music. I'll get to that presently.

It's a strange thing that cruelty has a life of its own, transferring its attention from victim to victim, making brutes of the brutalised. I was five and the only living things I could hurt were me and the family dog, a lovely, affectionate cocker called Judy. As a lover of animals, I wouldn't be able to live with myself if I'd hurt her seriously but I am ashamed to say I made her yelp with discomfort. I hated myself for doing it but gained a twisted relief from it. I also experimented with a razor blade on the inside of my thigh. Childhood innocence lost to abuse, fear, pain and guilt. Three years of it. Three years is eternity to a child.

I've never told anyone this: soon after the abuse started, I raided the family medicine cabinet and took away bandages and safetypins. Why? I must have seen someone with a bandage and the attention and sympathy they got. But my bandaged hand and arm attracted only bemusement from the adults, not the attention, the warmth, the love I imagined I'd get. My unknowing metaphor for trauma had failed.

Did I tell anyone about Miss Hucker's abuse? Not for decades. At the time I didn't have the vocabulary or the confidence to describe it. Maybe if I hid it, it would go away. Although I knew what she did was wrong, I didn't know how it was wrong, how it transgressed the boundaries of trust, how much of an abuse of power it was, in short, how it was bloody well criminal. It still angers me.

There was always music in the East Belfast bungalow, recorded music, mostly jazz played on 78s on a wind-up gramophone. Mum had been a piano teacher and loved the songs from 1920s and 30s Broadway shows, the music of her youth. Dad had been a semi-pro musician in the late 1920s, playing banjo in a Dixieland band around Belfast. He bought me a ukulele when I was six, maybe sensing that I was somehow troubled, perhaps hoping that music might help. Then he brought me to the Smithfield markets to buy sheet music. Smithfield was like a wonderland, a huge covered market with hundreds of stalls. Books, old instruments, magic tricks, clothes, furniture, tools. A treasure trove and a source of wonder for a six-year-old.

I escaped into the uke and by the time I was seven, I could play and sing dozens of old tunes like 'Up a Lazy River' and 'Chattanoogah Choo Choo'. Alone in the tiny dining room, I'd figure out the chords from the diagrams on the sheet music, try to remember the melodies I'd heard on records and practise the songs over and over. Whenever I'd got to grips with a new song, I'd trot across the hall to the sitting room where Dad, Mum, Philip and Grandpa would be sitting reading, and play it for them. My first audience. Nobody had a TV in 1952, so my singing and playing became the family's entertainment. Or was it? Fighting the fretboard with little fingers creating incorrect chords, making melodic mistakes, starting and stopping, a squeaky voice effortlessly destroying their favourite songs. How did they stick it?

The long-playing record, the LP, was invented in the late 1940s, and in the early 50s Dad bought a gramophone that you didn't have to wind up. Philip had inherited Dad's love of jazz and began buying LPs of big bands like Artie Shaw's and Benny Goodman's. I fell in love with their sound on clarinet and asked for one. But there wasn't much money around so they bought me a little wooden descant recorder instead. For the family this meant relief from my singing. For me it was a heaven-sent alternative to the hell that was school and I began to practise for several hours every day, figuring everything out for myself from a fingering diagram that came with the instrument. Nobody told me what to do. Even more importantly, nobody told me what I couldn't do. So I began working out the tunes that Benny Goodman played. I'd often have to transpose them to fit the recorder's limited range. It took ages but was the best ear-training money couldn't buy. After a few months I had learnt a few tunes but knew something was missing: I didn't have a name for it but I did understand that Benny Goodman would play a tune and then play something different but somehow related. It puzzled me.

I was out walking on my own one day, aged seven or eight, when a thought arrived in my head unbidden: if I can whistle an alternate melody, why shouldn't I be able to play it too? What my mouth does when I whistle is what my fingers will learn to do. It might have been the most significant thought I'd ever have.

I walked quickly back home to try it out. By counting the taps of my feet while hearing the tune in my head, I worked out little decorations that developed into snatches of alternative melodies that in time became full-blown improvisation. I was an eight-year-old jazz musician who didn't know it. I was driven by curiosity and the desperation of the escapee. When I left Miss Hucker's 'school' later that year, the only thing I could do was play the ukulele and the recorder.

In music I'd found an escape that worked for me, a refuge that afforded me some peace and relief from chronic tension. Lacking self-respect and confidence, I'd been given something I could excel at, an area of life where I had some control, something I could lose myself in, something to make the outside world fade away, something that was mine.

I was eight when I left preparatory school. I was sixty-three when preparatory school began to leave me.

2

You know Woody Allen's movie *Zelig*? In which the eponymous guy keeps popping up at hugely significant historical events? Sometimes I feel like Zelig's unlucky twin brother who keeps popping up in hugely dangerous situations. The list includes an earthquake in Yugoslavia, an avalanche on the Antrim coast road, falling masonry in London, the collapse of a theatre roof, a fall in another theatre, nearly bleeding to death in hospital, seven car crashes, two fires and falling through floorboards. Not much of it my fault either. I've stayed in ten hospitals, some of them multiple times. I've had more than a score of operations. My heart and lungs stopped for over two minutes. And that's only the headlines. No wonder I was diagnosed with lifelong PTSD. Here's an example of trauma and its effect.

One beautiful June day in 1956 my uncle Sidney took my cousin Christopher and me to an air display at Sydenham airport. A huge crowd ooh-ed and aah-ed as small planes swooped overhead and large planes droned by. One pilot, Squadron Leader Wally Runciman, the chief test pilot for Short and Harland, thrilled everyone as he skimmed low, accelerated, banked and returned. Then something went wrong, the engine sputtered and he plunged into the runway just in front of us. There was an explosion, a plume of flame, a pall of black smoke, an acrid smell and terrified people running in every direction like their lives depended on it. I lost contact with my uncle and cousin and it was ages before they found me and we drove home.

I thought nothing of it until decades later when I met Leo Barnes of the Hothouse Flowers backstage at a festival in Denmark where I was playing with the Danish band, Still B. Leo invited me to 'have a blow with the band'. After I'd guested with the Flowers, Liam Ó Maonlaí suggested he and I leave the dressing room and head out among the crowd to watch Bryan Adams. In amongst the huge throng I got a panic attack and I'm sure it related to the panic in the crowd at the air display.

I imagine, dear readers, that if you were asked to go on stage and perform in front of fifteen thousand people, without a minute of rehearsal, that you might run a fast mile away. You might even hide in that huge crowd. Some conditioning alchemy has made me your exact opposite: being invited on stage at short notice gives me a thrill of expectation that I will soon experience as a warm, familiar feeling of comforting achievement. If there's ego massage involved, it's the merest of sprinklings, like chocolate flakes on a knickerbocker glory. The main reward is the playing. I imagine sportspeople get the same feeling when they're performing well, like an out-of-body experience that derives from the purest of concentration and the consequent absence of anything negative like worry or fear.

When I was ten, Dad bought our first TV, a twelve-inch Bush black and white. Grandpa was surprised to hear its sound. He had thought TV would be like film and would start with silent TV before developing into talkie TV. To my shame, I laughed at him. (I was watching a TV programme in 2021 about the foundation of Northern Ireland a hundred years earlier when up popped a still photo of MPs, including grandpa. So he made it silently onto TV sixty-five years after he died. I think he'd have liked that.)

When I was eleven, Grandpa got sick and retired to bed, only getting up when Mum helped him to the toilet. Guilt consumed me for I was convinced that my constant rudeness to him had in some way contributed to his illness. All he could drink that winter was Lucozade and I spent all my pocket money on it for weeks. Maybe Lucozade will make him not sick. Bad little me. Poor dying Grandpa.

Then he was taken to hospital and I never saw him again. Nobody grieved openly and I wasn't taken to his funeral. For decades the slightest reminder, like the *Titanic* that I imagined him working on, or Westminster, gave me an unsettling sick taste of guilt. I was in my sixties when counselling helped me make sense of it: too many things that traumatized me coincided and at such a young age I had neither the vocabulary nor the experience or the intellectual tools I needed to cope. Grandpa's arrival in our house was within a month of my family's move from seaside to city, a stranger's probing fingers up my trouser leg and the blackness of the coal hole. Those concurrent threats initiated my sensitive five-year-old psyche into a pattern of expecting the worst, distrusting what was good and a guarded view of other people. Post-traumatic stress disorder. No wonder Grandpa and I did not get on.

What's PTSD like? If somebody gave you a lift in a car, you'd be grateful. When someone gives me a lift, I'll have the safety belt on immediately, will be a tad relieved if the car has airbags and will be silently, nervously assessing the driver's capability. Another example: to this day, it's one of life's best gifts when I see my daughter, Alex. I'll be driving away from her house with the warmth of love and affection coursing through me when my brain will start imagining bad things happening and I'll shout out loud, 'Oh just stop. For God's sake leave me alone.' And the warmth is momentarily gone. Apply that to everything and you'll understand how PTSD can suck all the good out of life and substitute a ceaseless, rattling expectation of disaster. The sufferer needs help to recover real enjoyment of what's good. I finally got great help in my seventies. I'll tell you about it later.

I had my first addiction experience when I was seven or eight. Dad, Mum, Grandpa and Philip had gone out somewhere for a couple of hours leaving me alone with instructions not to turn anything electrical on. Aunt Joan Catchpole happened to call and left a present of a biscuit tin full of fudge she had made, not rubbery like shop-bought fudge but delicate, almost flaky. They won't mind if I have a couple of squares before they get home, I thought. Ummm, delicious. Then I wanted more and more, until I was on a sugar high that was reinforced by the forbidden nature and adrenaline rush of more … until it was half finished. I'm going to be in trouble anyway so I might as well have just one more.

When they got home and I told them I'd eaten the lot, they merely marvelled that I hadn't got sick. If instead Dad had beaten the crap out of me, if he had said, 'Son,' slap, 'this is for your own good,' slap, slap, 'and it's hurting me more than you, but metaphorically,' slap, slap, 'and I'm slapping you now so that you won't turn into an addict or an alcoholic when you grow up, or even earlier. In fact, so that you will grow up,' slap, 'are you getting the message?' slap, slap, 'there's a downside to addiction, a price to pay, and every reward has a risk or responsibility attached. OK, son?' If my greed had been thus punished, would my addictive traits have been checked or delayed or interrupted? Or was addiction an inevitable destiny?

3

I changed schools when I was eight, moving to Strandtown Primary, a half-hour walk from home. No posh St Hilda's nonsense here, just a straightforward working-class school. So no more tiny classes where I stuck out as the sensitive country child I was, merely teachers controlling big classes where I could blend in.

Morning assembly at Strandtown was bizarre. While hundreds of children trooped outside and lined up in rows, two senior pupils carried a wind-up gramophone and a fold-up card table out to the tarmac quad, managing to maintain straight faces as they set up the table, wound up the gramophone and played a scratchy recording of 'God Save the Queen'. In all weathers we stood to attention in our short trousers and long skirts, mentally cursing the cold and the monarch while being carefully conditioned to send her victorious. Long to rain over us indeed.

I was an inventive child. I liked making up stories, working out what would happen, the what if? Although I could tell fact from fiction, the teacher couldn't, so she got in the habit of sending me to the headmaster, Mr Martin, for telling lies. He'd beat my hands with a cane. Finally it was fact that drove my creativity inwards. One day Mum and I were walking to the shops when an old Morris Eight got its skinny tyres stuck in the tram lines. The driver must have tried to steer out of it and the car suddenly flipped on to its roof and came to a halt a hundred yards later, sparks flying, a crashing grating noise getting everyone's attention. When I told that true story in class, the teacher sent me off for the ritual caning. But it's true, Sir.

When I was ten in 1955, Aunt Biddy told her next-door neighbour about her nephew who played jazz on the recorder. The neighbour was a BBC producer and I was invited to play on a children's programme. Over the phone, someone asked what I wanted to play and I said, 'Lullaby of Birdland', a jazz tune I had taught myself.

I thought about nothing except playing as well as I could and spent the journey on the trolleybus with my mother into central Belfast and Broadcasting House thinking about the tune and practising some improvisations in my head. I didn't take in the surroundings – the huge edifice that was the BBC, the corridors, the people, the studio, its equipment.

'Lullaby of Birdland' has complex chords but, in my naivety, I thought everyone would know it. Including the BBC pianist who didn't. I suppose she thought some ten-year-old was coming in to play a nice wee lullaby so she didn't ask for any rehearsal and I didn't bring any sheet music because I'd never had it. A recipe for disaster, especially as the show went out live to the province.

Someone gave me a hand cue, I launched into the tune and straightaway noticed the look of panic on the pianist's face as her hands hovered in indecision over the keys for ages. Then she had to either commit or else admit defeat. She began to play. Were we even in the same key? If anyone was listening they would have endured the most horrendous, cacophonous jazz ever broadcast, chords clashing with improvisation, the logical beauty of George Shearing's tune shattered crotchet by crotchet.

But I'd done something that people appeared to find remarkable. I had made my parents proud. It's possible nobody had ever heard jazz tackled by recorder and piano so they didn't know what to expect. Maybe the very fact of it happening made it OK, justified it.

Soon after the BBC, I got some blood disorder that confined me to bed for months, lying in a tunnel that Dad had made of wire so that bedclothes wouldn't touch my skin that had erupted with boils, all over me, up to ten at a time. They would start tiny and grow into excruciating lumps the size of a big coin. Then they'd pour blood that was almost black. Not nice but I made the best of it, reading book after book and increasing my recorder repertoire exponentially.

Mum was so good to me then. She was good to all of us, always, but my suffering and her caring created something very special between us.

The first of a long series of doomed romances happened in my last year of primary school when I was pre-puberty, ten years old.

She was Josie. Her face was more freckles than skin and she seemed determined to retreat behind her hair. But I liked the freckles so I asked where she lived and could I walk her home. Our walks to the Holywood Arches, near where she lived, became regular, at least once a week. Totally innocent, we'd chat about school and the people in it. Gradually she forgot about hiding her freckles. Then one day she asked me in and I met her parents, down-to-earth, friendly, working-class adults. This went on for months. We never held hands or kissed, probably because I never thought of it.

One afternoon I was walking out the school gates with a boy whose family milk business overlooked the school grounds.

'There's something I want to show you,' he said.

I followed him into the milk yard and we stood behind a line of electric milk floats, peering through a hedge into the school grounds. There was a circle of kids, nine, ten, eleven years old, in a sheltered grassy area. They were all cheering and shouting at something on the ground.

'They're here most days after school. What do you think they're doing?' asked the milkman's son.

Then the crowd parted momentarily and we could see two kids on the ground, a boy on top of a girl, fully clothed.

'I don't know,' I said, for I had no idea.

This was something I knew nothing about and did not like the look of. Suddenly we could see their faces and I felt pinpricks of shock all over when I recognised Josie's sweet freckled face laughing, revelling in the attention, having more fun than she'd ever shown with me.

'Are you OK? You look like you saw a ghost,' said my schoolmate.

'Yes I'm fine,' I lied, for there was too much to tell and I didn't know how to tell it, so I told nobody. My walks with Josie stopped. My interest in girls curled up and hibernated for years.

Some months later I had my first drink. I was eleven. Mum and Dad had a Christmas party for the neighbours and my aunts and their families. I was given the job of barman and waiter, taking drinks orders and ferrying trays of drinks from kitchen to sitting room. Curious, I added a couple of gins that nobody had asked for and took a detour to my bedroom. I downed them rapidly and carried on. Nothing much happened except I now knew I didn't like the taste.

Then whooooosh!

A wonderful physical rush followed by the removal of all cares. My customary tension replaced with social confidence. For the first time ever I felt at ease with people, even able to be funny around adults. Of course I took more detours, utterly prepared to tolerate the bad taste if I could get more of this anaesthetic cure-all.

I'd found another escape route.

Being abused as a child means you can never go home again, if home is a secure haven characterised by trust and love. The calmness of a good home is a state of mind that's now gone. You can't get home and it makes you edgy and rattled, not good with people, even less good with yourself.

Then along comes alcohol, and for a while it masquerades as a new home you can visit, an alternative home with fake warmth and treacherous affection, a new home that the addict mistakes for home home. Then you need more and more alcohol to get to the new home. And the journey home becomes dodgy, full of peril and unpredictable danger, riddled with insidious lies told by others and yourself. I see that now. When I was eleven, all I knew was that it helped.

4

'Donald, you attained 89 per cent in your French exams, 91 in Latin. Therefore you will study Greek.'

'Yes, Sir,' I said, it all being Greek to me, for I was only interested in music and everything else was a distraction. In a way, I'd become a victim of the eleventh commandment that was reserved for northern Protestants: thou shalt achieve.

Mr Bullick, the head of the Classics department in Methody, thus informed me I'd be studying Greek with him. What a life-changer those two percentage points were to become.

Methodist College Belfast, aka Methody, was the largest grammar school in the UK, with two thousand pupils and a campus that stretched from the girls' boarding department on the Lisburn Road to the boys' boarding department on the Malone Road. I started there as a day pupil in 1956, commuting on four buses every day. I worked hard in year one and Greek was apparently my reward. Not music, Greek.

I'd already started into ten years of studying dead languages when I was summoned to the music department to meet its head, Mr Willis.

'Your ability on the recorder has been brought to my notice. Really you should be studying music but it's too late for that now. But I can offer you a clarinet or a flute. Which would you like?'

Joy of joys. I can finally have a go at Benny Goodman tunes on the right instrument.

'A clarinet please, Sir.'

'You don't need to think about it? Consult your parents?'

'No, Sir, definitely a clarinet.'

He went on to tell me I'd have to join the school orchestra and that I'd need lessons. He gave me the phone number of a teacher, Mr Johnston.

That same evening I persuaded Dad to ring Mr Johnston and set up my first lesson. I forgot to mention I'd been selected to study Greek.

My parents had very little disposable income, never went to a pub or a restaurant and were the last I knew to get a TV and a car. But they were good to Philip and me. Paying for clarinet lessons was another example of that.

Methody gave me my first clarinet a week later, a new Boosey & Hawkes Edgware in a black wooden case with black velveteen lining. I couldn't wait to get it home and kept sneaking peeks at it between classes.

I started on my own at home that afternoon, figuring out how the five pieces of clarinet fitted together and how the reed and ligature were affixed by studying photos on Benny Goodman albums. Then utter disappointment: I tried for hours but couldn't get a sound out of it that even remotely resembled a clarinet. And it left me panting for breath.

Some days later Dad drove me to my first clarinet lesson in the little Austin he'd bought. I was so excited to meet Mr Johnston, a slim, wiry man in his early forties who was principal clarinet in the Ulster Orchestra and in the BBC orchestra. While I wanted to rush into tunes, or at least fingering and scales, he gently explained that it was going to take time. At the end of an hour I knew how to assemble the instrument without risk of damage, how to clean it, that I should buy Langey's clarinet tutor, where my fingers should go for a basic F scale and how to hold the mouthpiece between my lips. At the end of the lesson I wanted to hear a clarinet close up, rather than on record, so I asked him to play something. He chose a written piece from his library and played. It was fast, technical and thrilling, with the sound down low rich and woody and the sound up high pure and clear. Inspiring me on purpose I think. On the bus home, I was happy: this one lesson armed me with the basics. I could now assemble it and make a start on transferring jazz tunes from recorder to clarinet.

I was determined to master it. After two buses home from school, I'd assemble the clarinet, prop up Langey's tutor and escape for hours every day. It needed time: the recorder, like the oboe, flute and saxophone, ascends predictably, eight notes at a time, C up to B, then the next C up to the next B: octaves. On those instruments the fingering for a D in the lower octave is almost the same as a D eight notes above. But the clarinet ascends via an interval of a twelfth and then an octave into an area of unpredictable fingering known as the 'cross-fingered register'. So the fingering for a G in the lowest register (Mr Johnston's rich, woody sound) is almost the same as a D in the middle octave. And the next D (his pure, clear sound) is out on its own somewhere, stranded in a spaghetti of fingers. An ergonomic headwrecker.

My poor mum. I practised hard, squawking, squeaking, playing bum notes, repeating scales a hundred times, all in the room beside the kitchen where she'd be preparing dinner. Never once did she complain or ask me to go to my bedroom. As she was my whole audience, I wanted her to get at least a tiny bit of enjoyment out of it. I asked her what her favourite tunes were and learned them. Actually they were the first tunes I learned on clarinet. Then I'd do request time after the repetitive torture of scales played badly.

'What would you like to hear, Mum?'

And a thankful voice from the kitchen, 'Do you know "I'll see you in my dreams"?'

I'd concentrate hard on getting the phrasing just right for her.

Every Sunday evening I took two buses to Mr Johnston's house in the Galwally area at the top of the Ormeau Road. I had a one-to-one lesson with him for three out of four Sundays. On the fourth, there would be a group lesson that lasted a couple of hours. Mr Johnston always played the bass clarinet parts while four students moved from chair to chair playing the other parts in turn. The music we played was Mr Johnston's own arrangements of classical pieces by all manner of composers from Gabrieli to Gershwin.

Mr Johnston knew I was different. I wasn't a brilliant reader of music like many of his other pupils and he found it intriguing that when I got lost I could make up my part, never straying into a wrong key or playing something that didn't fit. He'd just smile and say, 'Well done, everybody. Keith you need to practise your reading, though some of what you played sounded like an improvement on the original.'

My passions now were Classics and the clarinet. I'd quit athletics and rugby even though I'd won races, been trained by the legendary Ron Pickering and the future Olympic gold medallist Mary Peters, and captained rugby teams. I simply didn't have the time to train properly and do sport well so I made a decision to run whenever I could, but not competitively.

Drink also had a bearing on my fitness. Between school and home, I'd sometimes visit the Spanish Rooms, a bar in downtown Belfast where teenagers in school uniforms drank alongside hardened, bemused drinkers in mid-afternoon. I'd often down three pints of scrumpy, a potent cider, before snoozing on the trolleybus home. I'd still get hours of homework and clarinet practice done before stopping around midnight. Funny thing: I never went near the scrumpy bar on days when I had an evening gig, already protecting the music from the drink.

Knight's Bicycle Shop on Great Victoria Street became a regular haunt. Dougie, the son of the owner, started a jazz and blues record shop on his father's premises. Effectively it was a library: if you paid fourteen shillings for an LP marked E for excellent and brought it back in the same condition, Dougie would allow you thirteen shillings off your next purchase. He was also kind enough to steer me to albums, musicians and tunes he thought I might like. Thus I built up a repertoire of tunes I loved. I even practised them on the buses to and from school: my fingers would find their correct positions on my school ruler while I heard the tunes in my head. If I was unsure, I'd check the melody on the clarinet when I got home. I liked to work things out for myself. It was the same as everything else about jazz: nobody told me what to do and nobody told me what I couldn't do.

I could almost say the same about drink, but it wouldn't be the whole truth. I loved the feeling of freedom from the past that I'd get after a few drinks, but even then, though nobody told me, I sensed danger: drink had to be dangerous because of what I'd seen it do to other people, including a much-loved uncle. But because of the temporary boost to self-confidence, the ease it gave me around people and the release from constant tension, drink was hugely attractive. So I'd have to live with the danger. Unknowingly, I was embarking on a thirty-year internal battle between attraction and revulsion, emotionally up when the drink kicked in, down when it wasn't available, the rollercoaster of addiction.

5

In 1959, when I was fourteen, I'd been learning clarinet for two years when a boy I didn't know, Chris Doran, stopped me in a Methody corridor and introduced himself.

'We're getting a wee jazz band together. Do you want to come along to a rehearsal?'

This was different. New and exciting. Up to this point music had been a solitary experience that had been instigated by a desire to escape from abuse, then from engagement with other people. My one public performance had been almost solo too, on BBC radio. Now music had dragged me into social interaction: you can't be a loner in a band.

At our first rehearsal there was Chris on piano and drums, Davy Shannon on guitar and banjo, Davy McKnight on drums and me on clarinet. We could all sing. Interesting that three of us went on to be professional musicians and Chris combined architecture and music throughout his life. We rehearsed in a room in school and played some gigs including a school dance, a musical and some private parties. We played on UTV's teatime programme *Roundabout*, just after the station opened and got a write-up in the *Belfast News Letter*, which gave us fleeting fame in Methody.

Were we brilliant? No. Could we play like adults? No. But what we lacked in ability we made up for in enthusiasm and energy. A teacher came to hear us and asked us to play for the school dance. We asked two musicians to join us, Tom King on trumpet and Jim Armstrong on trombone. All went well and the dancers seemed to like us.

Naively I sang alternative words to a song, words that might be construed as blue, but so innocent and funny they'd be deemed pastel blue. Next day we were getting congrats from our classmates for our playing when I was summoned to Mr Rose the viceheadmaster's study and threatened with expulsion from Methody if I didn't provide a written apology forthwith. Apparently the teachers who were supervising the dance took exception to the 'filth' I'd sung. That's conservative, Protestant 1950s Belfast for you. Some of those same teachers could be found falling out of the pub up the Lisburn Road, the Four in Hand, during school hours. Some of them had whiskey breath every afternoon. A couple of them even had illicit relationships with underage pupils. Hypocrites.

The Classics teacher, Mr Bullick, began to bring me to his holiday home in Cushendall on Antrim's glorious coast road, ostensibly for grinds in Classics, in reality to be a companion to his son Brian who was two years older than me but had a condition that left him looking normal but with the mental capacity of a six-year-old. Extraordinarily, Brian had taught himself to play hymns on a church organ. The Bullicks acquired a harmonium for Brian's older sister in the hope that she might be interested to learn how to play it. She wasn't, but Brian was. Without any lessons he began to press keys. The family ignored this but came running from other rooms when he began to play church hymns. Nobody could explain it. I got on great with Brian. Although he was older and bigger than me, he became like my little brother.

When I had finished the day's quota of Classics, Brian and I would head out on foot or on bicycles, often hanging out with a bunch of other teenagers on holiday. I used some of my jazz earnings to buy a canoe, which let me get away from everybody, often paddling far out to sea.

It was an innocent time until I was fifteen and some of us began drinking together in secret. One calm summer night, six of us stole a parent's car and drove to another village for drinks. The next day I was told that I had had eighteen drinks, nine glasses of lager and nine glasses of sherry. I tried to drive the car but they wouldn't let me. I went for a swim fully clothed. I didn't remember any of it. It was my first blackout and other people were around to hold up the mirror of their memory. I was shocked at myself but I didn't learn from it. Rather, I learned the wrong lessons: I never considered giving up drink but I did resolve to watch what I drank, never again marrying grape-based drinks with their grain-based first cousins. Was this the first move in a strategy of lying to myself? Was it the first time the disease of alcoholism manifested its devious, insidious nature?

Throughout my teens, Dad and I spent many Sunday mornings at the home of my Aunt Joan and Uncle Harry. I idolised my uncle. He was a very successful solicitor, witty, a great storyteller and the owner of a collection of cars when most families struggled to have one. I was eight when he put me on his lap and let me steer an MG TD. He taught Philip to drive in a Jaguar Mk VII. He even had a Bentley and an AC Ace but what I admired most was his understanding of car mechanics and his ability to fix them. They lived with two children in a six-bed red-brick near Stormont. It sounds idyllic but there was a problem that affected everything: my beloved uncle was an alcoholic who went on benders. A binge drinker who fought his illness all his adult life. The family kept his problem hidden, getting him to treatment in private clinics when they had to. I became aware only because I witnessed twelve-year-old cousin Owen trying to get his very drunk father up the stairs to bed one Sunday morning. It was pitiful. Owen was obviously embarrassed and I tried not to show my shock. When I asked Mum about it, she shook her head, stayed tight-lipped, merely muttering, 'Poor Harry.'

I felt an invisible, unspoken bond with my uncle: we were both secret drinkers.

When I played a jazz gig with the Embankment Six, I couldn't drink because those decent men had promised Dad they'd look after me. When I gigged with any other band I'd be playing with adult strangers who felt no need to look out for me. So I'd get drunk, coming home from gigs at three or four in the morning, making myself sick quietly in the kitchen sink before sleeping for a couple of hours until breakfast at 7 am and the buses to school. Why did I make myself sick? Because I'd got sick from drink in bed one night and was ashamed.

I remember a bunch of adult men making bets about how much alcohol their teenage clarinettist could hold. I remember another long night of jazz on a ship in the docks when I and four other musicians drank so many bottles we were able to line the stage with them, all the way round three sides. Like drink was a competition.

As Dad and I were preparing to head to Uncle Harry's one Sunday morning in 1960, a stranger phoned and asked for me. He introduced himself as Jimmy Compton. I knew him to be a famous trombone-player and bandleader. His clarinettist had an abscess on a tooth.

'Strange he didn't have it last night when the gig was in Belfast,' said Mr Compton who wanted me to play with his band in the Republic of Ireland that night. The divisive Northern education system never mentioned the War of Independence or Irish geography so I had never heard there was a republic in Ireland, but I said yes, being thrilled to be asked.

I was collected at 2 pm in a noisy, smelly Bedford van and introduced to the other musicians, men in their forties and fifties. Jimmy Compton himself was sitting in the front passenger seat and appeared to be sleeping soundly. To my surprise, the surprise of a Belfast Protestant boy used to men pottering with cars on quiet Sundays, a bottle of whiskey was already circulating in the van. When it reached me I went to take a swig but another musician put his hand on the bottle and said, 'I think you're a bit young for that, son.' The Bedford was almost clapped out and it was 7 pm when we finally stopped. I had a headache from the exhaust fumes that percolated up through the floor. One of the band said, 'No posters up,' and somebody replied, 'That's a bad sign.' There was no sign of a ballroom either and we parked opposite a phone box. I was surprised it wasn't red. They woke Jimmy and he headed off to phone his manager in Belfast. He took ages. Eventually he stormed back to the van.

'Do you know what it says inside that phone box? Dromore West. Which of you friggin' geniuses navigated us here?'

‘What’s the problem, Jimmy?’

‘The problem is I distinctly remember saying “Dunmore East” before we left. Which is near friggin Waterford. You managed to get us to Dromore West, out beyond Sligo, and there’s no way we’ll get to Waterford from here. It’s diagonally across the whole friggin’ island.’

‘Sorry, Jimmy,’ muttered the driver.

The musicians left the van and their fifteen-year-old clarinettist and headed for the pub. I sat alone and hungry for three hours, playing tunes in my head, reading their newspapers, not much bothered by anything except the huge disappointment of not playing with the band. Then they came back out in high spirits, climbed in beside me and handed me a doorstopper ham-and-cheese sandwich, their banter fast and funny. This time, when the bottles circulated, nobody stopped me from gulping some. One by one they fell asleep, their farts merging with the exhaust fumes, until there was just me and the driver awake. I gently prised a whiskey bottle from someone’s sleeping hands and was quite drunk when we pulled up in East Belfast at six in the morning. No point in going to sleep for an hour.

My first real gig: no music, no money, no meal, no sleep. Just a hangover that throbbed all day while I tried to master irregular verbs in a dead language in Methody.

Like every teenager I struggled to understand the world that presented itself to me. What’s OK? What’s not? Was it men circulating a whiskey bottle at lunchtime on a Sunday? Was it people doing a job where it’s acceptable to have a few before work? Where you’d be thought boring or even a threat if you didn’t partake? What’s normal to some might be surreal to others. I just know that the addictive me was happy to be camouflaged by older drinkers in our version of normality.

The world I was in was scarily adult. Abuse made me want to escape, first to solitary walks, then music, then drink. Music and addiction brought me to places no fifteen-year-old should be. Looking back I want to protect that boy but of course I can’t. Maybe nobody could have.

6

Jim Armstrong, the trombonist who had augmented the Chris Doran Band, rang me in 1961 and asked if I would come to a rehearsal with the Embankment Six. The rehearsal room was over Dougie Knight's record shop on Great Victoria Street and I was nervous ascending the bare wooden staircase. The band specialized in arrangements of ragtime music for a six-piece Dixieland band, especially pieces by Scott Joplin. I struggled through written arrangements and blew solos as well as I could in the hope of becoming a band member. My luck was in and they hired me, booking me for regular Tuesday and Thursday residencies in Sammy Houston's, the Mecca of jazz in Ireland.

My first jazz session as a semi-professional sixteen-year-old was an ear-opener. Dad drove me to the club on the second and third floors at 32a Great Victoria Street, four doors from the world-famous Crown Bar. It was all new to me and I tried to affect casual interest as Dad and I walked up the stairs and across the sprung dance floor, our movements reflected to infinity by walls of mirrors. I was really a wide-eyed ingénu, fascinated by new surroundings, excited to be in a place of jazz, wondering how the night would progress. I sat in the band room as the musicians arrived, nodding to me in an offhand, adult way while Dad took a seat near the stage.

Then the gig. I sat transfixed at the side of the stage as the five musicians, Billy Bosomworth on drums, David Smith on double bass, George Hayes on banjo and guitar, Jim on trombone and John Ritchie on trumpet started fast and got faster. In minutes it seemed the music was a licence for wild jiving, men throwing women under their legs, women twirling with speed and grace, nobody colliding, their bodies managing an unchoreographed, collective carousal. The whole place was soon blue with smoke and hot with sweat and smelly with perfume and powder and people.

I'm to wait to be announced. My stomach cramps. Three tunes pass until:

'And now, ladies and gentlemen, please welcome on stage a brilliant young clarinet player, Keith Donald.'

Dad claps harder than anyone. I'm shaking as I walk the few steps onto the stage. Jim points to a microphone and we're off. The first song is 'Sweet Georgia Brown'. Trumpet leads. I try to find spaces to weave in and around the trumpet and trombone, concentrating, eyes closed, listening hard. John sings and Jim nods for me to play obligato. I do it the way I've heard it done on record, playing between lyrics, contributing, not featuring. When John finishes the song, Jim shouts, 'Clarinet solo.' Off I go and it feels like the rhythm section changes gear. I'm flying as all my nerves leave. My ally the clarinet and I are one as it responds to my thoughts. Muted trumpet and trombone start a low riff behind me. Another couple of choruses. I don't want to stop but I know I should. Jim's trombone starts to solo. John leans towards me and shouts, 'Riff on third chorus, follow me.' Third trombone chorus and John's trumpet starts a new riff. I listen, understand, join in with a harmony. Feels good, like all my years of listening to, and loving jazz, all the years of figuring out complex stuff on my own, all the lessons with Mr Johnston, all the hundreds of hours of solo practice have coalesced to form me, a musician who can move people's bodies on a dance floor and connect with their emotions too, a kid who can get respect from adults.

They kept me on stage for their whole set and I had to maintain huge concentration: my playing, their playing, who was next to solo, my volume and closeness to the mic, all of it new and all of it crucial. After two hours I was exhausted but didn't realise it, wanting to play all night.

Compliments came in the band room. I found it embarrassing and didn't know what to say. Blushing just makes you blush more.

Outside. Cold air. Dad's car and home. I could sense his pride beside me.

I couldn't sleep at all. I replayed the whole gig in my head, hearing every note, playing alternative solos. I fell asleep after 5 am and got up for school at 7. It felt like winning an Olympic gold medal one day and going out training in the rain the day after.

7

I was consumed by jazz. Practising or performing, I could disconnect from the passage of time. I'd learn a new tune and an hour would feel like minutes.

Jazz can be better than sex. Sex starts, grows in intensity, reaches a climax and then you talk, pillow talk. Whereas a jazz solo can keep on growing and growing, reaching a plateau and you think it's over, but off it goes again, climbing more peaks. Later you talk about it in the band room, muso talk.

A jazz solo is the very essence of unpredictability. Nobody can tell what will happen next, not even the soloist. The players have no consciousness of time or space and focus exclusively on the music, hearing only one another and reacting, communicating in a fashion that transcends normal communication, expressing emotion that springs from the core of the musician and connects directly with the core of other musicians and then with the listener. A jazz solo is the ultimate art form, being at its best spontaneous creation, immediate and without promise or possibility of revision. Beethoven and Mozart were reputed to be great improvisers. In a different century they might have been writing for big bands and playing with them too. In a different century, Duke Ellington would have been composing for orchestras.

I didn't have to be on stage with a band to play jazz. I could hear it all in my head, sitting on the bus to school or staring out the classroom window.

'Donald, your thoughts please?'

'My thoughts, Sir?'

'Your thoughts on the text in front of you, specifically your opinion of Plato's notion of a philosopher ruler. Please?'

I want to tell Mr Harrison, a pleasant man with a great sense of humour, who was rumoured to have been a code-breaker in the war, the truth, my truth. I want to say, 'Look Mr Harrison, you're a man of the world. You have to understand that I'm sitting here in a Methodist College blazer with Plato's *Republic* in front of me in Greek, but last night I was in Sammy Houston's Jazz Club, in green corduroys, suede shoes and a white shirt, playing clarinet for dancers who could barely see me because of the smoke and the steam and the sweat in their eyes and part of me is still there …'

'It's about Socrates, Sir. He's talking about the ideal and the real, and if you want a perfect state, you have to have a philosopher running it.'

'Well bluffed, Donald! We covered that half an hour ago. May I remind you that there are exams just over your horizon, exams that may change the course of your young life?'

'Yes, Sir. Thank you, Sir.'

And I return to my own private ecstasy, hearing something inaudible, feeling something indescribable and therefore in absentia, only present in body, my spirit elsewhere.

Jazz is a language without definitions. Every player and listener has their own understanding of it, built up through years of listening and practice. The notes are words, the melodies sentences in a syntax of chords. Every so often along comes someone like James Joyce who uses language differently, somehow extending it. Like Armstrong, Parker and Ellington.

You cannot compose a jazz solo because writing contradicts the very essence of improvisation: spontaneous creation. In Bronze Age Greece around 900 BC, bards trekked from village to village to tell stories, often of historical happenings. It usually took several nights to finish a story, the bards able to remember thousands of lines of verse, continually refining the story with each new recitation around a fire in the open air. They were the jazz musicians of their time, always on tour, always experimenting with language, listening to other tellers of stories, incorporating new advances in their art. Then Homer began to put his *Odyssey* and *Iliad* into writing and other bards followed suit until their ability to remember huge tracts of poetry was gone, their prodigious memories undermined forever. It was literature's gain but the fireside jazz clubs of ancient Greece were never the same.

All this I knew as I walked on stage each night in Sammy Houston's. There would be enthusiastic applause in the packed, dimly-lit club but I'd barely be aware of it as my natural, accustomed focus took me over. Minutes later, we have played the theme, a Scott Joplin tune called 'Thriller Rag', arranged for trumpet, trombone, clarinet and rhythm section. It's my turn to solo. I have no foreknowledge of what I will play and that's good, for the solo will be truly spontaneous and I will briefly live on the edge without preparation or parachute. The guitar, bass and drums and my clarinet are speaking the same language, speaking as they listen, inspired and guided by one another. We are sparking off each other's knowledge and wit, building a combined thing that comes from deep inside while being far outside of ourselves, that is greater than the sum of the musicians, that relies on intellect but emanates from a place that is not intellectual but instinctive.

We are flying though earthbound. I do not have conscious thought: I don't think, 'That's a B flat seventh chord, therefore I should play notes like D, F, A flat.' No, I'm not thinking like that at all: at the same time as the guitar plays the chord, my fingers are choosing notes that may enchant or surprise us all, notes that link what preceded to what follows in a coherent stream of notes that comprise the solo, itself a new melody. No considered thinking is involved for it is coming from source to result, from core to fingers, from emotion to emotion, from player to listener, from history to immediate. If conducting an orchestra gives you the exhilaration of flying a plane, I am an astronaut now, gone beyond flying into a realm where few venture.

8

I'm writing about music and addiction as positive and negative escapes. It occurred to me as I woke this morning that, for me, sex was another escape and I ought to mention it.

It might be unusual but, for this naive youth, sex preceded masturbation. I was seventeen when I first had sex. That first time was awful. It was like a really bad gig: nobody came. I didn't know anything about intercourse and hadn't the confidence to admit it and ask what I should do. It was years before I had sex again.

I was eighteen and a student in Trinity when I worked masturbation out, its method and outcome (pun intended). Once I'd started it I couldn't stop. Up to four times a day. I masturbated everywhere: in the loo on a train, in the back of a speeding bandwagon while conversing with mates up front, in a plane, in a field, even while driving a new car on the motorway out of Belfast. Monkeys in the zoo have it right: they're not embarrassed by it and neither am I. It's only conditioning, usually of a religious nature, that tells us the spilling of seed is wrong. It would actually be better for the planet if more seed was thus spilled and the insane growth in human population was curbed. For a short while it proved an effective antidote to tension. Then it stopped working as an escape and I got bored.

A lot of musicians took advantage of fans' adulation and had post-gig liaisons. Most of the married musicians didn't. I had a few such encounters. One reason my tally is small relates to early abuse: something deep inside me would get freaked out if a woman came on too strong. I could feel the rattling start up inside me and I'd find an excuse. Running away I suppose, like in childhood.

I've also been in a few steady relationships that lasted longer than a year. Fine women all, but I could never make it stick, no matter how much I tried. I never felt relaxed in a relationship. Either edginess or distrust would always win. I suspect it may be Miss Hucker's sole remaining legacy. So at the time of writing, I've been celibate for fourteen years and it suits me. There's also an additional rationale for staying solo: women may be better off without the risky venture a relationship with me would be.

9

Mum was apolitical, never expressed bigotry or bias and accepted people for what they were. Dad was a very pale shade of Orange. His father had been a Labour Unionist MP in Westminster and in the first Northern Ireland parliament, so Dad had grown up in an atmosphere of careful, righteous unionism in Belfast and London. His one annual exercise in public fence-sitting was the tying of red, white and blue bunting from tree to tree in our wee garden, while choosing not to march in the Twelfth parades. Nothing of importance was ever discussed in the family, not religion, not the recent world war, definitely not politics or Irish history. We didn't listen to the news on radio and no decent newspaper managed to cross the threshold and spark debate. So I grew up unaware of anything outside of athletics, classics, music and secret drinking, in a carefully woven, divisive, Protestant cocoon.

I don't therefore know if Mum and Dad were proud or apprehensive when, aged sixteen, I answered an ad in the *Belfast Telegraph*'s musical instruments section, looking for clarinet players for the Twelfth. As I dialled, I wondered what kind of a band it would be and if I would know their music or have to learn it.

'Hello, b-b-Billy Argue here,' stammered a friendly voice.

'Hello, Mr Argue. My name's Keith Donald. I saw your ad.'

'G-g-good. What is it you play?'

'Clarinet, Sir.'

'Good. C-c-come to my house for a wee chat, s-son. Here's m-my address.'

So I got on a trolleybus and found his house. He met me at the front door and showed me into the front parlour, the good room, stammering welcomes. He seemed nice and I felt sorry that he had a stammer.

Before I opened the clarinet case he asked if I was a reader or a busker, meaning did I need music to play (like Mr Johnston and most classical musicians) or could I play by ear.

'I play by ear mostly, Sir. I taught myself to play the recorder, then I got a clarinet teacher, so I read simple stuff OK too.'

'G-good. Who do you play with?'

'The Embankment Six, every Tuesday and Thursday in Sammy Houston's Jazz Club.'

'Very g-g-good. You read and you busk. That's two out of three. Are you P-P-Protestant?'

'Yes I am, Mr Argue.'

'That's three out of three. Alright, son, bring the clarinet and wear a white shirt and black trousers. B-b-bring a pacamac. Half-six in the morning at York Street station. OK, son?'

'When is that, Sir?'

'The Twelfth, Son! The twelfth of July. Don't let me down now,' he said, rising to his feet.

The clarinet stayed put in its case and the audition was over.

Dad checked me into his car at 5.45 am on a clear and cloudless twelfth of July morning.

'Are those the clothes you're supposed to wear? Pacamac? Lunch? Check, son?'

'Check, Dad.'

Then he gave me a lift to York Street railway station. We seemed to be early. I was on my own. York Street was deserted. No sound except the fading rattles of Dad's Austin A35. I was nervous.

Five minutes passed before two men with Scottish accents and accordion cases joined me on the pavement. We exchanged nods and stood together while they conversed between themselves in impenetrable Glaswegian.

At 7 am, we were twenty or so men and youths. I was youngest by at least five years. Then a very old single-decker bus parked in front of us, the smell and smoke of its partially burned diesel poisoning the clear morning air. The door opened and Mr Argue addressed us from the passenger step.

'Good morning m-m-men. For those who don't know me, I'm Billy Argue. C-c-climb aboard and we'll get started.'

Many of the men had played together before and the bus was soon of nostalgia and reunion stories:

'Aye, fifty-five was a good year …'

'D'ye remember Sammy in fifty-six? Never saw anyone lower pint bottles like Sammy.'

'He's dead now. Ticker got him.'

I felt young and alone, neither talking nor being talked to. An outsider. The bus lumbered along at a steady 25 miles an hour before parking at the foot of a hill in a housing estate. Mr Argue stood up and faced us.

'Right lads. Instruments ready. Leave your p-p-pam … pacer … raincoats and lunches and form up.'

A couple of minutes' silence while everyone assembled instruments. I had already exchanged nods with three men carrying clarinet cases, so I stayed close to them. The eight accordionists, one of whom was Mr Argue, went to the front, followed by two lines of flute players, us four clarinet players, then three side drummers and a bass drummer.

We were twenty-four musicians without so much as a crotchet of rehearsal together. We stood alongside the bus, shuffling into an approximation of the rectangular shape of a marching band.

Mr Argue's instructions regarding uniform had been interpreted liberally: our white shirts ranged from white through cream and yellow to pastel blue, while our black trousers included midnight blue, chocolate brown and shades of grey. Billy Argue moved slowly among us, stammering helloes and distributing red ties and berets. We had nothing in common except the ties and berets and presumably our religion.

Taking station at front right, Mr Argue strapped on his accordion and shouted, 'She'll b-b-be coming round the mountain in B flat.'

BOOM went the bass drum, and again BOOM. RAT-A-TA-TAT, RAT-A-TA-TAT rattled the side drums and we were off, all fervently sticking to the melody, nobody risking a harmony on this hackneyed standard, all trying to get in step as we half-marched, half-straggled up the incline between the neat, white semi-detached houses.

After five minutes of the melody repeated over and over and over, we shuffled to a halt at the top of the steep hill, outside one of the small, Union Jack-bedecked houses. The older men were breathing hard, coughing, hitting their chests with their fists and lighting up cigarettes. The younger men were merely smoking, no doubt looking forward to the coughing fits that would come later. I was the only non-smoker.

The front door of the house opened to reveal a large man in a suit and bowler hat with an elaborate sash across his gut. I heard my clarinet colleagues muttering.

'Deputy Worshipful Master.'

'Aye. Always puts on a good spread.'

'Not a bit tight with the stout either.'

Following Mr Argue's lead, we trooped past the householder shaking his hand, filing through the house, straight through the kitchen where a crew of women and girls in aprons smiled demurely at us as butter, cheese, onions and Spam were added to white bread in a mass production line. Out the back door into a little back garden lined with trestle tables of sandwiches and cakes, between stacks of Guinness in crates. I picked up a pint bottle of stout, my first ever drink at breakfast time. Although I hung around the edge of several groups of hard-drinking, small-talking men, nobody spoke to me or asked my name. After three pints, I gave up hope of interaction and went inside to find a toilet.

When we left the house, it was still only 8 am. We got into formation again, Mr Argue yelling, 'Long way to T-T-Tipperary in G,' as we set off down the hill. Some of the residents came out to stand on pavements and shout thoughtful words of encouragement like 'Kick the Pope' and 'Up King Billy,' laughing while their children waved little Union Jacks, getting conditioned early.

Then we were back on the bus, arriving in some side street near Carlisle Circus, half a mile from the centre of Belfast, at half past eight. Mr Argue yelled, 'Back here, lads. Nine-fifteen on the b-button. Don't be late now.'

Not knowing the area or anyone amongst the thousands thronging the narrow streets, I stayed put, parking myself on the window-sill of a red-brick terraced house. After a few minutes, the front door beside me opened and a woman in dressing gown, slippers and curlers screamed at me, 'Hey you. Shift yerself. We can't see nothin but your fuckin arse.'

Freaked out by this shrieking apparition, I scampered to a position where I couldn't block anyone's panorama of hundreds of men, identical in suits, bowler hats and sashes, gossiping and guffawing.

The skies stayed blue. The men kept talking. Suddenly, at exactly 9.15 am, we were forming a band again. If anyone had warned me of the physical ordeal I was facing, I would have bailed and gone home. From 9.30 until 1 pm, we marched and played, our multicoloured troupe never entirely in tune or in step. Mr Argue stammered and shouted the names of every worn-out, played-out song he could think of in his efforts to find the lowest musical denominator we might have in common. Often, he'd give up and yell, 'The Sash, lads, the Sash.'

Every mile of the route was lined with cheering, flag-waving people, many of whom were on first-name terms with my fellow bandsmen. The noise was so deafening and constant that I could often hear nothing except the drummers behind me. Sometimes Mr Argue's instructions were inaudible and the front row of accordions would start off on their own while the rest of us would fumble with our instruments, trying to identify the song and the key, the tune taking a hundred marched yards to filter back to the bass drummer.

As the morning wore on, I found myself trying to get in tune, in time and in step, not with the rest of the band but at least with some of them. Every mile I kept playing on automatic while thinking, 'Please God, let it be over. End it now. Even an accident I'll settle for. We must be nearly there.' After ten ear-shattering miles, we were.

When we arrived at the field in Finaghy that was known as The Field, Mr Argue stopped us without much difficulty.

‘B-b-back here at two,’ he ordered.

My colleagues scattered amongst the thousands of Orangemen and bandsmen looking for pals and drink. I sat on the grass and took my shoes off. My feet felt twice their normal size from the miles of hot tarmac. I ate the sandwiches that had been neatly flattened in my pocket. Then using the shoes and pacamac as a pillow, I fell into an exhausted sleep with the clarinet on my chest for safety.

Mr Argue’s voice woke me.

‘Right lads, form up.’

It took time to wedge my feet back in the shoes. My face felt like the stretched skin of an overblown balloon from hours of blistering sunshine. My lips were caked with salt. It was like I had been pegged out in the desert in a Western. As I found my place, I realised we had the whole ten miles to march back. And everyone seemed to be drunk except Mr Argue and me.

With formation finally achieved, Mr Argue yelled, ‘When you’re smiling in E.’

Strange key, I thought and when we started to play it was beyond strange. If you start ‘When you’re smiling’ on an E note, you’ll be in the key of C, which is what Mr Argue meant. Unfortunately, as we left The Field, most of the band were trying to figure it out in the four sharps of E major while Mr Argue and the front row of accordions were in C. We four clarinettists didn’t know what he meant and whether we should transpose or not. The band began playing in C, E, D and F sharp. The resultant cacophony ruined anyone’s chances of identifying the song and the resemblance to an orchestra tuning up stunned even the most ardent of the cheering crowds into respectful silence. Bela Bartok met ‘Bitches Brew’ on the road from the Field in Finaghy.

It took two embarrassing rounds of the whole tune, with musicians shouting to one another, before we were all playing in C major and by then, any confidence we might have had that we were a band was destroyed. Utterly. So much so that Mr Argue’s stammered instructions were now treated with suspicion by most of the band who were drunk and completely disregarded by those of us with any degree of sobriety. Anyone who started straight in after the tune was announced did so at their own peril, likely to be stranded in a different key to the rest of us. After utter discord happened a second time, we let Mr Argue go for it on his own, joining in when we heard what key he was in.

The accordionist on the left wing was so drunk that he was in his own one-man band, never quite unravelling the mystery of Mr Argue and the Key Signature. This particular musician, a Scottish virtuoso whose playing in the morning had drawn admiring glances from his accordion colleagues, was now so disabled by drink that he often had difficulty controlling his instrument. He was so taken with the occasion and his contribution to it that he spent most of The Long March Back shouting to spectators, doing little dances of his own devising, clapping and cheering and sometimes singing along with us in fluent Glaswegian in a voice that could scratch steel. Danger threatened when he transferred his attention and enthusiasm to his instrument. The accordion requires physique and balance because its volume is created by compressing something the size of a set of encyclopaedias to a mere couple of dictionaries. Unfortunately for him and for some of the rest of us, Scottish Jimmy was trying to combine ebullient crowd communication with accordion-at-its-full-extension when he lost his balance and followed the long end to the tarmac. As did the accordionists behind him and two flute players behind them. While the five of them were floundering on the ground like dying fish and drunkenly trying to regain their instruments and their dignity, the band played on and lurched around them. The crowds loved it.

The ten miles back to Carlisle Circus felt like something Chairman Mao would have been proud of. I was glad it was all over. Except it wasn't, because we had to get back on the bus and visit the original crime scene, the Deputy Worshipful Master's house. Some of the musicians passed out on the bus and it was a much depleted band that limped up the hill to play outside his house. The bus finally pulled up at York Street at 9 pm, where Mr Argue paid us four pounds each and said, 'S-s-see you next year.'

I doubt it, I thought for I was aching all the way from my tomato red face to my swollen feet, while my lower lip had begun bleeding.

Dad had been waiting for me for two anxious hours. When I finally slumped into the passenger seat of his car, he asked me how I got on.

'OK, Dad,' I said, realising it was the first conversation I'd had all day. 'I got four pounds and some free Guinness.'

'Four quid! In one day!'

His astonishment was real. Back then four pounds would have bought a return ticket to London.

'You need to watch the drinking,' he said.

Good advice that I ignored. Thoroughly and for three decades.

How do I feel now about marching on the Twelfth parade? I'm not ashamed or embarrassed by it. First of all, I was a naive teenager who knew nothing of the parade's wider implications. Secondly, I marched as a musician, not someone who was holding a banner that celebrated bigotry or a distant triumph in battle, although I realise that simply being there implies some level of support.

I would never consider banning the Twelfth but Stormont or Westminster should insist on its triumphalist bigotry being reined in. Permission for it to continue should be dependent on it becoming more of a cultural celebration.

I know that the Orange Order tries to curtail the overt triumphalism of some of its members' activities but it should try a lot harder. Only a couple of years ago an event in an Orange Hall appeared to glorify the murder of a young Catholic newlywed. The Orange Order should start a compulsory education programme as a condition of membership. The headings for modules in the curriculum would be bigotry, history, the similarities in Catholicism and the Protestant beliefs, misogyny, racism and discrimination. The children I saw being conditioned on the march might be re-conditioned by such an initiative. Can't happen too soon.

10

I want to give you a sense of the two lives I was living when I was seventeen. I was a normal schoolboy who wore a Methody blazer, was a prefect, played in the school orchestra and studied English, French, Latin and Greek, getting top marks in three of those subjects.

I was also a semi-professional musician, with the Embankment Six and with other jazz bands who needed a clarinet player. I bought my own clothes and dressed with a style that would have been considered a tad bohemian – suede shoes, corduroys, patterned shirts.

I learned a new word that year: beagler. It describes someone who hunts foxes by running alongside beagle dogs. Hunting without horses. Did some horseless idiot wake up one morning and say, 'Pity I've no horse. I'd really like to see a pack of bloodthirsty dogs tear one defenceless, exhausted mother of cubs to pieces. I know! I'll get some beagles.' I heard the word on the way to a gig that was fairly typical of my second life, depping in a four-piece Belfast band at a function for some upper-class beaglers in County Tyrone. I took the trolleybus into the city centre where I was met and driven for two hours by the bass player. No problem there, you'd think. The car was small and his double bass was mostly inside it. I had to sit sideways in the passenger seat holding the bass and preventing the thin end from sliding further out the open window. I arrived outside a palatial house in Tyrone with a severe crick in my neck and a freezing hand that had gone into rigour. We ate with the guests and I wondered how so many people with marbles in their mouths had landed up in rural Tyrone.

The drummer and the pianist arrived late. To my utter disbelief, the drummer had fallen off a horse the previous weekend and proposed to play drums for four hours with one arm in plaster.

The piano was a semitone flat so I had to transpose every tune twice. The bass player and I went through four hours of, 'What key is it in, in concert? D, that means I'd normally be in E so it's E flat for me and C sharp for you.' The drummer added drink to his list of problems, saying to me, 'The bleddy arm is killing me. Get us a couple of double Bushmills when you get a chance, there's a good chap.' Upper-class twit. Judging from his drumming at the end of the evening, he might as well have had two broken arms. I would have been happy to provide the second one. And I had two hours with the neck-wrecking bass to look forward to. For four hours of dubious music, the uppermost thought in my head was *Gimme the money and let's get home.*

I could control my drinking at gigs like that. I'd heard about musicians who had reputations as problem drinkers and knew they didn't get many gigs. It wasn't going to happen to me. But away from gigs, I had difficulty socializing. I had no confidence and felt alone and stranded in crowds of people. If I didn't have a clarinet in my hand, I needed a glass in it.

Charlie, a pal from Cushendall, asked me to a dance in the centre of Belfast, saying, 'We might get lucky and score a couple of chicks.' This was my idea of a waking nightmare, hating dancing and not knowing what to do if we did 'get lucky'. We paid our way into a large hall, a kip with no atmosphere, or bar. It was full of teds and rockers: drainpipe trousers, jackets to their knees, winkle-picker shoes, dancing like dervishes with women in taffeta with beehive hairdos. I stood at the edge trying to blend in, and failing, so I left the place and snuck off to a bar to have a few quiet drinks. Then back to the dancehall and a bouncer who put up his arm and said, 'You're not getting in here, Sonny. You couldn't dance, sure you can barely walk. Fuck off, there's a good boy.'

I'm not sure what happened next. A total blackout? With only a vague memory of being in a police car, a memory I didn't trust, I began to sober up in a holding cell in Queen Street police station, the vicious poison assaulting head and gut as I sat on a concrete bench, looking at bare walls by the harsh light of an overhead bulb, my nostrils assailed by the sins of previous prisoners, cursing myself.

At 2 am, a policeman assisted a staggering old man into the cell and slammed the grey steel door. Through hungover eyes I viewed my drunken companion as he lolled on the bench opposite.

'Whatsh time?' he demanded.

'Two.'

'Whowhowho're you?'

'Keith.'

'Fuggin' nancy boy. What sort of stupid name is Keith?'

I didn't answer, feeling only pity and some curiosity.

'Fuggin' eejit Keith … what are you in for anyway?'

'Same as you probably.'

'Fuggit, you're only a kid. Drinkin, were ya?'

'Yes, and don't ask me where because I've no idea.'

It took him a while to digest this, holding my gaze with rheumy, expressionless eyes.

'You're fuggin' stupid, kid.'

'Why do you think that?'

'Because you're only going to end up like me and you won't like it. I don't fuggin' like it but it's too late for me. You'll not survive though. Quit while you can. I wish I had. Goin to sleep now,' he finished, turning his back on me, snoring minutes later.

I thought about this for four hours, looking at the greasy raincoat on his back, the worn-down heels on his shoes, the long hairs that punctuated the scabby baldness of his head, wondering if his prediction had the truth of his experience behind it, unsettled by him as if he were my ghost, come from the future to deliver a warning.

II

At 6 am, the sergeant explained that I was being let go. My name was now in their caution book and I should be of good behaviour in the future. I walked out into a silent city centre feeling filthy and hungover. It felt like I was seeing the world through a dirty plate glass window and I was the only person on my side of it.

My schooldays continued like this: classics, gigs, clarinet lessons, binges. I'd found another escape: non-stop activity and its by-product, achievement. Good results in school and my jazz life hid my drinking from everyone, including my parents.

A gig might finish at 11 pm and I'd hang out with some drinkers, musicians or fans, for a couple of hours. Often we'd leave a bar after midnight to find smog outside. Dense, lethal, impenetrable smog, caused by Belfast's topography, industry and coal fires. We'd take turns sitting on the bonnet of a car shouting, 'Straight … slow down … bear right … you're coming to a junction, sound the horn and go slow …' for hours. I'd have sobered up when I got home after 4 am.

Even now I get reminders of my early drinking days. I happened to meet a man in his seventies recently who had been at Methody. He thought I'd find it funny if he regaled me with stories of my juvenile wildness – at a party, lying on the floor, singing, 'I'm in the nude for love,' – falling down a flight of stairs and crashing through a floor-to-ceiling glass panel at a party in Antrim – stories that scare me now. It was only when I got sober that I came to realize that alcoholism had determined much of the course of my life: civilized people actively steered clear of the flake I'd become. Unconsciously I gravitated towards people who accepted the unacceptable. Inevitably they were themselves drinkers with drink problems. We camouflaged each other.

The head of Methody's music department asked if I'd perform the Mozart clarinet concerto at the 1962 school prize-giving in the Grosvenor Hall, a venue that held around eight hundred. I practised it for hours every day and spent every lesson with Mr Johnston refining it. Then Mr Johnston said I should go hear a visiting virtuoso perform it. So I headed to the Ulster Hall to hear Gervase de Peyer and the Ulster Orchestra. That Friday I was in the back row downstairs taking it all in: up front Belfast's glitterati, all dicky bows, furs and jewellery; at the back, a score of Mr Johnston's clarinet pupils. As the orchestra tuned up, it seemed like culture was making a bid for the hearts and minds of the people in our bombed-out, industrial city. All went beautifully until Gervase and the orchestra were half way through the wonderful adagio, one of my favourite pieces of music in any genre, with the clarinet and orchestra interplay seemingly suspended in slow motion in mid-air. Young Mozart must have been crying with joy when he wrote it. No coughing, no rattle of jewellery, everyone transfixed and transported when, in the distance, I heard a door bang. Then another one, closer. Then the double doors beside me burst open. Two Teddy boys stood framed there, all Brylcreem, drape jackets and drainpipe trousers. One of them split the quiet.

'Come on outta here, Sammy. I tould ye the fuckin' boxin' wasn't on tonight.'

Suppressed laughter in the back rows, craning of necks and rattle of jewellery up front, de Peyer playing on as Belfast's best got the better of culture.

Some months later I played the allegro from the Mozart concerto with the school orchestra augmented by professional musicians. I got lost just once, busking Mozart until I found my place again.

Another month passed and I played with the Embankment Six to six-hundred jazz fans in the Whitla Hall at the first QUB Jazz Festival on Monday, 3 December 1962.

After those two gigs, the Mozart and the trad jazz, the size of an audience never bothered me again, either way: it wasn't of interest to me if I was playing to a fifty-thousand crowd, which I often did at festivals, or to five individuals, as I once did at a jazz gig. I'd still get the same level of nerves, the churning in my stomach only settling when I'd been absorbed in playing for a few minutes.

That same year, big brother Philip and his lovely wife, Mary, invited me over to London. Philip took time off from work as a civil engineer on the M4 flyover to show me the sights.

On the third evening, they brought me to the West End to see *My Fair Lady*. Both of them having an early start the next day, they left at the interval after explaining how to get back to their place in Catford. With no great interest in *My Fair Lady*, I left almost as soon as they were gone and made my way to Chelsea to try to find a jazz bar I'd read about in *Melody Maker*, the Six Bells. As I got there, the band was announcing their last tune. Damn. I got a bus and found Soho and Ronnie Scott's Club at 39 Gerrard Street. Excited to be at the Mecca of jazz in Europe, I charged down the stairs to the basement. The man on the door said, 'Sorry, son. Can't let you in. You're underage.' I told him I was old enough to play two nights a week in Belfast's Mecca of jazz but I don't think he believed me. So I hung around at the top of the steps and was able to hear snatches of the Stan Tracey Trio every time the door opened below.

Then a pretty young woman, framed in a doorway across the narrow street, beckoned me over. Curious, innocent, naive, stupid, I crossed the narrow street.

'Fancy a drink, love?'

'OK,' I said, 'where?'

'Here if you like. Downstairs.'

We went down into a dingy room, thick with smoke, loud with London accents, smelly. She guided me to a table.

'What's your name?'

'Keith. What's yours?'

'Shelley. What's your poison, Keith?'

We ordered two lagers and two double Scotches. After half an hour of Shelley asking me questions about my life and diverting my questions about hers, we ordered the same again. I guessed she knew about having sex properly and I wanted to learn, but we lapsed into silence.

'Shelley, where's all this going?'

'We can sit here all night if you have enough cash, love.'

'But why did you ask me across the street?'

'To have a drink with you.'

'This isn't going anywhere. I'd better leave.'

Shelley signalled to a squat, burly man and left the table without a goodbye. The guy slapped an enormous bill down.

'You can't charge me that!'

'We can. We're all legit here, Sonny. Pay the bill or face the consequences.'

I was raging, with Shelley, with him, with myself, with Ronnie Scott's, and took some money out.

'That's all I have.'

'Have it your own way,' he said, beckoning two heavies.

The whole room fell silent as I was dragged from my chair and up the stairs, bouncing off everything en route, and thrown far out onto the cobbles on Gerrard Street.

I was bruised, grazed, dazed, confused, angry, somewhat drunk and somewhat aroused. I saw a strip club called the White Monkey and paid to get in. I sat on a wooden bench amongst silent men in macs and could now add depressed to the list. After seeing one bored woman take her clothes off to a scratchy record, I left.

I wandered Soho for ages, bought a hot dog and some chocolate without thinking about money. Suddenly I realized there was no public transport and I hadn't enough for a taxi. I'd have to walk. I asked people for directions every mile or so until I had been walking alongside the same man for ages.

'Where are you going, young man?'

He sounded like Peter Sellers' impression of an Indian.

I told him and he suggested we share a cab to his place, 'Lewisham, not far from Catford. I'll give you a cup of tea and then you can walk the rest of the way.'

In his flat, he said my feet must be sore after all the walking and I could take my shoes off. He turned on heaters and made tea for himself, coffee for me. We chatted some more as the room got very warm.

'Why don't you take your jacket off, Keith? Even your pullover?' he said in his perfect, Indian-accented English.

In my innocence I did as bid and it was only when he sat so close to me I could almost taste curry that I became uncomfortable and said I'd have to go.

'Oh no, you don't know how lonely I get, Keith.'

I got to Philip and Mary's around 6 am and never told them I'd experienced two jazz disappointments, a clip joint, a strip club and a nice homosexual man. I was still utterly naive with no understanding of any of it.

Soho is different now. It has lost its edginess. Nowadays 39 Gerrard Street is a Chinese restaurant called the Top of the Town and the basement that housed Ronnie's historic club is now kitchens. The clip joint across the narrow street has become two Chinese restaurants. Soft porn is carefully controlled in today's Soho. Ronnie's, now in Frith Street, features easier jazz. Tourists buy wee Union Jacks and think they've been to Soho. It's not the Soho I saw.

Part of any addict's story is the shame that fosters secrecy. I kept my sad night of Soho madness secret until now. Although I was just a naive kid, some part of me felt that this night was not normal and I should be ashamed. Looking back, I'm not ashamed. I feel sorry for that kid and wish he could have known the ways of people. I want to protect him from the problems he was just beginning to face, warn him of the opportunities he's going to miss, the loves he's going to lose.

Drug addicts don't care about much except the next fix. Most of them can't have a proper life outside of their addiction. Whereas many alcoholics can engage with some semblance of life outside the bottle, the half-life of an alcoholic. That's what I was embarking on.

12

Now it's 1963, I'm eighteen and I'm at one of those turning points you look back at later and wonder, what if? I'd used classics as one of my escapes for six years and my exam results were good enough for me to go to Oxford, Cambridge, Queens or Trinity. Mr Harrison, my Methody Greek teacher, whom I liked a lot, said, 'I went to Trinity. I'd recommend it and I think you'll like Dublin.' Dublin it is then, the words 'career' and 'guidance' not having met yet.

That meant saying goodbye to Mr Johnston. I did and he shook my hand with obvious affection. Down the years I've often thought of him, usually when I was playing a big gig abroad. Just before I'd step on stage I'd think, *Mr Johnston, I know you're with me. Help me get this right.* I still do that. I heard he died when I was in my forties.

When I was fifty-four, with about six thousand gigs played, I was busking on Grafton Street with Máire Breatnach, raising money for Amnesty International. The crowd around us came and went, some contributing money and moving on, some lingering and clapping. I noticed a middle-aged man hovering on the edge of the crowd for ages. He caught my eye like he knew me. When Máire and I took a break, he came shyly over to me.

'Hello Keith, you don't know me. I'm an amateur clarinettist. I was a pupil of John Johnston, about five years behind you.'

I shook his hand and we chatted. Before he left, he gave me something precious: a memory.

'You know, Keith, when you left and went to Dublin, I was having a group lesson with Mr Johnston. Before we started playing, he was chatting and sorting out some music. I watched as he put a bundle of music into a file and wrote on the label, "For Keith Donald". Seems there was a lot of pieces he didn't want to play with anyone except you.'

I thanked him and shook his hand again before he headed off. Maire came over to me.

'We should start again,' she said. 'What's wrong? You look like you're going to cry.'

'No worries,' I said, 'tears of happiness. I just got a lovely message from my clarinet teacher.'

Back to 1963: although I was good enough for the Mozart concerto and for semi-professional trad jazz, the world was moving beyond me. Young people didn't dance to trad jazz bands now, they danced on the seats at Beatles gigs. If I wanted to keep playing, I'd have to play something else, so I bought a saxophone and taught myself.

What had Methody taught me? Greek and Latin and English literature. Nothing else: not the history, geography or politics of Ireland or the War of Independence, not how to be a man, certainly no mention of procreation, fatherhood, responsibility or fidelity, civil rights, how business or society work, not even what I could do with my outstanding results in Greek and Latin.

Between school and Trinity I went to Greece with nine other guys from Methody, overland in a tiny Bedford with camping and cooking gear roped onto a roof rack. Ten of us in a space that a child on its way to school would share with a parent nowadays.

By the time we were in the July heat of Yugoslavia, I'd given up pitching a tent and was sleeping in the open on a groundsheet. One night we were camped in woods when I was woken by the tinkling of tiny bells just before a shepherd drove his flock of sheep and goats over me. Curled up for protection, I wondered why he was moving them in the middle of the night. Next morning we packed the Bedford and set off, soon puzzled by a convoy coming towards us, carts drawn by oxen, people seeming dazed, some of them with limbs in slings and bloodied faces. Next we were passed by a convoy of army vehicles. Then we saw fissures in the road that got wider and more dangerous the nearer we got to the next town, Skopje. We finally found a policeman with some English who told us there had been a massive earthquake during the night. The drive through Skopje was chaotic and terrifying. Older buildings were rubble that blocked streets. Newer buildings were precarious, with masonry still falling. There was a sporadic rumble of entire buildings collapsing.

My guts weren't the best and I needed a public toilet. In the midst of their confusion and loss, kind people gave us directions. The toilets were in utter darkness and there was liquid up to my shins. Bodies kept bumping into me. The smell was sickening. When I got out of there I couldn't bring myself to eat or to touch anything until I had immersed myself with a bar of soap in the sea at Thessaloniki after a hundred and fifty miles of roads and unmade tracks across the border.

I found out later that it was one of the bigger earthquakes in Europe in the twentieth century and that over a thousand people died.

The rest of the trip was wonderful: to Delphi, Athens and its museums and Acropolis, Olympia where I ran the original race track, Mystras, the theatre at Epidaurus and ten days when I slept on the beach at Vouliagmeni. Five weeks away, total cost forty pounds in advance and twenty spending money, all of which I'd earned playing jazz.

While I was away, Dad and Mum moved into the only house they ever owned, a new bungalow in an estate in Dundonald. My mother seemed dismayed at all the stuff I wanted to bring to Dublin. Maybe she was sad that I was going. So we got out Grandad's trunk and in went Classics books, a mountain of sheet music, the clarinet that Methody made me a present of, the Conn alto sax that Mum had gone guarantor on and some decent clothes. I boarded the train to Dublin, Mum in tears on the platform.

1963: I was eighteen. Like one of those Henry Moore sculptures with a hole in the middle. There was so much I didn't understand, about Northern Ireland and the tension that simmered constantly, tension that a lower-middle-class Protestant boy could never have understood. Tension that touched our family when Philip married a lovely woman who happened to be Catholic. Mum and Aunt Joan flew to London for the ceremony. Dad and I stayed in Belfast. My only sibling's wedding and I didn't even know it was happening. Did they think I'd never find out? But I did, as soon as Mum came back and I heard raised voices and saw Mum's eyes puffy from crying. To this day I hurt for her, and for Philip and Mary.

Back then I was either naive or deliberately uninformed about almost everything of importance: politics, Irish history, British colonisation, sex, psychology, human behaviour. Music saved me. Music and the people I met there. Plus a decent education by three progressive girlfriends. Thus I became a non-judgmental adult, never classifying people by social status, skin colour or religion, only by the presence or absence of threat. So I couldn't fathom why people looked down on me because I played jazz, and up to me because I could read Greek.

There was so much I couldn't do. Did you ever see a dog that wasn't socialised as a pup? It doesn't sniff other dogs and let them reciprocate. In its uncertainty of what's expected, it barks and tries to get away. I was like that, hopeless at mixing with people, usually masking my shyness and desire for escape with the fake confidence that drink allows. I could read Homer and Virgil but I couldn't read people. Nor could I dance, make small talk, cook, shop or use an iron. My experience didn't include anything outside of playing music, drinking, reading Greek and Latin and driving fast. On the outside I was a scholar and musician who could earn good money. On the inside there was a big hole where real knowledge should have been.

13

I was young and unworldly when I arrived in Trinity, which was old and stuck in the past. Women couldn't live there, not students, not teachers, not even women professors. All students had to live wherever Trinity told them to. Thus I found myself in digs in Drumcondra with three strangers: Maisie Tipper, our landlady, and Don McNeilly and Rodney Rice. I had a lot of adjustments to make. Here's one:

In my second week in Dublin, the sole on one of my shoes came adrift. I went into a shoemaker's tiny workspace.

'Morning. Can you fix this?' I said, holding a foot up.

'No problem. Take it off. A bit of tread will soon have you right.'

He's going to put a piece of car tyre on my shoe.

'Tread?'

'Aye, tread.'

'But you can't put tread on a shoe!'

'Do it every day, son. Look at all those shoes up there – all mended with tread.'

I looked but couldn't see any tread.

'Won't tread make it look different to my other shoe?'

'No, son, a little piece of tread like this and you'll never notice,' he said, showing me a spool of thread.

Not everyone speaks with a Belfast accent. I had a lot to learn.

Dublin was Catholic, 98 per cent Catholic. Maisie Tipper had religious pictures on every wall of the digs. The only pictures I'd ever seen on a wall were either art or family photographs, so at first I thought the picture of the Madonna and child was a picture of Maisie's relations. Maybe Maisie was the baby. Then her bedroom door was ajar and I saw pictures of the Pope and John F. Kennedy and thought, *she can't be related to all of them*.

At breakfast one morning she had dirt on her forehead.

'Maisie, you got something on your forehead when you were cleaning the fire out.'

She smiled and gently explained Ash Wednesday.

What was Dublin like in the early sixties? I liked the buildings. Maybe your eyes stay down in your home town because you might meet someone you know. Away from home I was freed from hellos and could look up and see the winter sun glinting off Trinity's granite, the Georgian streetscapes that reminded me of Bernard Buffet's paintings of Paris. I liked it that everyone drank all the time, liquid lunches moving from pub to pub until they became evening sessions, permanent camouflage for this apprentice alcoholic. I was amazed at the variety and number of Dublin's eccentrics. The well-dressed old woman who talked loudly as she walked the pavement on Nassau Street, stopping only to jerk her leg high like a dressage horse. The statuesque woman who bellowed Christianity while she handed out colourful tracts at Nelson's Pillar. Trinity's junior dean, R.B. McDowell, who sped around the campus in a gown and pork-pie hat, muttering incessantly, gliding like he had castors for feet. Brendan Behan in the Bailey: I saw him just before he died, holding court in the front snug, his purple belly visible through his unbuttoned shirt, in his forties but looking done. Less traffic than Belfast, with only the occasional traffic jam on Grafton Street when a large lorry and a bus would struggle slowly past each other. American tourists in flamboyant clothes that you'd never see in Belfast, loud and lardy.

There was a jazz scene, with sessions in cafés and a basement on South Frederick Street. There were eccentrics there too, like George Hodnutt, aka Hoddy, who wrote a jazz column for the *Irish Times*, puffed on

Black Russian cigarettes while telling jazz stories, and Andy Cole who played Thelonius Monk tunes obsessively. I went to his basement flat on Landsdowne Road to play some Monk with him and Kevin Fryer, an English bass player. Initially I was intrigued by Dublin, seemingly full of possibility.

On Friday 22 November 1963 I took the Enterprise train up to Belfast to collect the prizes I'd won in my last year at Methody. I was standing at the side of the stage in the Grosvenor Hall with my former classics teacher, Mr Harrison, and couldn't understand why the normally chatty teacher was standing as if dumbstruck.

'Everything OK, Mr Harrison?'

'I just heard President Kennedy has been assassinated.'

'Jesus wept!'

'I know. It seems only yesterday that you and I had a conversation in class about the three Kennedys and if they could stay in the White House until 1984.'

'That was when he won against Nixon.'

'OK Keith, they're announcing your name. You're on.'

I walked on stage not thinking about Kennedy but instead really pleased that Mr Harrison had called me 'Keith'. Like recognition of maturity, like respect.

The classics professors and lecturers in Trinity – W.B. Stanford, Donald Wormell, J.V. Luce, Herbert Parke and Alfie Hinds – seemed a decent bunch of men. Bedell Stanford was exceptional. Although he'd written countless books and translations and was a world-renowned scholar as well as a senator in the Irish parliament, the first thing you'd notice about him was his blue hair and deeply tanned skin. The tan was from spending summers in Greece, the blue hair was from a bottle. Another eccentric.

Trinity was full of characters, both teachers and students, including the sons of Larry Adler, Yul Brynner and Robert Mitchum. My law student cousin, Owen, pointed out a student in a gown traversing front square with a pile of books in her arms.

'That's Mary Bourke, law student and Trinity Scholar. She'll go far,' he said.

She did, becoming a significant human rights lawyer and then President Robinson.

The novelty of the place and the people soon wore off and I felt I'd lost my way: no jazz gigs, and subjects that had become irrelevant and boring. I was so shy and socially inept I didn't have the wherewithal to make new pals either. So I escaped again, drinking through my savings in the Pearl Bar, near the *Irish Times* in Fleet Street. At Easter I quit the digs, breaking Trinity's rules, but I was beyond caring, and moved to the first flat I saw advertised in the *Evening Press*, agreeing to rent it sight unseen. Such naivete. The flat was in a condemned building in Blessington Street and was one windowless room on the first floor. Cooking was to be done on a grease-encrusted cooker on the landing one floor up while the communal bathroom looked as if animals regularly used it. I asked for my deposit back. The landlady is probably still laughing. She certainly was when she closed the door in my face.

I played a few dress-suit gigs that winter, in a trio with a guitarist and drummer around the yacht clubs and tennis clubs of north County Down, hating every beat and bar of the music, only there for free drink and a decent pay night. Any subtlety in the music was wasted on the crowds dancing in front of us: rich young men with their own tuxedos, bow ties undone, lascivious faces greasy with sweat, the young women with recent expensive hairdos and designer dresses, looking bored and oozing haughty confidence. As Samuel Beckett once commented, 'The cream of Ulster society, rich and thick.' To them we were people who provided a service, whom they might have smiled at while tipping. They had no respect for us and I hated myself for taking their money.

I played just one jazz gig during my freshman year, the Trinity Ball with the Bill Somerville-Large Trio on 29 May 1964, playing a rented tenor sax in a packed, steamy Buttery. A great gig but the only one. After Belfast and well over a hundred gigs a year for three years, Dublin wasn't working out for me, and I didn't have the confidence to change it. I'd have been much too nervous to approach a band and say, 'I'm a clarinettist from Belfast, can I sit in?' or 'Evening, know of any gigs for a clarinet player?'

I was losing everything I had in Belfast – running, jazz gigs, the satisfaction of solving the intricate puzzles of classics, the run of myself. I was becoming a lush who drank more and more.

As bad if not worse than any of those losses was the impending loss of my first love. We'd been together in Methody and had both come to Dublin and Trinity. Diana was blonde, gorgeous, had a progressive, activist social conscience and was studying French literature. My opposite!

Poor Diana – she hadn't a chance. Try as she did she couldn't pull me back from disintegration. She spent many a night in the Pearl Bar trying to understand me. Her innocent love was pitted against the legacy of Miss Hucker: my inability to trust women and my growing reliance on booze. I remember the warm promise of first love in Methody, the excitement of holding hands, where we first kissed and the electricity of it. The great times we had in Belfast and London. And I remember how I destroyed it.

Poor Diana. My apparent accomplishments made me seem mature. She'd heard me play Mozart, and jazz. She'd watched me win races. She knew I could read Homer's *Odyssey*. What she could never see was the view from the inside, where all the so-called accomplishments were based on escape, where I was gone beneath low self-esteem, where I had no understanding of the world or how to find my place in it. Utterly immature, I distrusted other people and became obsessively jealous without reason.

Poor me too: I lost her.

14

Then it was the summer of 1964 and I went back to Belfast. Every student in Ireland had taken summer jobs abroad. I forgot to. So I stewed in my parents' new house, moneyless, jobless, friendless and without drink, until I saw an ad in the *Belfast Telegraph*, 'Sax player wanted for showband', and rang the number. I wasn't much of a sax player, never having had a lesson, but I hoped to figure it out as I went along. Learning on the job, I suppose.

Next day I met and rehearsed with the Federals, a nice bunch in their late teens and early twenties. I was impressed when they collected me in a new van. We parked outside a rusty World War Two Nissen hut in Sydenham. I thought we might be collecting equipment but was told the band's guitar player, Eddie Campbell, had lived there since being orphaned.

Eddie came out of the hut smiling. I took him in: five foot three, smiling eyes, cheap denims, professional-looking guitar case in hand. I liked him before he even got into the van. Over the next few months, I pieced together Eddie's early years: born into a working-class family, he had one sister; they watched their father die of cancer before they were teenagers. Then their beloved mother got sick and died, also of cancer, when they were in their mid-teens. They lost their house and were moved into temporary accommodation in the Nissen hut, which was basically a short tunnel of corrugated iron without insulation, windows or warmth. Eddie never once complained about living there. In fact, Eddie never complained about anything. Or anybody. Placid and smiley by nature, he simply got on with living. Eddie and I were to become great friends, gigging in four bands, recording number one singles, living in a caravan for a year.

The world of showbands was new to me in every way. All the music was in sharp guitar keys, unlike jazz. We had to wear uniforms and do easy stage moves known as 'the steps'. There was a huge fraternity of showband musicians who knew each other and drank in the same bars, and there was a lot of money to be made. Not easy money. In fact it was hard earned, but there was indeed a lot of it. I now had new pals, particularly Eddie and the singer, Geordie Sproule, who could sing 'I left my heart in San Francisco' as well as Tony Bennett before launching into the soul music of Sam Cooke or Wilson Pickett. A young Van Morrison loved Geordie's singing and told me so. I also had money for drink and clothes and was learning tenor sax, probably a good thing since nobody wanted to hear the clarinet any longer, it being associated with a previous era of music played by men in stripy waistcoats and funny hats.

Already, mates, money and drink began to outweigh jazz. I didn't know it but all my choices in music, relationships and career were increasingly being determined by the short-term dictates of addiction.

We gigged two or three times a week around Belfast before getting a residency in Romano's Ballroom on Belfast's Queen Street, on Wednesdays, Fridays and Saturdays, performing before the main attractions, famous showbands who often parked expensive cars outside in a show-off, showband line. When summer ended, I stayed in the band and began commuting twice a week, Dublin to Belfast to Dublin, hitchhiking or driving borrowed cars, bubble cars and motorbikes. The BMW Isetta that Diana's father had given her was the most interesting: its brakes required written notice, it had no reverse gear and you got into it by opening the entire front. I used to play jokes on passengers by pretending the brakes were so bad I couldn't get stopped, finally lurching to a stop with the front almost touching a wall.

'Fuck, that was close,' they'd say.

'We're stuck now,' I'd say.

'What do you mean?'

'There's no reverse gear and the only way out is now jammed up against the wall.'

'Jeez. What'll we do?'

'I usually wait for a passer-by and shout to them to push it backwards. If you're in a hurry you could clamber out the sunroof and do the pushing.'

'OK then. Suppose I have to.'

There was one Federals gig that still gives me the shivers. We were booked to play in a hall in a Territorial Army camp north of Belfast. There was a set of double doors at one end of the hall, a stage at the other end and padlocked emergency exits on one side. We'd been playing for half an hour when a fight broke out. Bands always played on when there was a fight as bouncers would quickly sort out the protagonists. On this occasion, the bouncers rewrote the rules and joined in. Women were screaming as men produced weapons. A woman clambered onto the stage for safety, followed by all the other women, at least forty of them. Geordie, John McGaffin and I put our saxes on their stands and built a barricade of tables and chairs in front of the stage. The band played on. The men fought on. Half an hour later twenty policemen arrived and put the remaining combatants in handcuffs. We sat exhausted among shocked, sobbing women. Every ambulance from a twenty-mile radius came to take the injured and unconscious away. It was lucky nobody was killed because the men had used chairs, baseball bats, knuckledusters and knives. A policeman told us it was planned, with one gang putting their own chains and padlocks on the main gates into the camp before tackling another gang inside the hall. Surprisingly, we got paid.

There's an excitement that comes with being in a commercial band: your first photo session, your first press, your first radio interview, being in a TV studio, decent money, and because you experience new stuff together, there's a closeness. Hanging out in the Hercules bar with Eddie and Geordie, I felt relaxed. I was more comfortable with talented, working-class musicians than I could ever be in Trinity's academic world. Music, drink and camaraderie felt real. Ancient Greece and Rome did not.

Between Trinity and the Federals, I'd contrived a life that required me to be in Dublin, then Belfast, then Dublin. Perpetual motion. September 1964 was when life on the road started. Sixty years later it hasn't stopped yet, though now it's more *Antiques Roadshow* than Jack Kerouac.

15

After the summer came the exams for honours students in September. I studied in the library in Queens, often with Diana. We both passed and moved into senior freshman year. I found a new flat at 319 Harold's Cross Road, a red-brick house in a long terrace. A classmate, Tom Bennett asked if he could stay for a few days until he found a place of his own. We left for college one morning in Diana's bubble car and were halfway into town when we realised we'd forgotten our gowns and wouldn't be admitted to lectures without them. I did a U-turn and sped back to the flat, put my key in the front door of the house and walked in. I fell five feet. There had been floorboards when we left. Now there were none. It was almost dark down there and very dusty but I could see a fat man staring at me.

'Holy fuck!' he said, before clambering up a short wooden ladder, straddling the joists to use the pay phone in the hallway.

'Yes, boss, he fell in amongst me. No, I'd only just got the floorboards up.'

I screamed from below, 'Get an ambulance you bastard. Can't you see I'm hurt?'

I heard a car door slam outside in the street.

I screamed, 'Tom. Stop. There's no friggin' floorboards.'

Tom's face appeared above me.

'Get that bastard off the phone and ring for an ambulance.'

'I've no money,' he said, searching his pockets.

'You don't need any for a 999 call. Get him off the phone now.'

As Tom tried to commandeer the phone above me, I lay in shock, realising that I couldn't seem to get my legs to move.

After the jangling noise and speed of an ambulance, I spent most of the day on a trolley in the Meath Hospital, with one trip to the X-ray department. A nurse came by and told me I had severely torn muscles and ligaments in my back and left leg, but no breakages. She came back at regular intervals, always kind, always adjusting the blankets at my feet. In the evening I was alerted to feeling in my leg by an itch. The next time the nurse came by I asked would she mind scratching my foot.

'Thank goodness,' she said, going on to explain that a severe knock to the lower spine can cause temporary paralysis. They hadn't known whether my paralysis was temporary or permanent so they had to wait and see. She had been tickling the soles of my feet every time she came by and was beginning to think I'd be leaving in a wheelchair. She seemed as relieved as I was.

I was in a lot of pain and on crutches for six weeks before I could limp along without them. I sued the Dublin Gas Company, got the price of a motorbike and carried on commuting, now on an Ariel Leader 250cc.

I was now in my seventh year of learning the languages and everything else about two influential old cultures and I was bored beyond measure, but I didn't want to quit because of the disappointment my parents would feel. I found out the absolute minimum number of lectures I could attend without reprimand from college and stayed just above the limit. Because of all the grinds from Mr Bullick and the year in Methody in a class of one with three teachers to keep occupied, I'd amassed a lot of classics, so that my time in Trinity wasn't about how much I could learn. It was more about how little I'd forget, so I passed exams by dint of cramming and a good memory.

I'd invented my own university challenge: a full-time university course and a semi-professional band, with a hundred miles between them. Plus I still drank for Ireland. I can find a myriad of reasons for drinking too much: shyness, lack of confidence, tension. Addiction is reason enough but hasn't been analysed or defined comprehensively. Nature or nurture?

Both? Genetics or conditioning? Maybe they'll find a singular cause lurking in the human genome and create a cure.

For a troubled teenager, drink is dangerously attractive. The attraction comes first, the danger later. The attraction is the relief you get from deep-seated problems, the freedom you feel and the fake confidence you suddenly find. The danger comes later when you can't function without a drink, when one drink is too much and it's also never enough, when addiction makes all your decisions and forces errors of judgment. Sometimes I really wished I'd never had a drink and could revert to the innocence of not drinking, of not feeling compulsion to drink. But I didn't yet have the wherewithal to stop: you need information, support and techniques to stop, especially support, and I didn't have any. Nor did I know where to find them.

I was still having fun while drinking and had enough control not to fall about the place or pick fights. So I hadn't hit rock bottom, which is deemed necessary by those in the know. It's tragic that for many alcoholics, their personal rock bottom coincides with their death. Then their friends say, 'Wonder what was wrong. Why did the poor divil drink herself to death?' While the sober alcoholics say, 'Poor divil. Pity she never got help.'

The moral of all this is get help if your drinking causes problems for you or the people you love. Go to the phone book and look up the relevant organisation. The number is right there on page one. Wherever you are, in any city in the world, you'll find a sympathetic person on the other end of the line who has suffered the same shit and has achieved sobriety. Just ring. I didn't and I regret it.

Please forgive the bold print – it's there because I want to shout this info loud. If you show any paragraph in this autobiography to someone with similar problems, let it be this one.

16

After a year and a half with the Federals and the twice-weekly commute to Belfast, often writing essays for Trinity on the Enterprise train, I was asked to join a well-known Dublin-based band, the Greenbeats. I was sorry to say goodbye to all my mates in the Federals but I did stay in touch with Eddie and Geordie.

In the showband world, the Greenbeats were several rungs up the ladder, even having their own satirical show, *Not So Green* on RTÉ radio every week. They were a great bunch: John Keogh on Farfisa organ and lead vocals, Peter Bardon on bass, Paul Williams on Gretsch guitar, Bob Kelly on guitar and vocals, Pinky Green initially and then Dave Pennefather on drums, Liam O'Sullivan on sax. The band members starred in *Not So Green* alongside professional actors David Kelly, Aidan Grennell and Brendan Cauldwell. Eanna Brophy wrote the scripts. We spent one day every week recording the show in the O'Connell Hall opposite the Gresham Hotel on O'Connell Street. Political satire meets the Goons.

Gigs were exciting in a way I hadn't experienced before. The band had fans all over Ireland, people who would drive through several counties to hear us. John was a real showman, sometimes riding the Farfisa like a bronco while singing a Jerry Lee Lewis song, often climbing up a perilous PA stack (decades before Bono thought of it), always communicating hard with his audience.

Stupidly I thought I'd get some relief from the commutes to Belfast. Wrong! The Greenbeats played four or five nights a week all over Ireland and I'd often get out of the bandwagon after travelling from Donegal or

West Cork in time for a change of clothes, a bar of chocolate and a Trinity lecture at 9 am.

The phenomenon of showbands was unique to Ireland, mainly because of the lack of music business infrastructure like music publishers, a choice of top-class recording studios and record labels. So if you were a songwriter like Jimmy Kennedy or Van Morrison or Rory Gallagher, you'd have to go abroad. The world's teenagers were dancing to beat groups and rock 'n' roll, but Irish teenagers weren't allowed that choice. While the world's musicians were becoming songwriters, Irish musicians went through an intermediate stage between jazz bands and rock groups: the showband era, a form of musical purgatory. It was an industry that employed around four thousand full-time musicians and the same number of semi-pros. Plus all the drivers, managers, box-office staff, bouncers and the rest, about ten thousand in total.

The people who controlled the whole show were the ballroom owners. Their edicts were rigid and stifling: you had to have a minimum of seven on stage, at least two of whom played brass and reed instruments, your repertoire had to be the current hits from British and American charts, you had to wear suits and you were expected to do 'the steps', a continuous side-to-side movement that involved everyone bar the drummer. If you chose not to abide by these rules, you got no gigs. Thus beat groups were confined to tennis clubs, rugby clubs and a few night clubs in the cities.

One result was an almost total lack of creativity. Showbands were human gramophones that rehearsed and learned three new songs every week. We got very good at being other people.

At the time I didn't realize how much damage this was doing to me. Where was the ten-year-old who rehearsed improvisations in his head on the bus to the BBC? Where was the sixteen-year-old who could get an adult audience on its feet with his clarinet? Indeed, where was the clarinet? I was losing a lot that was precious, swopping it for the instant gratification of cash, sex if I wanted it and fleeting, empty fame.

Goodbye real creativity. The only creativity in the whole industry was the constant invention of practical jokes that played out in the rehearsal room, on the road, in the bandwagon some of it dangerous, much of it hilarious.

I want you to experience just how different from 2025 everything was in Ireland in the 1960s: country ballrooms were big caverns made of unplastered breeze blocks. Some of them held several thousand dancers. How did they hear anything? It's a mystery, because twenty years later you could buy a car with more watts than a showband PA. Toilets were basic. Bands' dressing rooms were spartan, often boasting an unconnected toilet bowl full of builders' piss and fag ends. All ballrooms were unlicensed, with counters that sold soft drinks and crisps. Women weren't allowed enter bars in the '60s (except, presumably, to clean them) and could drink only in the lounges of pubs that had them. Men tanked up in pubs before heading in posses to the ballroom. You could get away with drinking and driving so everyone did. If your driving was outrageous you might get stopped and then, if you could talk without slurring or getting sick over the policeman, you'd drive on with his words of caution fading away, drowned out by your own laughter.

In the summer marquees were erected all over Ireland, huge areas of canvas stretched on six poles the size of telegraph poles over a maple floor and a thousand or more dancers. It being Ireland in the summer, the dancers often trekked through mud up to their ankles to get to the marquee.

Yet there was always an air of excitement in a ballroom. Apart from Mass on a Sunday, it was the only place where boy could meet girl. There was a smell of rampant hormones, sweat and cheap perfume. Ireland was coming out of the bleak 1950s, dragged into a multicoloured sixties by modernizers like Whitaker, Lemass and Browne. Plus, a generation of women was coming into adulthood aware of progress abroad and unafraid of showing rightful indignation at a totally male-biased society at home.

Dances lasted four or five hours, starting at 9 pm with a relief band, local musicians who'd play for a couple of hours to give the main attraction some relief from having to play the whole gig. It was often a relief when they finished. Dancers chatted while the relief band played, men on one side of the hall, women on the other. When the main band came on stage it was a cue for a chaotic scrum as men raced across the floor to bag the women they wanted.

When fights broke out, the band was expected to play on.

No matter what happened, the band played on. Once we Greenbeats were playing some dive in the west when there was a power cut. The whole village was in darkness. The ballroom owner appeared on stage with a torch and told us to keep playing if we wanted to get paid. We argued. He was adamant, stomping away by torchlight. With no power for the PA, guitar amps and John's Farfisa, I was forced to play for two hours, busking our entire set on tenor sax in an unmusical duet with Dave Pennefather on drums as dancers soldiered on round the ballroom that was now lit by car headlights shining through the double doors at the side of the kip. Soon it was freezing and stinking of exhaust fumes but the 'band' played on. If you put that scene in a film it wouldn't be credible, but it happened.

When Lent came around, I discovered that ballrooms closed and that our manager, Kevin Dunne, had organized a tour of town halls and community halls with a version of *Not So Green* that had sketches written for just us musicians. We were like the fit-ups of the early 1900s, touring shows that came with music, scenery and actors. One of our sketches started out with John sitting in a pram, fully kitted out as a baby with frilly bonnet and a soother in his mouth. When the curtains went back the audience would laugh and applaud the famous singer and presenter of *The Showband Show* on television. Each night Peter Bardon would walk on from the wings and have a very funny dialogue with his baby son. Until the night John got bored and tipped us off to stand in the wings. We all watched as Peter approached the side of the pram in which, out of the audience's sight lines, John had managed to have a full hard-on. John kept saying, 'Yes, Da,' while Peter stammered and giggled until he finally gave in to hysterical laughter and had to give up. As the curtains closed, the audience could hear baby John saying, 'What's up, Da?' while daddy Peter replied, 'You bastard, John.'

One night in 1966 we were playing in the Metropole Ballroom in Dublin's O'Connell Street when we heard a noise like muffled thunder and thought nothing of it. As we came off stage, manager Kevin appeared and said, 'Come with me lads. You'll never believe what just happened.' He led us up back stairs onto the roof. Below us O'Connell Street was like a war zone, dust beginning to settle on granite boulders and wrecked cars. Like a war documentary it was in black and white, dust making the trees monochrome. No traffic, just emergency vehicles everywhere. Then we realized that Nelson's Column was now a stump and the granite boulders were all that remained of the rest of it.

'Me and Isobel were driving along the street when there was an explosion and all of a sudden it was like driving in thick fog. I got the car stopped just as Nelson's sword landed in front of us,' said Kevin.

Later we were told nobody had even been injured.

Three weeks later we were asked to leave Lord John's club on Sackville Place, off O'Connell Street, while the army blew up the stump. We stood on O'Connell Bridge and clapped.

Why didn't somebody think of leaving the stump intact? Maybe frame it in a huge perspex case. It would have been a large sculpture that said more about Irish history than any book, a metaphor for colonization and partial de-colonization.

In my fourth year in Trinity, 1966–7, I lived in rooms in college, became president of the college Jazz Club and gigged all over the country with the Greenbeats.

One Monday night I was playing tenor sax in the club with Andy Cole on piano when I noticed a tall, tanned man enter the far end of the room. A minute later, a note was handed to me: *Gerry Mulligan wants to know if he can play with you*. So I said, 'Ladies and gentlemen, please give a warm Trinity welcome to Gerry Mulligan!' The students all laughed, thinking I was kidding, not believing that a giant of the US jazz scene could be in our humble jazz club, until Mulligan walked forward and there was a second's silence before everyone stood and applauded. He played his baritone sax with us all evening before we went to an impromptu party in Wordsworth Jones' flat on Grove Road, Rathmines, where Mulligan played piano, drank Jameson and told jazz stories until dawn.

One evening playing in Trinity with the great Gerry Mulligan meant more to me than the degree I got from the place a few months later.

I had to take on extra subjects to get honours, choosing Sanskrit, comparative philology and Plato because a classmate was doing them and I could borrow his notes. I bought textbooks and studied hard, either in the library or in the back of one of the Greenbeats' Volkswagen minibuses, mostly because I wanted to please my parents and reassure them I'd have the 'something to fall back on' they wanted for me.

The very last thing I had to do in Trinity was the viva voce, Latin for 'in live voice', in other words, an interview. I entered a room in the Rubrics wearing my gown and a serious expression to find four old men sitting behind a table facing me, wearing their gowns and even more serious expressions. It looked like a stage set. All that was missing was dust and fake cobwebs. I spent an hour with them, mostly reviewing my exam papers, mistakes I'd made, the thesis I'd written on Plato, mistakes I'd made in it, on and on until I wanted to make a really big mistake and run out of the place screaming. Then one of them said in a plummy accent, 'Well Mr Donald, you'll get your degree alright. I suppose it just remains for us to ask what you intend to do with the rest of your life?' I wanted to say, 'No more damn classics, that's for sure,' but I didn't have the heart for it. Instead I said, 'I'm actually touring with a great bunch of lads – you know the score: records in the charts means more punters at the box office – so I'm going to stick with that and maybe get a wee jazz gig going on the side.' There was a silence, baffled glances exchanged on their side of the table. After four years parsing the minutiae of their languages, I'd finally found a vernacular they had no clue of. The plummy accent stammered, 'Eh, well, thank you Mr Donald and congratulations on your success here. May we wish you luck in your, eh, chosen career.' And off I ran. Smiling, not screaming.

A week passed before it occurred to me that classics might provide a route back to jazz, so I asked Trinity's Careers and Appointments Office if they could find me a teaching job within fifty miles of London. A week later they said no. On such insignificance one's whole life balances: if I'd got a job near London, I'd have spent weekends there, hopefully gigging jazz on clarinet. I'd have had a totally different set of experiences, maybe no better or worse, just different.

We think we control our lives but we're wrong. First of all, the major factors are decided for us: gender, our parents, skin colour, the stability of the country and society we're born into, books or no books at home, opportunities in education and employment. When fate has decided all those, we think we decide the rest. But it's minimal.

My teachers of classics were admirable in many ways but they missed some big-picture issues: I studied Greek and Roman history for ten years but nobody thought to mention the flaws in Greek democracy: no votes for women, slaves, poor people or foreigners. Nor did anyone mention the bloodbath that passed as entertainment in the Coliseum: men fighting lions, tigers and even a rhino, criminals being executed while people ate lunch, pairs of gladiators fighting to the death. Why was it all sanitized, idealized for students?

Four years in Trinity gave me an honours degree in classics but it was a relief when it was over. No sense of achievement and no pride. My interest in classics had vanished in year one and I'd struggled on through three more years, juggling classics, some jazz, full-on professional music, the recording studio, the road and the drink. My real achievement was as a juggler. A juggler on a tightrope over the abyss that drink was about to open up for me.

17

Bob and Liam left the Greenbeats. We recruited a trumpet player, Dermot Cullen, and I recommended Eddie Campbell as a replacement guitarist. Eddie moved to Dublin and Paul Williams offered to rent us a twenty-six-foot caravan he owned. It was in a walled courtyard of a junior school for boys in Monkstown and we would have use of the school swimming pool, on the other side of the wall from the caravan. Eddie took the tiny room at one end of the caravan while I had a double bed that folded down from the wall at the other end.

This arrangement worked well as Paul lived nearby and drove one of the band's estate cars, a big Vauxhall that was so crammed with drums and amps that the back seats were removed and the three of us sat up front on a bench seat. Paul and I shared the driving. He was a lovely guy in his mid-twenties and a fine guitar player. Like me he had studied while playing in a band and had an MSc in entomology from UCD. He was gentle and smiled a lot. Eddie and I got on great with him.

On 22 November 1967, two months after I finished Trinity, we left Cruise's Hotel in Limerick in the early evening to drive to our next gig in County Waterford, Paul taking the first driving stint. It was a damp evening and had already been dark for a couple of hours when we reached Hospital, County Limerick, a village less than an hour from Limerick City. We saw a road sign that indicated a Y-junction ahead. We drove into a patch of dense fog and could suddenly see nothing. As Paul began to slow from fifty miles an hour, the car hit a bank of stones and earth that formed the horizontal top bar of a T-junction.

The road sign had been wrong.

I can't move. All the gear has shifted. We're wedged in. My head was where the windscreen had been. The bonnet had been blown off by the force of the crash and the engine was so close to me I could smell petrol and hear all its dying, hissing noise. We're going to burn to death. All this in a couple of seconds.

'Paul, can you hear me? Eddie?'

Silence from left and right.

I can barely breathe. Paul began to make gurgling noises and I tried again to get a response from him. He was unconscious. Is he dying? He can't just die, sitting shoulder to shoulder here in the middle of nowhere. I can't help him. I can't do anything.

Eddie came to and seemed to be trying to hold my hand. I took his hand and he squeezed before lapsing back into unconsciousness. We sat trapped and time stood still. Soft rain began to dampen my face. I was sure we'd all die and yet I was calm, a sense of acceptance and serenity enveloping me.

Ever since that long moment so many years ago I've believed that one is looked after in extreme circumstances and that death doesn't have to be scary. I don't know whether it's spiritual or chemical, but something takes us over and looks after us.

Help arrived: a lorry driver who was brilliant, asking me to make sure the ignition was off. I reached over but couldn't do it because my hand got soaked with Paul's warm blood. He immediately disconnected the battery and forced open the rear door. People shouting: 'I'll go ring for an ambulance' – 'Hang in there lads. We'll get you out' – 'I'll ask in those houses if anyone has a fire extinguisher.' The lorry driver asked me to tell him how to get the back unloaded and what should come out first. Maybe he needed my help, maybe he was trying to keep me occupied. I was asked if Eddie was breathing and said he was.

I had felt Paul die, his last breath a sigh.

After an hour or so, an ambulance arrived and, as Eddie and I were being stretchered into it, I saw Paul lying on the grass on the lane, his face shining, lit by headlights in the drizzle. He looked so peaceful, almost smiling. Why is nobody minding him? I couldn't understand why he wasn't coming with us.

That was the last time I saw Paul. Because Eddie and I were in the Regional Hospital in Limerick, we couldn't go to his funeral. To this day, Paul's death is a loss and I think of him often. It is utterly unjust that a kind, sensitive, accomplished 26-year-old should be killed through somebody's carelessness with a road sign. We could have been lifelong friends.

The ambulance brought us to Limerick, Eddie still unconscious. A junior doctor told me that my left leg and ankle appeared to be broken, as well as several ribs.

'I'm going to cut up the side of your boot so that I can get it off and have a look at your foot.'

That's when the pain kicked in, every minute movement of his scissors shooting pains up my leg.

'OK, you'll have to be brave. I'm going to try and snap the boot off.'

I was determined not to yell and didn't, despite the hot shock of pain that shot through me from foot to head.

'I'm afraid your boot came halfway off and snapped back on again.'

It came off the second time he tried it and I'd say my scream was heard in the next county.

I don't remember this happening but was told later that I woke next morning to hear a man and woman debating whether they could save Eddie's arm or would have to amputate it.

'Excuse me,' I said.

'We'll be with you in a minute,' said the woman.

'But you don't understand,' I said.

The surgeon, an avuncular man named Mr Kennedy, came over to me.

‘What don’t we understand, Keith?’

‘Eddie is an orphan. All he has is his guitar. Take his arm off and you might as well take his head off too.’

Apparently that’s all I said before I conked out again. Eddie’s arm stayed attached to Eddie. He was meant to play more gigs I guess.

Later that day we were moved into a two-bed ward. Eddie’s broken arm and shattered shoulder were wired into an elaborate contraption that ensured he could not move his upper body or arm. They told him he wouldn’t be leaving the bed for at least a month. My left ankle and lower leg had multiple injuries. I would have to stay in bed too, in traction, until they could start operating.

The crash was the main item on the front page of every Irish newspaper and regular updates were given about Eddie and me on radio and TV. My mum and dad drove from Belfast and stayed overnight, Mum’s face showing strain and signs of crying. Every band that passed through Limerick came to see us and the nurses were rightly impressed to see all these well-known faces in the corridors. Famous musicians and sportsmen played a football match for Eddie and me. It felt like all ten thousand people in the industry were rooting for us.

Eddie and I now had an extraordinarily close relationship. We’d soldiered through the highs and lows of two bands and had shared a caravan for months. Being with him all day and every night in the same small room, both of us avoiding talking about the extreme pain we were in, neither wanting to talk about Paul lest it bring us down to a place we might not know how to escape from made our bond like tempered steel. I’m guessing people who go through war together or suffer in a refugee camp would have similar feelings. Put simply, I loved him.

After five weeks Eddie and I left hospital following fond farewells to the nurses who had been so good to us, Eddie moving in with John Keogh and his family while I went back to the caravan. I managed to drive my car, a VW Beetle, by lifting the substantial weight of my left leg, in plaster from hip to toe, onto the clutch pedal, getting going in first gear, taking my hands off the wheel to lift the leg back into the passenger footwell and changing the other gears without using the clutch. I had no money, no possessions except the car and my instruments, and no work. I borrowed from Dad and spent most days that winter on my own. There was no heater in the caravan and I often couldn't see outside because of the ice on the inside of the windows. Without heat, TV and radio, I stayed in bed most of the time, reading, drinking, playing the clarinet.

Every Sunday I collected Louis Stewart and drove to the Fox Inn in Ashbourne where I had the privilege of playing jazz with him. Apart from that I was on my own, the freezing caravan becoming solitary confinement. The high walls around the caravan might as well have been the boundary of a private gulag. Plus the leg wasn't mending, needing a new plaster every couple of months.

No music, no work, no money, freezing, little human contact: I became very depressed. I needed some sort of a boost, some relief from the everyday negativity and bought the ingredients for Irish coffee, hoping it would cheer me up and warm me up too. I had never learned to cook and knew nothing about making an Irish coffee except what a barman once told me, that the glass had to be warm. So I was suspended on crutches heating a glass over the naked gas flame on the cooker when the glass exploded in my hand and I fell backwards in shock and landed on my bad ankle. Before I hit the floor I registered the sharp crack inside the plaster and felt a familiar pain start to surge. I lay for a minute, breathing hard, before reaching up for the bottle of Powers and drinking half of it. Then I dragged myself out to the car and drove to hospital, occasionally yelping from the pain every time I lifted the leg onto the clutch.

For six months I was in pain, either low level that allowed me to get to sleep, or pain of a different magnitude that kept me awake, often for twenty or thirty hours at a stretch. Like a lot of people I had to learn to live with it. I don't remember crying because of it. I do remember drinking to oblivion when I could afford it.

The Greenbeats went back on the road in April but nobody's heart was in it and we decided to play the gigs remaining in our diaries and pack it in for good. Eddie and I were wondering what to do when Tom Costello asked me to his office for a meeting. He was starting a new band with Peter Bardon as its manager. Would I like to be its bandleader? Yes I would. Who would I keep from the Greenbeats? Eddie and Dave Pennefather. The Greenbeats played their last gig on Friday 12 July 1968 in Omeath and the Real McCoy played its first on Thursday 25 July in Wexford.

Post-Traumatic Stress Disorder (PTSD) has symptoms such as alcoholism, drug addiction, poor sleeping patterns, jumpiness, memory loss, panic attacks and irritability, all of which I've suffered from. PTSD was called shell shock until GIs started coming back from Vietnam and US psychiatrists renamed it. My experiences were not unlike war: injuries, constant pain, hospitals, medics, uncertainty and helplessness when I felt a very close friend dying beside me. It's not surprising that I had the hallmark symptoms of anxiety and aggression. PTSD is an illness of information storage and processing, the trauma being too much for the mind to accommodate. Here's an example: six months after gaining an honours degree in classics, I was being driven in Dublin and saw some basic Latin on a church. I hadn't a clue what it meant. Six months earlier I could have translated Virgil's *Aeneid* without a dictionary and now I couldn't make sense of a simple phrase. After six years in Methody, all the grinds in Cushendall and four years of study in Trinity, it felt like my brain was playing tricks on me or some malign enemy was messing with my memory and making me distrust reality. I didn't talk to anybody about it lest they think I was nuts.

18

'It's an E minor seventh.'

'Nahtatall. It's a G something.'

'It's definitely E minor. Listen to the fuckin' thing again.'

Silence, then the needle scratched across the record to nearly the right place and started to inflict Bobby Goldsboro's 'Honey' on us yet again.

'Why are we doing this crap anyway? The song is fuckin' awful.'

'We're doing it because it was number one and the punters love it.'

'It's crap. It should be called Treacle.'

'Or Syrup.'

'Imagine calling your girlfriend Syrup!'

'Shaddup. We've missed the fuckin' chord now. Play the fuckin' thing again.'

We were in the hangar-like Arcadia Ballroom in Bray, suffering the joys of rehearsal. When a showband was on the road, they would rehearse one day a week to top up their set with whatever was new in the charts. Because the Real McCoy was starting from scratch, we needed to rehearse for three weeks. Like any classroom, people learn at different speeds and the more accomplished musicians get frustrated with the slow learners. And the thing about any band is it's not like a cocktail party: you don't choose people who will be great company. You choose them because of the instrument they play, as in, 'We need a trumpet player. Joe Bloggs is a good player and word has it he's not a total nutjob.' So strangers become colleagues and part of the work is ignoring their idiosyncrasies.

In the first week of rehearsals I was at a party in a basement flat on Waterloo Road and bumped into Davy McKnight, the drummer from my very first band in Methody. Davy was now with the hugely successful Freshmen and drove a big car, a Humber. I invited him to stay in the caravan 'for a swim in the morning' and we drank on for hours before driving to Monkstown in convoy. Unfortunately Davy misjudged the width of his car and demolished the fence around the school swimming pool, screeching to a halt with the front wheels dangling over the shallow end.

Two denouements: Davy paid for the damage, and I was given my walking papers and had to move, finding a nice top floor flat in a Georgian house overlooking the canal at Huband Bridge. I wrote to Mum and Dad to tell them of my change of address, reassuring them that my leg was mending, the Real McCoy was getting bookings and that I was happy I'd got the degree and had their 'something to fall back on'. To this day I'm glad I wrote that letter.

On the evening of 3 July I was drinking with Johnny McEvoy and the English record producer Peter Lee Sterling, aka Daniel Boone, in a hotel on Kildare Street. I excused myself and went to the phone booth in the lobby to ring home. I couldn't get through and forgot to ring again. Very early the following morning, Peter woke me in the flat. 'Dave Pennefather is down below ringing the bell. Will I let him in?'

'Throw the keys down.'

Dave came into the flat, breathless and pale.

'You have to ring your uncle's house in Belfast, Keith. Do you know his number?'

With a dread feeling in my gut, I trekked downstairs to the payphone. Uncle Harry told me my mother had died during the night.

That morning I drove north, stopping when I couldn't see for the tears. My poor mum, fifty-nine years old, dying unexpectedly when she was just beginning to have the life she deserved with her own house at last, my father finally in a job he liked, financial security, both sons doing OK. Not fair. My quiet, reserved, decent, loving mum, dead. She was endlessly supportive and uncomplaining. In my case, she'd suffered through me squeaking on recorder, thrashing on ukulele and practising for hours on clarinet, destroying all her favourite songs along the way, and never once asked me to move to my bedroom. Sometimes, after a couple of hours battling Mozart, I'd ask what she wanted to hear. A relieved voice would call from the kitchen, 'I'll See You in My Dreams', a beautiful, wistful song that she loved. I'd play it as well as I could, for she was my best audience, ever.

The last time I'd seen her was at my conferring ceremony in Trinity in May. Mum and Dad had driven from Belfast, full of pride and anticipation. They arrived late to find me pacing up and down outside the Exam Hall in gown and mortar board, feeling like a total impostor. I roared at them for being so late. The arrogance of it. How dare I give out to proud parents when they should have been hearing my gratitude for all the support and sacrifices that got me to graduation. What a shit I was. And how I've regretted my self-absorbed ignorant behaviour for five decades. Maybe I wrote to them in June to make amends. I'm not even sure of that.

The post mortem found that Mum had a stroke followed by a heart attack and that she had undiagnosed cancer. I saw her for the last time in a funeral home.

When I'm really lucky now, I see her in my dreams.

19

We were hitting the road soon so we needed stage clothes. Showbands wore suits, shirts and ties, often with Cuban-heeled Beatle boots. Tom wanted us to look more like a pop band but realized we still had to wear suits. He sent us to a trendy tailor in Capel Street. Whenever somebody wasn't needed at rehearsals they'd go for a fitting. Thus we never saw each other in the suits until they arrived in the TV Club on Dublin's Harcourt Street, minutes before we were due on stage to play to 1,200 punters.

'What the hell is this?' said bass player Liam McKenna, who was six feet tall. His suit jacket seemed to be well over a yard long, finishing between his knees and his hips. He looked like a highway robber and we began to laugh. Meanwhile Eddie, who was broad-shouldered and five feet and three inches, was slipping on a small triangle of cloth that stopped just below his waist.

'I've got a bum-freezer,' he announced.

The rest of us were cracking up. This was not a band uniform as we knew it. The cut of the suits was anything but uniform. Then somebody opened another package.

'Look at the friggin' shirts and ties they've sent.'

The shirts and wide, wide ties were made from the same flower-patterned material in a wild riot of yellows, browns and gold that might have looked passable on curtains. Or on the autumn.

'Holy fuck!'

'Friggin' tailor couldn't make two handkerchiefs the same.'

'There's enough material on this to cover the Mourne Mountains.'

'I'm not going on stage looking like a waiter.'

'This thing's like an overcoat.'

'At least your balls are covered. This thing's for flamenco dancing.'

'We have to keep them on. There's no choice,' I said.

Still grumbling, we took the stage. There was a second's stunned silence from the packed dance hall. Then the front couple of rows of standing punters started wild applause and wolf whistles and soon twelve hundred people were clapping like we were fashion icons.

After the gig, manager Peter asked if the people who had made the suits could come into the band room to meet us and we realized the seamstresses and assistant tailors were the punters who had been lined along the front of the stage. No wonder they were clapping madly: they were applauding their own work.

We asked them why the suit jackets were different lengths.

'The boss thought it would look well if the bottoms of the jackets formed a straight line across the stage.'

'He thought what?'

The following day I was called out of rehearsals in the Arcadia to meet a nervous employee of the tailor, come to collect the suits.

'I've come to collect your suits. I hear they might need some alterations?'

'You'd be right there. We thought, maybe naively, that our suits might resemble one another,' I said, handing over two big plastic rubbish bags.

'Sorry, what do you mean?' he said.

'It's a band uniform. The clue is in the word "uniform".'

'They should have looked the same?'

'They should but they didn't, much. Tell you what,' I said with a straight face, 'why don't you start again? Use the same material and make us seven identical straitjackets?'

'Straitjackets? Like in an asylum?'

'Now you have it. It's like a friggin' asylum in here so we might as well be honest about it. Best of luck now,' I said, heading back into rehearsals.

The Real McCoy had been founded and financed by Tom Costello and had Tom's considerable financial backing. So manager Peter hired the best photographer around, Roy Esmonde, for publicity shots, mostly out on locations like Portmarnock Beach, and soon we featured in newspapers and magazines. Peter booked us into a recording studio with my old jazz pianist pal Bill Somerville-Large engineering, and Peter Lee Sterling over from London to produce.

We arrived at Eamon Andrews' studios on Dublin's Henry Street before ten that first morning. It was like a secret place, just a door on the street with a clever logo that had Eamon Andrews' initials entwined in lower-case *e a* like a spool of tape. We trooped upstairs into a suite of rooms on the first floor. This was where everyone recorded: Johnny McEvoy, Dickie Rock, Brendan Bowyer, Butch Moore and Joe Dolan had all sung hits here. I'd been there before, recording with the Greenbeats and as a session musician, but some of the band had never been in a studio and they took it all in with wide-eyed silence.

Peter Lee Sterling wanted our first record, 'I Get So Excited' to have its own unique sound for radio and wanted to create a phasing effect throughout the track. We were given the morning off while Peter and Bill rewired the recording desk. Then it was time to record the backing track. With today's multi-track recording technology each musician can record separately, on an individual track, before all the tracks are mixed together and it sounds like all the musicians played together. Back then, they had to play together and recording was challenging, especially for recording virgins. You could know your part so well that you could play it without conscious thought on stage, but as soon as you were set up in a studio and the red light went on, you knew it was going to tape and you'd make mistakes, different mistakes every time. Then you'd get it right but somebody else's mistake would ruin it. It got to everyone's confidence.

'That's the best I've played it.'

'We have to do it again. I played an E instead of a B.'

'Damn it to hell, I'll never get it as good again.'

'Didn't sound that great to me.'

'It's you that keeps making mistakes.'

We'd have to take a break to let everyone get calm before we started again at square one.

The record got a lot of attention, radio listeners phoning RTÉ to find out what was wrong with their reception. The phasing effect plus the sticker campaign on car bumpers – *I Get So Excited by The Real McCoy* – kept the record in the charts for eight weeks, reaching number ten on 5 October. We were doing alright but not brilliantly at the box office.

Then Dave Pennefather came into Tom's office one Monday with a song he'd heard, 'Quick Joey Small', about a prisoner escaping from a US penitentiary. It was very catchy and we decided to take a chance and record it. Peter Lee Sterling flew over from London to produce it and we had the same team in the studio. Peter wanted a backwards guitar at the intro and Bill made that happen too.

Before the record's release we were to tour Ireland for a couple of months before heading to England for the Irish circuit there. A tough schedule, with gigs in Bundoran, Ballybunion and Dundalk one week and Waterford, Limerick, Belfast and Cork the next. Like throwing darts at a map. Once again my life was more about miles than music.

'All over the place like a madman's shite,' observed lead singer Mike dourly.

Despite the miles, the charts and the punters, I wasn't making enough money to live on. I'd negotiated a deal with Tom that had a percentage built in, but the band would have to do a lot better at the box office for it to kick in. I was taking home about half as much as my bandmates.

In September we were booked to play in Castletown House, a mansion in County Kildare, at a fundraiser for the Irish Georgian Society. We set up in the afternoon and mingled with guests in the grounds, surprised to see Marianne Faithful and Mick Jagger amongst Irish society's finest, him rattling a collection box while doing an impression of an East End barrow boy, 'Come on people, I know you can be generous, cough up now, cough up!' – clearly having fun while she wafted beside him, a pale thin waif in white.

We began playing at nine and were beginning to finish at midnight when a stout matron appeared at the front of the stage.

'Which one of you is the band leader?' she said imperiously.

Dave Pennefather was off his drum stool in a flash and matched her West Brit accent: 'That would be Keith Russell-Donald, ma'am,' waving her towards me.

'Well, Mr Russell-Donald,' she said, turning to me, 'would you mind awfully playing for more dancing? The young people seem to be enjoying your music so much.'

'Yes, ma'am,' I said, trying to ignore band giggles behind me, 'but the chaps have run out of cigarettes and their drinks are low.'

'Of course,' she prattled, 'and I expect I'll have to renegotiate your fee. I'll send someone for your drinks order, shall I?'

'That's awfully decent of you, ma'am,' I prattled back.

Minutes later a waiter arrived. I got off the stage and told him if he looked after us, we'd look after him. He came back with a two-tier trolley, the top deck with glasses of stout, beer and gin and one cigarette packet, the lower tier with bottles of spirits and cartons with two hundred cigarettes in each. I slipped him two pounds, probably as much as he was getting for his night's work and loaded the booty into Dave's drum cases. The waiter kept coming back. I kept tipping and unloading. Ma'am returned every couple of hours promising an ever bigger fee. The band played on … and on. We finished as dawn broke. We were so exhausted that Eddie appeared to be playing while dozing on an amp. We had to carry Dave's drums out without packing them as his drum cases were full of booze and fags.

The band toured the Irish ballrooms in England just before Christmas 1968. When showbands toured abroad, it was mostly to Britain and North America and they encountered few foreigners, audiences generally being Irish emigrants. In England, as we rapidly discovered, our audiences seemed to have left Ireland en masse in the 1950s and were under the impression that Ireland was exactly as they had left it.

Our first gig was in the Irish Club in Liverpool. Not for this audience the Liverpool of the Beatles, Cilla, Gerry and the Pacemakers and the Cavern. They were still firmly rooted in fifties Ireland and wanted any song with an Irish place-name in it or anything maudlin enough to stir their dewy-eyed nostalgia, even Nashville country songs, which we received requests for, scribbled in lipstick on cigarette packets. Needless to say, our repertoire of bang-up-to-the-minute UK and US pop and soul songs fell on deaf ears: this audience's ears must have been painted on. I felt despondent as we spent the evening being totally ignored by an audience that drank itself into green oblivion, danced to their own tempo and handed up increasingly bizarre requests. It was like two separate events with nothing in common except a coincidence of location.

While we looked smart in our new suits and Beatle boots, the audience's apparel owed nothing to fashion. The women wore cardigans and dresses below their knees and respectable shoes, presumably all specially imported from rural Ireland. Many of the men appeared to have come straight from work to the dance via the pub: they wore navy donkey jackets with McAlpine and Costain in big yellow letters across their backs and had cement on their boots. They evidently had no need of spades or hard hats on their building sites for they had hands like shovels and reinforced skulls, which they used to good effect in the fight that broke out towards the end of the night. The standard bar-room brawl in a Western was a mild altercation compared to this bunch of alcohol-crazed giants who bashed each other to bits before buying one another more drink.

On the way to the hotel afterwards, the mood in the van was subdued: whereas audiences in Ireland seemed to appreciate us, in Liverpool we were a background noise, which was tolerated as long as it didn't interfere with their peculiar form of bonding, the men exchanging injuries, the women knitting patterns.

Unappreciated? I felt we were lucky to have escaped unharmed.

Driving to London the following day, we discussed the Liverpool gig.

'Will all the gigs be like that?' I wondered.

'They might get worse,' said pianist, Kevin McAlea.

'The only way they can get worse is if they forget about dancing and go straight to the main event,' said Liam.

'Then it'll be like a boxing tournament with a soundtrack,' said Dave.

'Did you see the guy that threw the first punch? Must have been six foot six,' said Eddie.

'I never knew Irish people came in those sizes,' said driver Ken.

'Maybe they'll bring boxing gloves tonight,' said Eddie.

Some days later I rang the office in Dublin from a phone box on the King's Road in Chelsea.

'You're not going to believe this,' said Peter Bardon, 'every kid in Ireland is singing "Quick Joey Small". Looks like it'll be number one over Christmas.'

It was, replacing 'Lily the Pink' by the Scaffold and being replaced by 'Ob La Di, Ob La Da' by Marmalade on 25 January 1969. We were a sliver of musical meat in a gimmicky sandwich.

After our last gig of the tour in Cricklewood, we partied until dawn, celebrating the news from Dublin. Without disturbing our B&B beds, we boarded the van, the guys sleeping all the way to the ferry at Liverpool while I read the *Sunday Times* and *Observer* and sipped a naggin of Jameson.

Our number one meant that the office telephone never stopped ringing – gigs, radio interviews, TV, magazines, press. The fees went up and our debts were paid off. Tom began recouping his investment and my small percentage kicked in. Within weeks I was making so much money I felt I was trapped in crap music. No exit plan, no escape route and it was hard to even consider them because, for the first time in my young life, I had plenty of money. I was twenty-three and I was making more than the Taoiseach.

When 'Quick Joey Small' became a hit, we could gig six nights a week or even seven if we played the TV Club on a Monday. Here's a typical week and its numbers:

Monday afternoon: sometimes a fitting for new suits or a photography session or press interviews. I also had a weekly meeting with Peter Bardon and the band's accountant, Denis Byrne.

Monday evening until well into Tuesday morning: drink enough to be a party person, not enough to be a party bore.

Tuesday: a seven-hour day of rehearsals with a hangover you could photograph. In the evening, kill the previous hangover and drink enough to start a new one.

Wednesday: 3 pm call and drive to Galway. Play to 1,200 students in Salthill. Home at 6 am after a fifteen-hour day.

Thursday: 3 pm call and drive to Derry. Home at 5 am after a fourteen-hour day.

Friday: 1 pm call for drive to Tramore and local press interview and photographs. Stay over. Bed at 4 am after fifteen-hour day.

Saturday: If dry, game of football on Tramore beach. If wet, drive to Cork and go to a film. In the evening, play to 2,000 in City Hall. Stay over after ten-hour day.

Sunday: 1 pm call in hotel lobby and drive to Blarney Castle for photo session. Drive on to Castlebar via Limerick. Play to 1,200. Home at 6 am on Monday after eighteen-hour day.

Totals: 82 hours minimum. If you add time getting to band calls and my meeting with management, it's over ninety hours.

1,200 miles.

6,000 punters.

Well in excess of £1,200 band income. That's half the price of a semi-detached house in Dublin at the time.

After paying my income tax, I could have paid cash for a brand new car every couple of months with my share of it.

The first thing I bought was the tenor sax of my dreams, a Selmer Mark Six. Any musician will tell you that getting a new instrument gives you a boost. I was soon practising whenever I could, but after a month or so I realized I was practising for nothing and stopped, already gone way beyond the proficiency needed for our repertoire.

When you start making good money, you get a sense of relief: at long last you don't worry about bills and you can actually save. Then you get unsettled when you realize you're not any happier because of the money, but, and it's a very big *but*, you don't fancy being broke again and you think comfort plus unhappy beats broke plus unhappy. Equals trapped. A wise and confident person might have come to a different conclusion: I'm not happy so I'll play music that I like and find some way of surviving. I had neither the wisdom to think that nor the confidence to put it into practice.

The Real McCoy were in the charts three times in 1969, with 'Round the Gumtree', 'Many the Memories' and 'Guitarzan', respectively bubblegum rock, a ballad and a piece of gimmickry. The non-stop activity meant that I didn't have the time for extended binges, just for manic Mondays and occasional toxic Tuesdays. I drank every other day but kept it under control. One Monday I was heading for bed, quite drunk and wanted to read something in a newspaper first. I fell asleep in a chair in pyjamas and bare feet, in front of a two-bar electric fire. Neither the pain nor the smell of burning flesh had the power to wake me in time. I had to get a taxi to hospital in the middle of the night. Even the blisters had blisters. It was weeks before I could walk without dressings and a limp. I even played gigs wearing sandals. When I look back on that, I think I was mad. At the time, it was just my madness and I was surrounded by people – drinking buddies, colleagues – all of whom had their own brand of madness and didn't judge me. We all accepted one another, laughed and got on with it.

20

Stuff happens to me. I don't invite it but it happens nonetheless. My flat was broken into in early 1969.

The burglar was coming out of my flat just as I got home one afternoon. I thought he might have stolen the silver picture frames and other stuff that my mother had left me so I ran after him, every step hurting my fragile left ankle. I made the mistake of shouting 'Stop thief' and he ran harder, reaching the corner beside the Pepper Canister Church while I was a hundred yards back. A van pulled alongside me.

'Were you robbed?' shouted the driver.

Breathless, I nodded.

'Get in,' he shouted and we took off.

We were right at the thief's heels down one of the lanes off Upper Mount Street when he cut right over wasteground where the van couldn't follow.

'Thanks,' I said, taking off on foot and in pain again.

At the other side of the wasteground, back by the canal, a motorcycle was revving. The pillion passenger got off and motioned for me to get on. The bike roared along the canal and I could see the thief getting into a four-door Ford Cortina. He tried to ram us as we came alongside. The car sped off, turned left onto Baggot Street Bridge and got stuck in traffic.

'Follow if you can,' I yelled and ran to the Cortina, climbing in the back door.

A large Labrador jumped from the front seat, landed beside me and tried to lick my face. The lights changed, the car took off, turned left into

Haddington Road and gathered speed. I kept the dog at bay and shouted, 'Stop the car!' The thief drove even faster so I slipped over behind his seat and grabbed him from behind in an armlock, effectively removing him from all the car controls. The car mounted the pavement and hit railings as we wrestled. The motorcyclist appeared beside my window.

'Get the cops!' I yelled.

I had my left arm around his neck and was pulling him hard, his back arched, his hands trying to pull my arm away. I took a bunch of keys out.

'Calm down or I'll stick these in your eyes.'

He went limp. I held onto him. We stayed like this, him begging me to let him go, me telling him to keep quiet, the dog curling up beside me. Ten minutes later the motorcyclist was back, followed by a squad car.

They took him and his dog away. I thanked the motorcyclist – never did get his name – and hobbled home in drizzle, suddenly deflated and exhausted.

There are two denouements: a young Garda called to my flat some months later, gave me back the stolen money and told me the thief had got probation.

Six months later I was on one of my very rare visits to a nightclub when I saw the thief on the other side of the dancefloor. He was studying me. I got ready for more action. He crossed the dancefloor.

'Mind if I join you?' he said.

I pointed to an empty chair.

'Look pal, I'm sorry I robbed you.'

'Are you?'

'I want to explain what happened.'

'Go ahead.'

'My mam gave me money for stuff she needed at home. I really was heading to the shops when I stopped for a drink and got a tip for a horse. Friggin horse wasn't even placed, probably started from a kneeling position …'

Despite myself, I smiled.

'… so I went to the house you were in to borrow some money from the chicks that lived in the flat under you. They were out. I must have snapped – I never robbed before. I won't do it again either – you put me off it for good. So it was my one and only time, right?'

I leaned forward and shook his hand.

'Thanks pal,' he said and I never saw him again.

21

That summer the British army was sent into the north. Kevin McAlea and I drove north to visit our families. We arrived one fine August day when the rioting and house-burning was at its height. The smell of smoke hung in the air, particles constantly drifting in the light summer breeze, particles of people's lives and family heirlooms. It was deeply unsettling to see the city in so much torment. Kevin and I drove past a smouldering bus, burned-out cars and smoke-blackened shops. We didn't dare drive into the Lower Falls where whole streets of terraced houses had blazed the night before. The thugs who set the fires had made sure brave firemen couldn't do their jobs. The politicians and police did nothing to protect vulnerable Catholic areas. Kevin and I suspected they'd have saved the Lower Shankill if it had been ablaze.

I wondered what I would have done if I'd been a kid whose family was burned out of house and home by gangs of self-righteous bullies. I imagined the helplessness of parents who couldn't protect their families.

That day served to awaken something in me. As a child in a lower-middle-class Protestant household where politics, human rights and discrimination were never mentioned, I grew up unaware of the problems I'd have had in a similar Catholic home. A Catholic boy would have expected to find it more difficult to get a job, to get promotion, to buy a house. If he was in Derry, he'd have been up against a rigged system of gerrymandering that kept local power in Protestant control. I grew up without knowing any of that, so I'd marched on the Twelfth parade in Belfast, innocently playing tunes that could stir bigotry and celebrate oppression.

If I'd stayed in Belfast, maybe becoming a student in Queens, some of that naivete might have stayed unquestioned in me. I would have got a job teaching in a Protestant school and had Protestant colleagues and friends. At a deep level inside me, nothing would have fundamentally changed.

Three things ensured I questioned all my early conditioning: moving to Dublin and becoming aware of a different way of looking at the Northern Ireland system of society. Secondly, the civil rights movement made a lot of Protestants start to ask questions of themselves and their attitudes. But mostly it was being in bands and having great pals who were Catholic that opened my eyes to the injustices of the North.

22

I look back on life and my feeling is one of amazement that I had so many experiences worth the re-telling. So here's a couple of road stories:

We were intrigued to be invited to play on the opening night of a new ballroom in County Mayo that had Ireland's first revolving stage. We had to ask for directions several times before we found it, a huge barn of a place surrounded by fields and hills in every direction.

'Nobody will ever find this kip,' said driver Shay, pulling up near a door at the back.

'You might be surprised. They might come from miles around,' said Dave.

'And wonder why they bothered,' said Eddie.

The place was barely finished, part of its car park a builder's dump, its interior unplastered breeze blocks. But it did have a revolving stage that worked fine. We tried it out in the afternoon with the relief band playing out front as we started 'Quick Joey Small' in the back before the stage revolved us into view and the relief band out of sight. We did it a couple of times and headed to the nearest town for a meal and a game of darts.

When we came back in darkness we couldn't find space to park. Dave had been right. We changed into our suits and took our places on stage, facing the bare block wall behind the stage. The ballroom owner arrived and, shouting over the noise of the relief band, proudly told us he had posters up over three counties and well over a thousand people had shown up, all wanting to see the modern miracle of a revolving stage.

He asked if we were ready and we started playing while he walked to the stage controls and pressed a large knob. Nothing happened. He jabbed at the knob. Nothing. The relief band finished a song some of them knew and seemed uncertain what to do next.

'Play another one,' he shouted.

They couldn't hear him over the noise of our hit. The audience fell silent. We cut our hit short and waited. He was now jabbing the knob frantically.

'Play another fucking song,' he yelled. Out front the audience heard him and began giggling. He signalled for us to wait before scurrying off. Minutes later he returned with two burly bouncers carrying a piece of metal in the shape of a starting handle of a vintage car. The bouncers inserted it into a slot beside the knob. We started playing the hit again. For half the song, nothing happened. We played while watching the bouncers heaving and straining, the ballroom owner goading them into more effort. Then BANG. Something seemed to give. The starting handle had a mind of its own, bucking violently as the bouncers fell back. The stage gave a jolt, gathered speed and accelerated until it fairly whizzed round, Dave's drums rolling off their stands, all of us thrown to the floor, the mic stands and leads getting entangled and falling to the floor with us. The relief band's lead singer was catapulted off the stage into the crowd in the first recorded instance of involuntary crowd-surfing. The audience was crying with laughter. Our carefully choreographed showbiz entrance was so chaotic it looked as if our instruments, amps, drums and ourselves had been dropped randomly from a height. There was no question of us regaining our feet or our dignity because we were all in hysterics. Eventually Mike O'Brien found a microphone and leaning on one elbow on the floor, said, 'Ladies and gentlemen, let's hear it for Ireland's first revolving stage.'

We were driving to a gig in the Royal George on Limerick's O'Connell Street when the bandwagon engine blew up. It was a dark night with pelting rain and we stayed in the wagon while our driver headed off to find alternative transport. Half an hour passed before he showed.

'Lads, I found a farmer with a van. There's no seats so you'll have to stand for twenty miles or so.'

'What about the gear?'

'You move yourselves and your clothes and bags into his van. He's going to give me a hand to get the gear into a trailer that's hitched on the back.'

When we drew up outside the Royal George we were running late.

'You guys go and get changed. I'll get the gear set up,' said our driver.

Thus we never saw the trailer. Or smelled it. It had been used to transport pigs and it's apparently hard to train pigs to use a toilet before they travel. It had been easy to slide the gear aboard.

That night in the Royal George, any dancers who came near the band did so just the once, and a big gap between band and audience soon developed. Not one punter came near us at the end for photos or autographs either. We imagined the word going around Limerick, 'They're a good band but there's a terrible smell of slurry off them.'

Finally, here's a story that spread itself over months:

One Sunday night we played in Bandon, County Cork, to a packed house. Afterwards we were entertained in a private bar by the ballroom manager, Ronnie Reynolds, a decent man. There was a weekly competition between ballroom and band and a drinking challenge was issued around 2 am with significant money riding on the result. What someone from the band had to do was bend backwards and operate the optics with his lips, in effect swallowing shots of Irish and Scotch whiskey, brandy, gin, vodka and rum in quick succession from the upside-down bottles. It had to be completed in under a minute. As the band's chief drinker, I was nominated. Band pride was at stake and I accepted, getting all six down within the time as my mates cheered me on. Lots of banter and shouting as money changed hands. As the band's chief practical joker, Mike O'Brien felt compelled to pee in a glass, top it up with whiskey, ice and a mixer and give it to me, of course tipping everyone off to watch.

I didn't remember the 180 miles home or getting into the flat on Palmerston Road. When I woke up, my watch had stopped and it was dark outside. I had to go to the flat next door to ask the time. It was early morning on Tuesday. I hadn't had a Monday.

At rehearsals, I told the guys how long I'd slept. They told me why. I took Mike aside and said, 'That was funny but really out of order. I will get you back. You'll never know when, but I will.'

A couple of months later our driver had the flu and I was driving the bandwagon to a gig in Derry when a truck threw back a stone that smashed the windscreen. Bits of glass started flying inside so we stopped and removed all of it. No windscreen meant I had to drive slowly and we got to Derry just in time to set up, eat and play. After the gig, the guys loaded out while Eddie and I rigged the interior with suit covers suspended behind the front seats. Eddie and I travelled up front with amp covers to keep the weather off us. While everyone slept behind the row of suit covers, Eddie and I battled the elements up front, slight drizzle turning into slicing, stinging stair rods of rain whenever I drove over 30 mph. As dawn broke, we were still forty miles from Dublin and a new problem arose: flocks of wood pigeons enjoying the warmth of tarmac on the Derry Road. I saw an opportunity and leaned over to tell Eddie, 'I'm going to capture one of those birds in the no windscreen. When it's coming in, hold the suit covers to one side and we'll see what the lads make of it.' Eddie grinned and nodded approval. A few minutes later, I made our speed coincide with the flight path of a drowsy, fat bird and Eddie ushered it in the back. We ducked as it flapped wildly in amongst the sleeping musicians.

'Holy fuck!'

'What the fuck is that?'

'Get the fuckin' thing off me! I have to get out! Open the door!'

'You can't. We're doing forty.'

'Keith, you better stop. Mike's not the best.'

After bedlam in the back and hysterics up front I pulled up, the bird was let out the side door and flew off unscathed.

Mike had fainted and was carried out to the side of the road. When he came to, deathly pale, he told us he was allergic to anything with feathers. I sympathized with him while secretly filing this info away for future use.

Another month elapsed and I was driving in Ranelagh when a sparrow bounced off the windscreen of the Beetle. I stopped and walked back to see if I could help it. As it died in my hand, I told it that, even in death, it might be of service.

The next night we were gigging in Beechmount in Navan, a ballroom where the only way into the band room was across the stage. Mike was the kind of showband star so image-conscious he probably blow-dried his blond locks before going to bed. He was never, ever seen in public without being carefully coiffured and dressed. For Mike, life was a photoshoot.

As he got ready for stage that night, he had one boot on and was in his vest with hair like a cornfield after a storm. I had tipped everyone off and we watched with carefully concealed interest as he struggled to get the other boot on.

'Must have left last night's socks in it,' he muttered, turning the boot upside down, shaking it vigorously. When a small mess of blood, beak and feathers emerged, he screamed, turned white and scrambled out the door and across the stage, sprinting as best he could on one boot through the relief band and onto the empty dance floor as his adoring fans looked on in silent bewilderment.

We had to go on without him and it was a good ten minutes before we saw our driver smuggling him through dancers in a borrowed overcoat and cap. When he finally came on stage in the middle of a song, I sidled over to him and said, 'Told you I'd get you back. Here's the deal, Mike: if you don't mess with my drink, I won't inflict any more Hitchcock on you. Right?'

'Right,' he grinned, 'fair play to you.'

A couple of pals and I began meeting in the Barge pub, beside the canal in Ranelagh. Soon a crowd of music business people would congregate every Monday, the showbiz night off. I spent Monday afternoons with Peter Bardon and the band's accountant in Tom Costello's office on Lower Leeson Street, handing over the wads of banknotes I'd collected all over the country at the week's gigs – amazingly I was never once robbed or lost any money – and receiving the details of the next week's work on the road. Then I'd get to the Barge in the late afternoon and stay until closing time, being joined by the regular Monday nighters: Johnny McEvoy and Odette Mathews, Norman and Susan Harris (Norman being Johnny's tour manager), Roy and Lucy Esmonde (who photographed bands in studio and on location), Shay and Dympna Healy, Brian and Carole Molloy (Brian managed successful bands including the Cotton Mill Boys), Jim and Phil McCann (I'd played on Jim's first album) and Dave Pennefather. Others might drop by too, like Luke Kelly, Danny Doyle and Frank Harte. The craic was unfailingly good, with news from the road and stories about other bands and artistes. After the Barge we'd head to somebody's house or flat nearby. I was a fully fledged, fully camouflaged problem drinker.

The road had become my life. I was either on it, recovering from it or preparing for it. Recording was the means of keeping us successful on the road. Drinking was relief from it but even then I'd be swapping stories like the ones in this chapter with other musicians, hearing their road tales too. Apart from manic Monday nights, my entire social life was on the road, with the same crew of musicians, meeting the same fans at the same venues, eating in the same cafés and restaurants, making the same pit stops at the same shops. On and on, while my bank balance grew and my spirit withered.

When I was twenty-five in 1970, I had 'everything': great pals, girlfriends, chart success, clothes that I bought in Chelsea, a degree, a Lancia Fulvia coupé and a comfortable flat on Dublin's leafy Palmerston Road. But I knew that inside, where my spirit should be taking shape and blossoming, there was nothing. I was disturbed and no amount of material success could make up for deep-seated unhappiness. As for self-knowledge and self-esteem, I didn't even make it to the starting blocks. I knew I needed help but had no idea how to ask for it, or who to talk to.

23

After my mother died in 1968, my father seemed lost. They had a long marriage and I can remember only one rocky patch when I was exposed to a lot of his anger and her tears. To this day I don't know what was temporarily wrong between them for a couple of years. Whatever it was, they'd got their closeness back when she died and my father was devastated. I tried to see him whenever I could, clearing out the house with him when Mum died, helping him adjust to digs, bringing him out for drinks whenever I was near Belfast and inviting him to gigs. He tried hard to hide it but there was a deep sadness about him.

In 1970 he rang me and said he wanted a chat. I said I'd be coming into Belfast airport and he could give me a lift to the train station in the city. Halfway there we stopped for a drink.

'Son, I wanted to talk to you about something serious.'

Oh God, has he got cancer or something?

I nodded encouragement.

'Keith, it's this: I've met somebody.'

'You mean a woman?'

'Yes.'

My big, brusque father seemed nervous, even shy. He needed approval. I jumped up, ran round the table and gave him a hug.

'Who is she, Dad?'

'Joan Willis. She used to play tennis with your mother and me when we were young. I bumped into her a few months back. She's a widow.'

‘I’m thrilled for you.’

‘You’ll like her. She’s a professional pianist. Shows, pit orchestras, cabaret gigs, all that.’

Later, he asked if I’d be his best man and a few months later I was. Between the church and the reception, I stopped the car and drank a half-bottle of gin in ten minutes. I was so socially inept I was terrified at the thought of making a speech. As soon as I arrived at the reception, I was careful to order a gin and tonic to disguise the ten that I’d effectively drunk neat. Nobody noticed my breath. During my short, rehearsed, funny speech I noticed my Uncle Harry grinning and nodding encouragement. I even had time for the thought to race across my consciousness that poor Harry was probably completely sober and craving a drink, whereas I ...

That evening four of us were in Joan’s house in Bangor. Joan played piano, her daughter, Carole, played banjo, I played clarinet and the three of them sang standards and show tunes from the 1930s and 40s. Magic.

During Real McCoy mark one, I didn’t drink to excess often when I was with the band. Most of the time I had too much responsibility: collecting large amounts of cash all over Ireland and getting it safely to Tom Costello’s office on Lower Leeson Street, peace-making between band members, keeping receipts for hotels, petrol and the rest. I managed to hold the drinking down to a couple before a gig and a few afterwards. I made up for it on days off, often drinking through the night. I thought I was invincible. After all, I’d persevered with a degree that didn’t interest me, I’d come through a couple of bereavements, I’d survived car crashes and injuries. I thought success would last forever.

I did make time for girlfriends and a few uncomplicated flings. Noel Redding, bass player in the Jimi Hendrix Experience once said to me, ‘Keef, you and I were born at the right time, even the right year, mate.’

‘How’s that, Noel?’

‘We came to maturity in that window of opportunity that started with the invention of the pill and ended with the discovery of AIDS.’

‘Being musicians probably helped our success rate too, eh Noel?’

'Yep. What would we be if we weren't musicians?'
'Dunno.'
'Virgins.'

Showbands took two weeks off every year. The Real McCoys' holidays were the first two weeks of September and, after gigs, rehearsals, binges and the rest, I wanted to chill on my own. So I bought a ticket for Malaga, intending to explore the south of Spain on my own for a couple of weeks. I was fortunate to be offered a small house to stay in by a friend's family.

At the beginning of September I flew to Spain on my own, hired a car and found the house in a tiny fishing village. I liked the little village, the deserted beach, the church in the town square, the lack of tourists and the variety of different drinks I found in a nearby shop, buying an armload of bottles like crème de cacao, crème de banane and the export Gordon's gin with its yellow and orange label. I spent the first two days drinking in sunshine on the roof garden before deciding I should take the hired car for a decent blast before returning it. I drove inland to Mijas and beyond, with careless speed on narrow, mountainside roads where a mistake meant plunging to certain death hundreds of feet down a ravine. I began dicing with a motorcyclist, the two of us seeing who could get around bends quicker. When I finally stopped at a T-junction, he pulled alongside. I rolled down my window. He reached in and took the ignition key. I hadn't realized he was a policeman. He left me languishing in a cell and I was almost sober when another policeman, a distinguished older man with perfect English, explained that I could either go to trial or pay a 'fine'. I paid. I found out later that he had extorted the equivalent of a fortnight's salary but, when you consider the dice I'd had with death, I got off lightly.

A lot happened in 1971: despite having the money for any house in any part of Dublin, I'd always hankered after a wee cottage up the mountains and that's what I bought in April. It had no running water, no kitchen, no heating, no telephone and a septic tank that kept malfunctioning. I didn't care – it was my place and over time I could fix its defects. After digs in

Drumcondra, rooms in Trinity, fifteen flats and a caravan, I finally had my own place. No more packing and moving, so the day after I moved in I took Grandpa's cabin trunk out to the garden and burned it.

I'd been living there for a week and had furnished the place with a camp bed and a fridge full of drink when there was a knock at the front door late at night. Ciaran Burke of the Dubliners and his wife, Jeannie, introduced themselves as neighbours and I invited them in. When we all got tired of standing and drinking we drove further up the mountains to their house to sit and drink. Ciaran showed me the porch he had built out of Guinness bottles and mortar. I left at dawn.

Without knowing it, I had bought a house that was two hundred yards from a bona fide pub. In the days before cars, certain pubs on the outskirts of cities were given a special licence that enabled people travelling by coach to freshen up before getting home. These pubs were called 'bona fides'. I now lived close to a pub that seemed to decide its opening hours as the mood took it. Certainly, if enough people wanted to keep drinking, the pub was happy to keep serving. The only thing that the pub had to do to stay legal was serve food. The owner kept a cupboard full of old chicken carcasses and, if he got a tip-off that the police were coming, he'd put a plate of blue-mouldy bones in front of you and say, 'If anyone asks, the chicken was lovely.' The place was potentially lethal, as it gave me the licence to drink to oblivion without having to worry about driving anywhere. Pals sampled it, usually once. They'd complain for weeks after a night up the mountains with me that they weren't the better of it for days. Dave Pennefather christened it 'Keith-lag'.

In May I crashed the Lancia and bought a dangerous VW Beetle with a big engine and a tendency to go straight on when you turned in for a corner at speed. 'Understeer' I believe it's called and I frequently thought I was driving straight to the scene of my own accident.

I left the Real McCoy and joined Billy Brown's Band the same month. Billy had left the Freshmen and chose a bunch of good players to work with. We were the first showband 'superband': Desi Reynolds on drums, Johnny Browne on bass, Tiger Taylor on guitar, Mike Nolan on trumpet and Paschal Haverty and me on saxes. We rehearsed for ten days. Truth is we interrupted drinking and storytelling to rehearse enough material to get us through an hour and a half. Showbands played much longer than that and Billy's plan seemed to be that the musicians were so good they could fill out the set with guitar solos, sax solos, trumpet solos, even drum solos.

Someone asked Billy what we'd be wearing on stage.

'Whatever you want.'

Freed from the banal civility of the suits I'd been forced to wear on stage for years, I went shopping. I bought a dress suit, threw the trousers away and wore the jacket and waistcoat with jeans and runners. For a while I became a *Top of the Pops* cliche. One day I was walking past C&A in Belfast and saw some shiny mini-dresses in the window display. They'd be like shirts on me. The dress suit is too hot for the stage. So I went in and asked a bemused sales assistant if I might look at a few of the dresses.

'Are they for your girlfriend, Sir?'

'No, I plan to wear them myself.'

She blushed. I laughed.

'No, Miss, you don't understand. I plan to wear them on stage.'

'Of course, Sir.'

She evidently didn't believe me and I realized that further protestations on my part would deepen the hole I had dug.

'Yes, these look the business. Where can I try them on?'

'We had to do away with the changing rooms because people were stealing so much so what we do is give you a receipt and if you come back later today, we'll change the goods or give you your money back. After today it's a credit note. Is that OK?'

'Yes, fine. But where can I try them on?'

'Maybe the toilets in front of the City Hall?'

'I don't think so. Look, I'll just buy three of them and find somewhere, OK?'

Ten minutes later I thought I'd have a drink and found a bar in Queen's Arcade, across the road from C&A. Two gin and tonics later I went into the gents and put a coin in the door of a cubicle. I stripped to the waist and put a new, shiny dress on. It seemed to be alright for length, ending just below my waist. But I wanted to see how it looked in a mirror. I knelt on the floor and studied the shoes coming and going until I was sure the coast was clear. Racing out from the cubicle for a quick look in the mirror, I heard the damn door slam behind me. Suddenly very sober. I've a beard. I'm wearing a dress and I'm in the gents' toilet in a bar called The Queen's. This is Belfast – they call them 'queers' here and they beat them up. My money is in the cubicle and I can't get back in without a coin. In seconds flat I became Ireland's champion limbo dancer, shredding the dress in the process.

This band was unlike any experience that any of us had ever had: Billy was really successful, a singer, arranger and pianist who drove interesting Alfas, Lotuses and convertible Mercs: he must know what he's doing! Then we went on the road and the audiences didn't know what to make of us. We seemed to divide them into those who loved the musicality of it versus those who hated the unfamiliarity of it. We never rehearsed again and life on the road became a long bout of drinking, car accidents, great meals, storytelling and good money.

Car accidents? Mike Nolan crashed into the wall of a police station and then wrote off his sister's car going to retrieve his own car. I crashed my new VW twice, the second time writing it off.

One day I arrived early in Billy and Angela's house for a band call.

'I feel scruffy as hell,' I said.

'A shower will freshen you up,' said Angela. 'Down the hall, second on the right.'

I undressed and pulled back the shower curtain. I nearly fainted when a huge seagull flapped its wings in the shower tray. I pulled on trousers and shirt and went back up the hall.

'Angela, do you know there's a big bird in the shower?'

'Gosh, you're really pale,' said Angela. 'You must have got a shock.'

'A wee bit. How did it get there?'

'It's called Nelson. Billy found it in the garden. We're trying to save it. There's another shower in our bedroom you can use.'

Some days later, Billy told us that Nelson had died and was now in the boot of his car, in a shoebox. We decided that burial at sea was appropriate and so it came to pass: on a fine summer's day we drove our cars onto the Tarbert to Killimer car ferry that runs between County Limerick and County Clare. It was jammed with interested tourists. We gathered around as Billy held the shoebox and opened the Bible at random to read something for the service. Then Mick Nolan played 'The Last Post' majestically as Nelson slid into the Shannon. Some of the tourists applauded, no doubt thinking they had witnessed some wonderful Irish tradition. A couple of priests barged through the crowd and came face to face with us to remonstrate.

'We've never seen anything that bad. That was utter sacrilege.'

'Fuck off,' we said.

'You should be ashamed of yourselves.'

'Fuck off,' we reiterated.

The tourists seemed unsure if this was part of the tradition.

The fun and games, the twenty-minute drum solos while the rest of the band went to the pub next door, the practical jokes, the great meals in the best of restaurants, the all-night drinking and storytelling sessions all came to an abrupt end after six hectic months. We were at Billy Brown's birthday party in the ranch-style house he was renting. The whole band was there and maybe forty other show-business people. Around one in the morning, Billy and Angela retired for the night, telling everyone to feel free to party on. Desi and I were talking with a promoter from Limerick who stopped us dead when he said, 'Sorry to hear about the band lads. I hear last night was your last gig.'

'What? Are you sure?'

'Absolutely. Billy's been getting a new band together.'

'Nobody told us. Do you mean he let us buy him presents for his friggin' birthday when he's planning to sack us?'

We went to find the rest of the band and Desi and I were sent to Billy's bedroom to ask him if we still had jobs.

'Go away,' said his voice from the bedroom.

'Billy, this is serious. We have to talk,' I said.

Billy opened his bedroom door, pointing a shotgun at my chest. He cleared everyone out into the street before slamming the front door. Thus he gave notice to a loyal bunch of guys, some of whom had wives and kids and mortgages. The first shotgun divorce.

A couple of days later I heard that Billy wanted me to join his new band, which was shortly heading off on a six-month tour of Canada. Of course I said no. How could I betray mates like Desi Reynolds and Mick Nolan for money and a job in Canada? I wasn't that insecure.

Billy Brown's Band was the only band I ever joined where drink took precedence over everything. It crammed six years of drinking, partying, storytelling, car crashes and mischief into six months and it was inevitable that it would end badly. Billy and I never spoke again.

24

In 1971 Desi, Mick and I started a jazz band called Jump in Slattery's of Capel Street on Monday nights, with Noel McGann on bass, Des Moore on guitar and Ken Stuart on piano and vibraphone. Sometimes we would be joined by great players who came to sit in, including Dick Buckley, John Curran and Ivor Carroll on tenor saxes, Brian Dunning on flute and Louis Stewart on guitar. Occasionally the wildly eccentric Dick Tabuteaux, nicknamed Dick Tappy Toes, would sit in on bongos. He lived in an attic in a condemned building and had no visible means of support. Rumour was that he would leave the skylight open and wait for a pigeon to fly in. He'd then chase it with a tennis racquet until he had killed or captured lunch. He couldn't really play the bongos, using the same flailing technique that he probably practised on the birds, but we felt sorry for him and let him sit in. He'd go home with some money too.

Jump played in the basement and, in our breaks, I'd often go to the top floor to hear Planxty who had also started a residency. Planxty were Christy Moore on guitar, bodhran and vocals, Donal Lunny on bouzouki, guitar and vocals, Andy Irvine on vocals and almost everything with strings, and Liam og O'Flynn on uilleann pipes, maybe the first folk-trad supergroup. Over the next decade I'd play with all of them. One evening Christy Moore came downstairs in Planxty's break to hear us, and he and I got talking, among other things about saxes and uilleann pipes.

Dublin was awash with fine players then, with jazz and folk bands in many pubs and big bands of up to eighteen musicians in Clery's Ballroom, the Metropole, the Gaiety Theatre, the Olympia, the Shelbourne and

Gresham hotels and Laurel Park, while rock groups played in Sloopy's, the Five Club, the Revolution Club, the Moulin Rouge, the Scene, the Caroline Club, tennis clubs and rugby clubs, and showbands still filled ballrooms like the TV Club, the Ierne, the Olympic, the National and the Crystal. On a Friday or Saturday night, more than three hundred musicians would be earning good money in Dublin.

A lot of musicians came to my Good Friday party in 1972. I had the perfect set-up: a house with no neighbours to complain and no furniture to wreck. I set one bedroom up as a darts room complete with mat and score board and a bench seat. The other bedroom was for those who smoked joints. I borrowed a piano and a drum kit for the sitting room and bought several barrels of drink and proper bar taps. Altogether a hundred and twenty people came, some arriving with kids during the day before sorting out babysitters and returning at night. All the great jazzers played: John Wadham and Pete Ainscough on drums, Jimmy McKay on bass, Louis Stewart on guitar, Noel Kelehan and Jim Doherty on piano, Brian Dunning on flute, John Curran and Dick Buckley on sax, Mick Nolan and Davy Martin on trumpet. Afterwards, there were hundreds of spirits and mixer bottles to be dumped. There wasn't a single breakage or disagreement. The first to arrive was Brian Dunning at noon and the last to leave was Louis Stewart at eight on Saturday morning. Twenty hours of drink, stories and jazz but I was still no party animal: my shyness and ineptitude took over halfway through the party and I climbed up on the roof with a full glass and straddled the apex where I could see people arriving and leaving on one side and be a tacet part of the party on the other.

For me, drink was a medicine whose dosage I could self-prescribe. It was a medicine that enabled me to bury trauma and postpone dealing with it. I could remember what Miss Hucker had done to me but chose not to think about it or its consequences. Drink enabled that suppression of bad memories. But if drink were merely medicine, there'd be fewer alcoholics. Drink also enabled me to be a gregarious partygoer with a huge circle of friends. I had some of the funniest times imaginable when I was drinking. And I have drink to thank for giving this serial loner several friendships that were warm and genuine and have survived for decades.

25

After Billy's band, I was a bit shell-shocked. I'd never been sacked from anything before. Or looked down the barrels of a shotgun. Then Peter Bardon made me an offer that I had to consider: 'Come back to the Real McCoy with its new lead singer, Tina. I'll also introduce you to a bank manager who will help you with investments.' I rejoined the band, met the bank manager and bought a second house, in Ranelagh, from my pals Norman and Susan Harris. I was no sooner back with the band than we had a hit, 'I Don't Know How To Love Him', which went to number one in December 1971. So I was back to being successful in an area of music I didn't want to be in. But they were a pleasant bunch, Tina, who was vivacious and happily married to my mate Desi Reynolds, Johnny Browne from the previous band, John L. Sullivan on sax and flute, a funny, friendly man, Tommy Walsh on trumpet, with whom I drank and played darts every night, Dave Pennefather our band leader, and my best pal, Eddie Campbell.

Tina and the Real McCoy played five nights a week throughout 1972, including three weeks in the Maple Leaf ballroom in Toronto and two weeks in Chicago. (I got lost in Toronto airport, went out a wrong door and ended up on the tarmac. An Irish-Canadian man driving a baggage train gave me a lift to a door that would let me back into the main concourse. We yelled about Ireland over the noise of a jet engine while I sat on other people's suitcases.) The band rehearsed in my cottage up the mountains one day a week plus I had two jazz gigs on Mondays in Slattery's and late at night in the Revolution Club, playing the music of jazz fusion bands like Blood, Sweat and Tears, and Chicago, with the wonderful Colm Wilkinson on vocals. Tina charted again in July with 'Tell Me What's the Matter'.

That Christmas Marian was in my cottage early on Christmas morning. There was snow on the ground and, as we were standing silently taking in the wonder of the snow-covered hills, an open landau drawn by four black horses sped past. Aboard were a few Christmas revellers and Garech de Brun, the famous Guinness heir, dressed as Santa Claus.

'Quick, Marian, open the back gates,' I yelled, running to assemble the clarinet. Five minutes later we drew alongside the landau and I stood up through the sunroof of my Fiat 500 to play 'Jingle Bells'. Garech de Brun shouted and applauded his approval while his driver struggled to control the horses, presumably not used to snow and a mad clarinettist.

At this stage of my drinking, I rarely got caught out. Having trained myself not to slur my speech, not to lurch or stagger and never to get involved in arguments or pick fights, nobody was aware how much and how constantly I was drinking. Since I had started drinking every day when I was eighteen, I'd built up a tolerance for alcohol that now seems scary to me. I never quit for so much as a single day and could down a bottle of gin before anyone knew I'd been at it. I had my own rules: only a couple of pints of Guinness before a gig; eat well and regularly; never let social drinkers slow me down; never mix grape and grain. Of course I woke up in strange places or with strangers with no knowledge of how I'd got there, but I never let details like that deter me from the absolute necessity of escape. And I neither knew nor cared about the danger: what one thinks of as tolerance is actually one's liver being able to process more and more of the poison that is alcohol, until it reaches a plateau and can't cope any more. That's the beginning of cirrhosis, which is incurable. Before alcohol, the liver has the consistency of jelly. As it copes with the poison, it changes and the liver of a dying alcoholic will be like leather. I couldn't have cared less.

And I had a plan for complete escape: I'd play pop music until I was thirty and had the Ranelagh house paid for. Then I'd get back to jazz and the rent from Ranelagh would subsidize me. Thus I rationalized playing music I had little interest in. I justified it as being like a student subsidizing their real life-long interest by working in an Icelandic fish cannery for the summer.

In 1972 I played one hundred and ninety-seven showband gigs, twenty-two jazz gigs, several recording sessions and around sixty rehearsals. In four countries. Three hundred days of paid music. Three hundred and sixty-six days of poison.

Here's my diary for June 1973, the month that changed everything: showband gigs in Talk of the Town in Galway, Castlebar, Athy, Enniscrone, Crossmolina, Stardust in Cork, Top Hat in Dun Laoghaire, Enniskeen, the Hibernian in Mallow, Ballybunion, Naas, Limerick, Waterford, Galway, Ennis, Bunclody, Clogherhead, Newport, the Noggin Inn, Killorglin and my last ever showband gig in Ballybunion on Wednesday 27th. I was also playing jazz on nights off. That left two free nights that month.

After Killorglin we drove the following morning to Ballybunion in Kerry. We had a great day, fitting in a quick rehearsal before a game of football on the beach. When the gig was over, we found Chase, our driver, so drunk he could neither walk nor talk. We loaded the bandwagon ourselves in silent annoyance while he fell asleep inside it. I was the only other person insured to drive, having been put on the insurance so that I could do all the driving and keep his job open for him when he was sick for two months earlier in the year.

We left Ballybunion after two that morning with me at the wheel. We had to get back because we were to stay in Dublin and drive to Wexford for the next gig on Thursday and I felt obliged to keep going. Soon after Limerick, the low rising sun was cutting straight into my eyes. I was driving steadily on the Dublin side of Portlaoise at a place called the Heath when I came over the brow of a hill at around 60 mph and, descending the other side of the hill, drove straight into the back of an articulated truck that was trundling along at 40 mph. Did I fall asleep momentarily? Was there a patch of early morning mist in the dip? Had I been blinded by the sun? I honestly don't know.

Out of control, the bandwagon slewed across the road, crashed through a fence and dropped several feet into a field. Before I blacked out, I heard our 'driver' whimpering and crying and told him to shut up. I asked Tommy Walsh if he could get everyone out. And he did, God bless him, except for Tina and me. She had somersaulted from sleeping in the back of the wagon, sailing over everyone else before getting lodged under my seat, a gaping wound pouring blood from her head. I was wedged in by pedals, the wheel and the dashboard, unable to move. I kept blacking out and coming to. I remember very gentle firemen and ambulance crew using oxyacetylene cutting equipment to get the two of us out. After some hours the whole band went in ambulances to Portlaoise Hospital and wound up in the care of the registrar, Charlie McCormack, a wonderful man and brilliant surgeon.

I was in and out of consciousness for the first week or so. I have flashes of memory like snapshots, unrelated to each other and only explicable by asking people weeks and months later. In one of my snapshots I see all the guys in the band in the same ward and we're all laughing and joking: this happened apparently, the day after the accident, before I began to go downhill. In another, I'm trying to leave Portlaoise but have no money. I want to write cheques to pay the different stationmasters on the line to Dublin. I know that cheques can be written on anything so I am tearing up paper into cheque-sized sections. That's in my head. What my colleagues in the neighbouring beds saw was unconscious Keith trying to tear up his bedclothes.

The third snapshot is of someone sitting astride me and hammering something into my chest.

I had broken bones in my right foot, knee and hand, all the ribs broken on my right side, a dislocated hip and a femur so broken that Charlie McCormack later described it as being 'like dry toast'. I also had fluid on my lung, which Charlie drained off by sitting astride me and driving a draining tube into the lung. My snapshot was accurate.

After a few days Charlie apparently noticed a reddening around my neck. He recognized the reddening as the sign of an incipient fat embolus caused by the release of matter from my smashed thigh bone into my bloodstream. He knew that it had the potential to stop my heart. So Charlie ordered medicine from the Eastern Health Board that enabled him to save my life when my heart and lungs did stop for two minutes and ten seconds.

My father moved into the Killeshin Hotel across the road until I was off the danger list, renaming it the Collision Hotel. He later told me that Charlie had warned him that I might have some brain damage from the heart stoppage. Dad decided to test me. When I was a kid at home, he used to reassure himself that all was well between us, especially after a row, by smiling and saying, 'OK, Keith? Check?' So now he said it to his comatose, possibly brain-damaged son and was thrilled with my response, 'Check, Dad.' He told Charlie that he was certain my brain was unscathed.

It was around ten days before I fully regained consciousness. All my bandmates had been discharged except for Tina. The nurses gave me daily reports on her progress. Despite our drunk roadie I felt personally responsible for Tina and was thrilled when I was told she didn't have brain damage.

After a few weeks I was being escorted down a corridor by a nurse who would come to help me learn to walk when her shift finished. I warmed to her and appreciated her personal crusade to get me moving on the crutches. She was making sure that I didn't fall, literally watching my back. We were making very slow shuffling progress down a corridor when I saw a poor wretch forty feet away who looked like one of those emaciated men you see in films about concentration camps. This poor man's pyjama top was open and you could see his ribs as he shuffled towards us. I was still feeling sorry for him when I saw the nurse beside him and realized he was me reflected in a glass door.

There's a shock you get, almost like sudden grief, at a disturbance of your body image.

'God Almighty,' I said.

'What's wrong?' she said, her arm tightening across my back.

'I didn't know I looked like that,' I said.

'Well, you are lucky to be alive. Don't forget your heart and lungs stopped for over two minutes. I was there. It was touch and go. You were lucky Mr MacCormack was nearby. He got you going again, you know.'

'I have to sit down. Sorry.'

'No worries, I'll get you back to bed.'

As we were shuffling back, she told me I weighed ninety-five pounds, under seven stone.

I had plenty of time to think in Portlaoise. One day a medical social worker parked herself at my bedside and we talked.

'Are you going back to playing in bands, Keith?'

'No way am I going to go back to playing pop music.'

'Are you one of those stars that has their money made?'

'I do have two houses alright but I owe money on both of them.'

'Is there anything I can help you with? Any information I could find for you?'

'That's decent of you. My plan was to be a jazz musician by the time I'm thirty but I'm not a good enough musician now.'

When she left, I thought about that and cried. I was devastated because, although it was something I had suspected, I'd never openly said it. It hurt like physical pain.

When she came back a second time I told her I'd remembered that two pals had finished a one-year diploma in UCD for graduates in other disciplines. It gave them the equivalent of a basic social science degree. The medical social worker said she would find out about it. A few days later she told me I would be too late for the 1973 academic year but that there was an introductory night course in UCD at Earlsfort Terrace. I thought that maybe something interesting and rewarding like social work would allow me to earn enough of a living to avoid crap music and play a couple of gigs. All I wanted was a few gigs to make me a better player.

I was in so much pain that sometimes I couldn't cope with the endless stream of generous people who came down from Dublin to visit me. I had to ask the nurses to put screens around me. Then I could hear familiar voices outside the screens – 'But nurse, I'm after driving all the way from …' – but the pain was excruciating and I was too exhausted by it to be any fun.

One day I said to the nurse who spent her time off getting me to move on crutches that I hadn't been to the bathroom since I came into the hospital.

'You mean your number twos?'

Embarrassed I said yes. Later a junior doctor examined me and told me I had impacted faeces because I didn't have the strength to move it out.

The nurse came back.

'If you like I can get that out,' she said.

'How?'

'Gloves and a mask. I've done it before.'

'Could I do it myself?'

'You could but it might be hard work.'

She brought me a few pairs of gloves and a silver dish and pulled the screens around my bed. Within five minutes I was crying from the pain, determined to finish the job, regretting my decision to go it alone because of embarrassment. It took over an hour and left me beyond exhausted.

After weeks and weeks in Portlaoise, I was utterly bored and wanted to get back home. I talked to the surgeon.

'Charlie, I think I'm well enough to go home. What do you think?'

'I think you're not.'

'Please, will you just think about it?'

Later that day he came to my bedside.

'Here's something for you, Keith,' he said, handing me a book. 'You can look at it later. You can go home next week ...'

'Oh thanks, Charlie. You're a star.'

'... but I have two conditions: you told me about your cottage and that you live there on your own.'

'Yes.'

'I couldn't be responsible for that, I'm afraid, so the first condition is you find somewhere to live with people around, OK?'

'Yes. And the second?'

'Is that you attend a rehabilitation clinic every day until you get some strength back. I've already made a phone call for you.'

When he left, I looked at the book. It was by Henri Charrière, entitled *Papillon*. Appropriately it's about an escapee. On the flyleaf Charlie had written, *For Keith. You too have shown extraordinary courage. Best wishes, Charlie MacCormack.*

26

A week later Marian's father, Frank Skeffington, took seats out of his estate car so that I could lie flat. He drove me to their home in Churchtown, a suburb of Dublin. For the next couple of months the Skeffingtons were extraordinarily hospitable and kind, Mimi making me snacks several times a day to build me up, Marian's brother, Ian, making sure I didn't fall when I attempted to walk a few yards outside on crutches and Frank bringing me to the pub in the evening. One evening Sean Pender called to tell me there was a benefit gig being planned for me by Dublin's top jazz musicians.

'It'll be in the Baggot Mooney. Everyone's going to be there,' said Sean.

A week later he visited me again.

'There's the money that was raised,' he said. 'You get the entire door. Nobody even asked for a taxi fare.'

I was near to tears.

Then he continued, 'You'll never guess who was there.'

'Who?'

'Benny Goodman.'

'How come?'

'Louis Stewart is going on tour with him all over Europe and he was in town, so Louis brought him along. Nice man, very quiet and unassuming. You'd never guess he's one of the all-time American greats.'

'And my childhood idol.'

When Sean left, I thought about this and felt a surge of anger: I was so weak I couldn't go and meet Benny Goodman. I hadn't the strength to play an instrument. I couldn't earn a living. I was dependent on the kindness of others. I was in shocking amounts of pain. And all because an ungrateful, stupid, irresponsible driver couldn't stay sober and drive us home. The fucker never apologised to me either. When I think about that, I don't know whether my lasting anger with him or my sadness for him is more powerful, because, fifty-two years later, I doubt if he sees the injustice or the irony. Or the years of agony and stress he caused me.

Five days a week I had to struggle out of bed, hang off the crutches and get into a blue tracksuit, taking half an hour to accomplish it. I was collected before ten by Eastern Health Board car and brought to St Anthony's Rehabilitation Clinic. The driver was a witty Dubliner salt-of-the-earth type who knew only one way to drive: at breakneck speed, as if tearing along to A&E with the siren on. There were the same four patients in his 'ambulance' each morning, various ages, all with different forms of handicap, all on crutches. I used to think that if he crashed, they'd never get the right bits back on the right people. For six hours each day I was in the gym or the physio room trying to rebuild my musculature. It was intense, hard work and painful most of the time and, try as I might, I could not get much movement from my right hip.

One morning all the patients, old people, accident victims, arthritis and cancer sufferers were given the morning off and told to be in the gym at eleven for some function that involved the Lord Mayor, women in fur coats and dignitaries in suits. All of us patients in our blue tracksuits stayed on one side of the gym. It seemed to be going well until an attendant who sported an intricate caliper went to bring a tray of coffees to the dignitaries. He tripped over someone's crutches and six black coffees landed in my lap. The low murmur of small talk was interrupted by my Northern accent, 'Oh holy fuck! Jesus wept!' The dignitaries all stopped chattering and turned to see one of the patients apparently having a seizure and tearing off his tracksuit bottoms. Three nuns were around me in seconds, two of them nurses, one a physio. I was being treated less than a minute after being scalded and had to act like it was normal to have three nuns attend to my genitals.

I have to say I was now permanently confused, maybe in some kind of constant shock at the turn of events. My plans were gone awry: I had no money so on a whim I sold the Ranelagh house. The slightest movement meant immediate pain and I had no morphine any longer so I was drinking a lot. I couldn't play music because I didn't yet have the physical strength. I dreaded going back to the cottage. I was deeply unsettled and unhappy.

When I went to sign documents for the sale of the Ranelagh house, still not sure if I should sell or not, my solicitor asked, 'Have you thought about suing somebody, maybe the band or management? After all, you were supposed to have a driver and you didn't because he was so drunk.'

'I don't know about that, Joe.'

'I'll find you a barrister who will give you advice free of charge providing you use him if you do have a case. No foal, no fee.'

'OK.'

Two weeks later I was called to a meeting with said barrister, a very pleasant avuncular man who said, 'Keith, I have two pieces of bad news for you.'

'Go ahead. Life can't get much worse.'

'Firstly, you don't have a case. I spent a fair bit of time in the Law Library researching precedents: sadly you don't have a case.'

'Ah well. What's the other bit of bad news?'

'If you had a case, with the injuries you suffered, I wouldn't have settled for less than thirty thousand pounds.'

That would buy four houses on Palmerston Road, in maybe twenty-four flats. That would set me up to be a jazz player for the rest of my life, I thought.

I thanked him, said goodbye and made slow progress on the crutches round the corner to the Barge Inn where I sat catatonic, nursing a double Jameson and peppermint, trying to dull a range of pains.

Soon after the barrister's bad news I asked Marian to marry me and she said yes. We got married in University Church on 1 December 1973 with me like Ratso in *Midnight Cowboy*, hobbling along on a stick beside my beautiful bride.

1. Raymond Donald, in Belfast, 1929.

2. The Amateur Quintet, Belfast, circa 1929 with Keith's father Raymond centre on banjo.

3. Keith Donald, Portstewart, 1948.

4. Methodist College, Intermediate Athletics team 1960.
Centre front row: Keith as Captain.

5. Keith Donald with matched clarinets and his first soprano saxophone, 1962.

6. Keith Donald and Rodney Rice on O'Connell bridge, 1963.

7. The Greenbeats. *Left:* Peter Bardon, Keith Donald, John Keogh, Dave Pennefather, Bob Kelly, Liam O'Sullivan, Paul Williams, 1965.

8. Keith Donald and mother Denise Donald at Trinity College Dublin, 1968.

9. The Real McCoy *Left:* Kevin McAlea, Eddie Campbell, Dave Coady, Dave Pennefather, Mike O'Brien, Keith Donald and Liam McKenna, 1968.

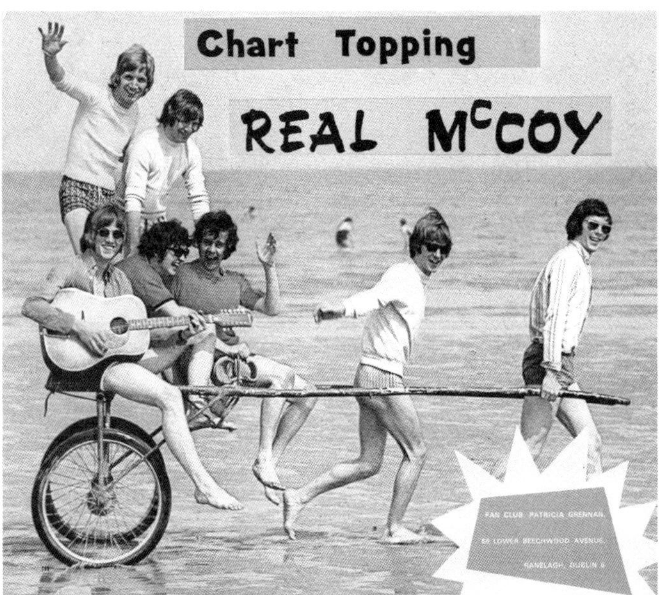

10. The Real McCoy. *Left:* Liam McKenna, Mike O'Brien, Eddie Campbell, Kevin McAlea, Dave Pennefather, Dave Coady and Keith Donald, Portmarnock beach, 1969. *Photographer*: Roy Esmonde.

11. Eddie Campbell, colleague and best friend, 1970.

12. The Real McCoy. *Left:* Eddie Campbell, Johnny Browne, Tina, John L. Sullivan Tommy Walsh, Keith Donald and Dave Pennefather in Keith's Fiat 500, 1971.

13. Philip Kinane, best friend since 1978.

14. Moving Hearts. *Left:* Donal Lunny, Christy Moore, Declan Sinnott, Brian Calnan, Eoghan O'Neill, Keith Donald, Davy Spillane, 1981.

15. Moving Hearts poster, Dublin ,1981.

16. Moving Hearts, Glastonbury mainstage, 1983.

17. Left: Keith Donald, Glastonbury, 1983. Right: New York, 1983.

18. Dunnes Stores Strike, 1984. Kathyrn O'Reilly holding her son Jonathan, with Keith Donald and Mary Manning. *Photographer:* Brendan Archbold

19. Keith Donald, Mary Coughlan and Greg Boland in Keith's back garden, 1985. *Photographer:* Frank Miller

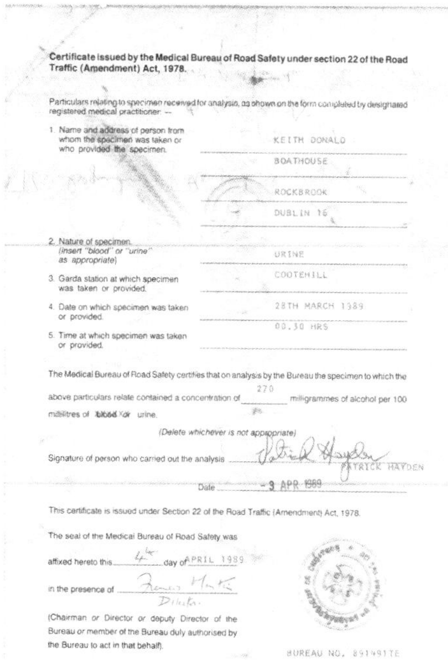

Certificate issued by the Medical Bureau of Road Safety under section 22 of the Road Traffic (Amendment) Act, 1978.

Particulars relating to specimen received for analysis, as shown on the form completed by designated registered medical practitioner: —

1. Name and address of person from whom the specimen was taken or who provided the specimen. KEITH DONALD
BOATHOUSE
ROCKBROOK
DUBLIN 16
2. Nature of specimen. *(insert "blood" or "urine" as appropriate)* URINE
3. Garda station at which specimen was taken or provided. COOTEHILL
4. Date on which specimen was taken or provided. 28TH MARCH 1989
5. Time at which specimen was taken or provided. 00.30 HRS

The Medical Bureau of Road Safety certifies that on analysis by the Bureau the specimen to which the above particulars relate contained a concentration of 270 milligrammes of alcohol per 100 millilitres of ~~blood or~~ urine.

(Delete whichever is not appropriate)

Signature of person who carried out the analysis Patrick Hayden PATRICK HAYDEN

Date —3 APR 1989

This certificate is issued under Section 22 of the Road Traffic (Amendment) Act, 1978.

The seal of the Medical Bureau of Road Safety was affixed hereto this 4th day of APRIL 1989

in the presence of Francis Martin Director.

(Chairman or Director or deputy Director of the Bureau or member of the Bureau duly authorised by the Bureau to act in that behalf).

BUREAU NO. 8914917E

20. Certificate Issued by Medical Bureau of Road Safety, 1989.

21. Larry Mullen of U2 and Keith Donald at the launch of the Rock School in Ballyfermot Senior College, 1989.

22. President Mary Robinson, Dermot Bolger and Keith Donald at the launch of MusicBase in Temple Bar, 1993.

23. Ronnie Drew, Rory Gallagher and Keith Donald at the Guinness Hopstore, 1993.

24. Keith Donald and Noel Redding of the Jimi Hendrix Experience, 1994.

25. Keith Donald and Paul McGuinness in Temple Bar, 1994.

26. Christy Moore and Keith Donald in MusicBase for one year anniversary, 1994.

27. Antonio Breschi, Ronnie Drew and Keith Donald who toured together in 1995.

28. Keith Donald with Yanigisawa curved soprano saxophone, 1998.
Photographer: Colm Henry

29. Alex Donald 1978 and Alex in London, 2006.
Photographer: the award winning Michael Donald.

30. Keith with his brother Dr. Philip Donald at the launch of Philip's book *Ireland's Civil Engineering Heritage* in Trinity College Dublin Provost's House, 2013.

31. Poster for one-man show in Brussels, 2016.

Charlie MacCormack rang me in early '74 and said I'd have to come back to Portlaoise for a minor operation to remove the fifteen-inch pin from inside my thigh bone. I got to Portlaoise the afternoon before the operation. Charlie introduced me to his wife, Monica, and their eleven children. Then he and I went to his golf club.

'What will you drink, Keith?'

'Gin and tonic please, Charlie.'

'A large gin and tonic and a large scotch and soda please.'

A man after my own heart. We had a couple and went back to his house where I ate with the thirteen MacCormacks. Then guests began arriving: nurses who sang, a young doctor who was a really good pianist, a barbershop quartet comprised of male nurses and a tin-whistle-playing retired doctor. Charlie surprised me by playing piano quite well. One of his sons played clarinet and loaned it to me. Every time I put my half-pint glass of gin and tonic down, one of the steps-of-stairs children refilled it. I noticed they were doing the same with Charlie's half pint of Scotch and soda. At midnight, just Charlie, Monica and I remained.

'One for the road, Keith? I've got you a room on your own, in the women's ward. I'm sure you won't mind,' he winked.

At six the next morning, I was woken up for a nurse to give me the pre-operation anaesthetic, which I'm sure I didn't need. For an hour I lay with morphine and gin doing their work and came to understand how people get addicted to that floaty, carefree warmth. Then I was wheeled down to the operating theatre at seven and chatted with Charlie who was ready to operate, dressed in green gown and trousers, just about to scrub up. As the anaesthetist put me under, the last thought I had was that, behind his gold-rimmed, half-moon glasses, Charlie's smiling eyes were bloodshot, very bloodshot.

I woke up at lunchtime. On the locker beside my bed was the fifteen-inch silver rod that had enabled my femur to mend (albeit more than an inch short) and a screw-cap tonic bottle with a medical prescription glued to it which read, *Keith, this is half and half Gordon's gin and Schweppes tonic. I recommend you don't start until evening. Best, C MacC.* Where else in the world would you get the likes of Charlie MacCormack?

He was funny, kind, a brilliant, life-saving surgeon and a good jazz pianist. I was so lucky to have met him.

A month later I was back in Portlaoise with Charlie for a last check-up.

'I don't understand why you can't move that hip. Bring this note down to X-ray.'

I spent a day limping up and down until he looked at the fifth series of X-rays and said, 'There's still nothing showing but every instinct tells me there's something lodged in your hip joint.'

Another operation by a hip specialist in St Vincent's Hospital proved him right. The surgeon there forecast that I would have problems later in life because of the tiny piece of bone that he had found in my hip when he dislocated it. No wonder I was in agony six hours a day, five days a week for months while I tried to get it to move.

One thing stands out from those two weeks in St Vincent's: around six every morning the matron would accompany a priest around the ward. He blessed patients with 'holy' water applied to their foreheads. I'd then lie awake pondering how water gets to be holy. It began to annoy me that I was being woken every morning by a priest's wet hand. One morning I happened to still be awake before the bugger got to me, pain having won its battle with painkillers. I kept my eyes almost shut and timed it so that I reared up in the bed when he was a couple of feet away.

'I'm a Protestant, you know,' I roared.

He turned out to be a fairly athletic priest because he leapt about three feet in the air like he'd just met the devil. He never came near me again, making a detour round my bed every morning like it was the ninth circle of hell.

One addendum to my experiences with Charlie that I found out about decades later: my father wrote to Charlie to thank him for taking care of me. He said, I *am deeply conscious of the fact that you doubtless saved his life*. Charlie's reply to my father was equally warm, saying, *Keith has great guts and I'm proud of him. When I've worked on a person as ill as he was and with success I always feel I own a little of them so to a small extent he's my boy as well as yours.* Two lovely men showing great style and humanity.

Accidents. I've had quite a few, some my fault, some not. I can't be blamed for the no floorboards injuries. I can't be blamed for being a passenger in four car and van crashes. In the other three crashes, I displayed bad judgement, like the guy in a Western who would circle the wagons and shoot inwards. By the time I was twenty-eight, I'd been on crutches five times, for a total of eighteen months. I deserved some sort of Golden Crutch Award.

I'm not going to beat myself up about the amounts of drink I had every night from August '73. Inside a few months I had lost my job in a band, good mates, my health, my physique, a house and the long-term plan that would enable me to return to jazz. I was in constant pain. I had been on and off morphine for weeks and used drink as a self-prescribed substitute. I had nearly lost my life. My lifelong companion, PTSD, was letting me know he'd not gone away.

27

The crash that had brought me as close as you can get to death took me off the road. No more endless touring. No more showbands trying and failing to sound like records. I had witnessed so many great songs being murdered that I should have been taken into some kind of musical witness protection programme.

In February I got a job playing clarinet and sax in *Joseph and his Amazing Technicolour Dreamcoat*. I began playing two or three jazz gigs on Sundays. With matinees in *Joseph*, I was playing fifteen gigs a week plus plenty of recording sessions for jingles and on people's albums.

I was in a hotel room abroad in March when Marian rang me to tell me my father had died.

My father had always been overweight, often weighing as much as seventeen stone. He was six feet tall and wore it well, but years of a sedentary job and little exercise caught up with him, and his heart gave out after an operation when he was sixty-eight. I had become very close to him after my mother's death six years earlier, even acting as his best man when he remarried. My stepmother, Joan Willis, was a professional pianist, and I got on famously with her. When I called to visit them, we'd often play music, Joan on piano, my father singing standards of the 1930s and 40s while I played clarinet. I'd helped him when he cleared out the family home after my mother died. I took him for frequent drinks and chats and he often came to my gigs. He confided in me and I in him. I was deeply shocked when he died and 'coped' with it in my usual fashion, drinking to oblivion. I drank all the way from the hotel room to

London, finishing a neat bottle of gin in a stranger's car. I made it north to his funeral in Bangor. By balancing the intake carefully, I managed not to feel much. I didn't know it then, but grief avoided is grief postponed. Like a stream blocked by a boulder, the grief will find a new route and will often surface in an inappropriate place. Unresolved grief and PTSD were now weighing me down like the psychological baggage they were. Add in the pain I felt every day, though thankfully not all day, and you'll have an idea of the mess that I'd become.

I escaped into as much work as I could manage to find, never missing a show or an opportunity to drink. When you're playing a pit show, you are playing exactly the same music for each show and there's no musical challenge. You are on automatic, getting it right every time, the only challenge being not to get so bored you fall off your chair. Sometimes I had fun though: one night I finished a pit gig, didn't bother packing the instruments and drove like a rally driver to the Horseshow House where some jazz pals were playing. I timed it just right, emerging from the back of the room, walking to the stage playing a hot solo in the right place. The band and crowd loved it.

I often found myself sitting alongside Joe Coughlan in the pit, a lovely, cynical, funny man who was twenty years my senior and a superb player and teacher of saxophone and clarinet. He once whispered a story to me that made me belly laugh and draw glares from the conductor. Joe had worked in the Theatre Royal, once Dublin's premier venue. It was so big they could have a circus on stage, an orchestra in the pit, show a film between live shows, and house all the circus animals backstage. Joe's then pit colleague, a competent sax player, made friends with one of the circus monkeys and would feed it nuts before the show. One evening the monkey thanked him by biting his finger. Much blood and several stitches. The sax player had to miss two nights and lost his wages for them. When he came back, he in turn thanked the monkey by feeding it some laxative chocolate. The monkey's act was to circle the stage on the back of a pony and it did, to the audience's horror spraying parabolas of monkey shit all over the stage. Worse was to follow: the next act on was the Royalettes, an all-female dance troupe. Nobody cleaned the stage or thought to tell them what awaited them and their act disintegrated into a series of skids, falls and loud curses. The audience hid their children's eyes. The orchestra couldn't play for laughing.

Despite having to shuffle along on crutches, I had attended the evening course in social work in UCD at Earlsfort Terrace (now the National Concert Hall, where I've played many times with different people). I learned a lot from the lectures so I applied to go to UCD, was interviewed and got into the diploma course that was designed to equip its graduates to be social workers.

I was almost thirty when I started in UCD. I wanted a job that allowed me to choose what music I'd play, work that might be useful to somebody, something that could provide me with some job satisfaction. I also hoped that social science and its psychology component might give me some clue as to what made me the bundle of contradictions I had become: an ebullient drinker with no self-confidence whatsoever, a natural loner with a gregarious life, a classically-trained jazz clarinettist who had worked for most of his career as a pop sax player. A bit of a mystery to myself.

There were twenty in the class in UCD, mostly people in their twenties and thirties who had a primary degree and wanted to get qualified for a career change. It appeared that the course had a lot of ground to cover and that we'd all be assigned 'placements', a word that was new to me. I looked forward to learning some child developmental psychology, urban and rural sociology, the delivery of social services, basic politics and economics and family law amongst other subjects. My first placement was in the Eastern Health Board in Tallaght, a town of 60,000 that had been a village of 600 a few years previously. Dublin's housing lists meant that families got points for the problems they suffered and the 'problem families' got more quickly to the top of the housing list. Then Tallaght was built and those families were the first to be assigned houses. All very well-meaning but poorly thought through because it meant that there were whole streets of families with serious problems that had to try and get by without the support of helpful neighbours. You'd be visiting a family and see the cars of half a dozen professionals from other agencies parked nearby. It was all a revelation to me.

There was an area walled off for caravans and temporary housing for Traveller families. I was talking to the mother of seven children who seemed to be coping well with huge numbers in a tiny space when I heard a noise I didn't recognize.

'What's that sound?'

'Rats inside in the wall,' she said with a sad shrug of her shoulders, as if to say, '*Nothing I can do about it.*'

Though I felt desperately sad for her, there was nothing I could do either. I had a lot to learn.

I was paying my own way through UCD so I had to keep working while studying. *Joseph and his Amazing Technicolour Dreamcoat* had finished an astounding run of ten months and I transferred to another Noel Pearson production, *West Side Story*. Word went round the fraternity of pit and session musicians that this was the hardest music they would ever attempt in a pit so everyone took it seriously. I bought the record, took the music home in advance of rehearsals and worked hard between UCD projects. The conductor, Ed Coleman, was an American who travelled the world conducting *West Side Story* and the plan was that it would run in the Olympia in Dublin for four weeks before transferring to the West End in London with the same actors and dancers but an English pit band.

There were twenty musicians and Ed at our first rehearsal, some from orchestras, some session musicians – a hand-picked band. We rehearsed hard for a week before moving into the Olympia to work with the cast, some of them Irish, a few American, most of them English. We worked like this for several days until we were due to open. The buzz about the show around Dublin and beyond was great with a lot of coverage in the press and on TV.

A final dress rehearsal was scheduled for 2.30 pm on the day we were due to open. The jazz flautist, Brian Dunning, rang me at home at lunchtime as I was preparing to leave.

'Are you able for a shock, Keith? Part of the ceiling in the Olympia has collapsed. Doubt if you'll be doing the show. At all.'

I drove into town to find bedlam in and around the theatre. Dame Street was blocked by emergency vehicles and the whole city centre was gridlocked. I picked my way over rubble through dozens of firemen, emergency crews and Dublin Corporation officials until I got to the stage and peered through a fine dust cloud, down over granite boulders and huge beams that had fallen where my colleagues and I would have been sitting two hours later. The proscenium arch had given way, bringing down lumps of stone, beams and plaster, burying Desi Reynolds' drum kit and an upright piano. There was no delineation between stage, pit and stalls, all being covered in rubble. It looked like a bomb had fallen. I began to shake with the realization that twenty musicians and most of the cast would have died that afternoon. Then it occurred to me that if the collapse had happened eight hours later with an audience in its seats, the death toll would have been up near a hundred. I went to the nearest pub and found the other pit musicians there, drinking hard to stop rattling.

The impresario Noel Pearson is an amazing man. Before the dust had settled, he had decided that the show should go on. He found a disused cinema, the State in Phibsboro, and sent everyone there. He had an Aer Lingus pilot friend go to Denmark Street in London and buy parts for the musicians, the originals being under six feet of debris. The pilot managed to get all the parts except for drums: Desi Reynolds would have to try and remember an extraordinarily complex chart. The show opened that night, without scenery, in a dusty old cinema to a crowd of first-nighters in furs and dress suits, with an atmosphere of collective relief and defiance and camaraderie that was unprecedented and palpable. It felt like the scene in *The Glenn Miller Story* where the band refuses to stop playing even though the Luftwaffe is overhead. The show stayed in Phibsboro and was sold out every night.

Then I was offered the job of clarinet, flute and sax in the pit in the Gaiety Theatre for the pantomime with Maureen Potter. In 1975 the panto ran for three months with two shows a day for the first month: I'd committed to six afternoons and six evenings in the panto, two jazz gigs on Sundays and five mornings a week in UCD. But I needed the money to support the studying and I was glad to be offered it. Marian suffered my absences stoically, spending a few evenings each week with her parents to vary the monotony of being up the mountains in a cottage on her own. Our marriage suddenly became Saturday mornings.

While the panto was still running I started my second placement, in the newly opened hostel for battered wives and their children at the top of Harcourt Street, Women's Aid. I don't think I was much use to them: the last person most of the women wanted to talk to was a man. Their little girls were nervous of me while all the little boys were somewhere on a spectrum of aggression. I was appalled at the state of some of the new arrivals into the hostel: burned, scalded, broken and bruised, and I was enraged by the men who still managed to instil fear by threatening to break in during the night. Eventually I was trusted enough by some of the women to give them a break and take a gaggle of kids down to the swings in Stephen's Green.

I sat the exams and passed. While I was looking for a post as a social worker, I took the three-month pit job in the Gaiety for the summer run of *Gaels of Laughter* with Maureen Potter again. The pit orchestra was a small band conducted by Thelma Ramsey, all of us determined to have fun because of the absence of any musical satisfaction. I liked them all: Joe McIntyre from Derry on trumpet who had been a star on the jazz scene in London for a decade or so, Joe Coughlan who sat beside me and played the same instruments as me, a great storyteller and a powerful drinker who never got drunk, Eddie Tighe, the bass player who was a postman by day, George Reilly the soft-spoken drummer. They formed the core of Thelma's band and were joined by others like Mike Nolan, Earl Gill, Benny McNeill, Dick Keating, Jack Bayle and Johnny Tate. I was quickly apprised of the quirks and survival mechanisms of a pit band. As the show settled down and no new dialogue or scenes were added, the musicians would mark their parts lightly in pencil: for instance, 4" or 8" or 11" would describe the number of minutes between music. Four minutes meant just about enough time to get out of the pit, race up the back stairs and get a bottle of beer or stout or a short in the green room, which would then be brought back down the stairs and sipped or gulped outside the pit while waiting for the next verbal cue from the stage. Eight minutes meant enough time to leave the theatre through the stage door, go in the back door of Neary's pub, conveniently located almost straight across Tangier Lane, get a quick drink, race back and hover at the little door into the pit. Anything longer, including the interval, meant that six or eight men in dress suits would come in the back door of Neary's, hold a finger in the air to the barman and walk out the front door to the pub across the road for a quick one. Five minutes later we would walk in the front door, collect a perfect pint of Guinness and take it out the back door without paying. I used to think that Nearys' customers, especially at matinee time on a Saturday afternoon, must have found this routine of ours very curious. I imagined Americans back home saying, 'Yeah, we were in this cute little bar off Grafton. Seems there's an Irish tradition that if you walk through a bar twice in a tuxedo, you get to drink for free.'

Of course, with the amount of drink we were getting through and the brilliant, crazy stories musicians tell, sometimes we'd miss the cue totally or think a four-minuter was eight and stroll in late. Thelma would give us a smiling telling-off and normal service would resume for a while.

My favourite pit story: I was playing in the twenty-piece band for *West Side Story*. There's a point near the end where dying Tony is cradled in Maria's arms as they lie on the street. Everything is silent at this climax of such a moving story of love failing to overcome alienation. She begins singing, her voice breaking, 'There's a place for us. Somewhere a place for us …' Finally she sobs and can't sing any more. But one night a drunk in the stalls thinks he'll help out and tries to finish the song for her at the top of his voice, 'Somewhere-a, somewhere-a,' while his friends shush him and all us musicians shake with barely suppressed laughter.

In my twenties and early thirties, my major achievement was surviving the drink. I felt no identification with the standard 'drunk' and his or her tendency to fall over, pick fights, cause rows and get sick. I had trained myself to do none of that. Thus I drank more than most and got away with it. Often, when it was my turn to buy a round, I'd say, 'Must go to the loo – I'll order the next round on my way back.' Then I'd have a shot at the bar, order the round, go to the gents, return to the bar, have another shot – maybe a double – and return to my mates. Thus I'd get three extra drinks on board and the warmth of a secret buzz. My major goal was to avoid pain, and drink seemed to take the hardness out of trauma, like people talk about a couple of drinks 'taking the edge off'. So I could bury all memory of childhood abuse and not really grieve at the loss of my mother, Paul Williams and my father as well as shrug off the injuries sustained at 319 Harolds Cross Road and in awful car crashes.

Although I'd been hoping that the study of social science and some psychology might help me understand myself better, I seemed to have added another contradiction to the list: I was now a fully qualified social worker who needed one.

28

I was still looking for a social work job when UCD rang and asked if I'd consider going straight on to do the 'post-grad', another diploma that gave its graduates the UK professional recognition, the Certificate of Qualification in Social Work, generally referred to as the CQSW'. UCD said they would be able to find me some financial support too so I said yes. On arrival in the new class, imagine my surprise and delight when I found that the only other man in a class of twenty was Bill Somerville-Large. I'd played Trinity Ball with his jazz trio in 1964, recorded in Eamon Andrews Studios in Henry Street and Radio Luxembourg Studios in London with him as house engineer, and now we were to spend a year studying together.

My first placement was in St Ita's, Portrane, a vast, forbidding complex of red-brick buildings in Portrane, north-east of Dublin. As I lived twenty miles away, south-west of Dublin and St Ita's wanted me to start at nine each morning, I asked UCD if they could find me something else and they said sorry but no. I asked them about the financial support they had promised. Again they said sorry but no. I wasn't happy, told them and resolved to get on with it.

In 1975 St Ita's had a population of two thousand souls. Eighteen hundred of them languished in its back wards, mostly forgotten and unvisited. The other two hundred were in the admission wards and were expected to move back into society after some weeks or months. It was this floating population that received some degree of attention and care. I was assigned to the senior social worker, Mrs Crowley, a pleasant woman in her fifties with a nice line in dry wit, a useful attribute in St Ita's as the place was ghastly.

British policy in the Victorian era had been to deal with social problems by hiding them, with the result that all the asylums in Ireland were built at a 'safe' distance from major cities. It seemed to me that St Ita's hadn't had the benefit of any maintenance or refurbishment since it was built in the 1890s. One day I was told that I should see all of it and I set off with a young doctor as he went on his rounds armed with lists and mountains of medication. In one of the female back wards he pointed out an old woman whose short legs dangled off a bench like a little girl's. She looked like some force had squashed her, compressed her so that her face was oval, her body truncated and her limbs short.

'She's a cretin,' he said. 'It's a thyroid problem caused by vitamin deficiencies. Doesn't happen nowadays. She's probably the last example of cretinism we'll get.'

We came to a children's ward where many of the youngsters were wearing crash helmets and some were in restraints and unable to move much.

'Why are they wearing all that gear, doctor?'

'In case they hurt themselves.'

'Why the crash helmets?'

'Because they would batter themselves against the walls into unconsciousness or worse if they weren't wearing them.'

'If they survive long enough to become adults, where do they end up?'

'You'll see presently.'

On we trudged, through ward after ward of heavily medicated people. Nobody was being helped, visited, engaged with, talked to. Lack of adequate staff meant that the few psychiatric nurses that were there could only keep eighteen hundred poor people in permanent sedation. I wondered who was crazier: the people who ran the system or the people in it. Finally we came to a wooden structure.

'This is a disgrace,' said the doctor. 'If you get a chance to write about it, you should. This damned wooden shed was erected as temporary accommodation for the workers who built St Ita's in the 1890s.

And now, eighty years on, it's being permanently lived in. Disgraceful, utterly scandalous.'

We went in, he unlocking and relocking big locks with huge keys. Ken Russell couldn't invent this, I thought. Twenty grey-faced men sat on chairs that were screwed to the floor.

'I've brought the wrong tablets,' said the doctor, 'back in a minute.'

No staff around so I was alone with them. For five long minutes they looked at me with dull, expressionless eyes. I was uncomfortable and tried smiling but got no reaction: maybe they'd never seen a smile before. I stood and waited. Some of them went back to picking at food on paper plates with their bare hands. Probably too dangerous to give them knives and forks. I would be able to communicate better with animals. *This is weird. Don't know what else I can do*. Finally the doctor came back, doled out tablets that they swallowed meekly and we left.

Outside in the fresh air with its slight saltiness from the Irish Sea, he said, 'See what I mean. It's an absolute horror, eh?'

'Yes. Do they ever get out for a while?'

'No, there isn't the staff to manage that.'

The place was like the negative of a photograph: everything was the reverse of what it should be.

Once seen and experienced it couldn't be unseen. Even when I wasn't there, I could feel its power seeping into my psyche.

One morning a week Mrs Crowley and I would sit on either side of the psychiatrist at the desk in her office while she reviewed her caseload. She'd start with an eighteen-inch pile of files in front of me. She'd take a file from the top of the file, scan it swiftly and call in its subject. The person would sit on the other side of the desk facing the three of us while the psychiatrist asked exactly the same set of questions:

'How are you this week?'

'Have you had any recurrence of your symptoms?'

'Have you heard voices? Have you heard your own thoughts spoken aloud?'

'Medication OK? Good, we'll continue you on that for another week.'

And get roughly the same answers from them all. After two hours, she'd have moved all the files over in front of Mrs Crowley and I think it was that successful movement of files, that depletion of one pile while building another that gave her the only job satisfaction she was likely to get.

One patient I got on with was a Traveller woman who self-harmed. She had been a beauty queen in her teens but years of self-harm, a rough life on the road and a brutalizing husband made her look fifty even though she was in her late twenties. Nuala gradually began to trust me and confide in me. I liked her resilience and her soft nature, and was happy to spend time chatting with her. I hoped the chats had some practical purpose but rationalized that even if they were just conversation, it would still do her some good to know that another human being had respect for her and was ready to listen.

Mrs Crowley had a daughter who was an established actress so she understood the logistical problems I had every day, racing between home, UCD, St Ita's, evening gigs and Wednesday matinees. She often asked me to do home visits in the afternoons, effectively letting me go early. One day I raced through a couple of home visits, spending just enough time to write a report because I had a wedding to go to with Marian and had to rush home to change. Around nine that evening I was having the craic at the wedding when I had a sudden flash: Mrs Crowley had asked me to look in on Nuala, who had recently been released. I said I'd be back in an hour or two, left the wedding and drove like mad to the Travellers' encampment where Nuala lived. There was a wake in full swing and everyone was drunk, swaying and staggering from caravan to caravan. Apart from myriad bonfires it was dark but eventually I found two young boys who were sober.

'Hello, lads. Do you know Nuala?'

'Nuala is my auntie, sir. She's in that van there, but you won't get much sense out of her. She's after taking tablets, sir.'

I let the boys bring me into the caravan. It wasn't big but there must have been twenty people milling around inside in semi-darkness. One oil lamp and cigarettes in everyone's hands meant the air was as dense as smog. I spotted Nuala lolling half-conscious, her eyes almost closed, nobody paying her any attention.

'What tablets did she take?' I asked the young lads.

'Me ma's.'

'Is your mother here?'

'That's me ma there.'

'Hello, I'm Nuala's social worker from St Ita's. Do you mind me asking: did Nuala take some of your tablets?'

'Aye mister, she helped herself to a right fistful of me Valium.'

'I think she ought to go to hospital.'

An argument started. Some of the people agreed with me while others disagreed vehemently and soon everyone was shouting at each other and at me. I held my ground for I was fearful about Nuala's life. Finally I got them to agree that Nuala's brother and nephew could come with us and that I'd accede to Nuala's mumbled wish to go to 'St Ita's, only St Ita's. They know me there. Right?'

We set off in my car. The weather knew the meaning of 'pathetic fallacy' and a full-on thunder storm was raging. They asked me to stop and get them all cigarettes. I got drenched. We arrived at St Ita's and I left them in the car while I went to the psychiatrists' staff room, dripping my way up the stairs.

'I've got Nuala down below in my car. Seems she's taken a fistful of Valium,' I said.

'Why on earth did you bring her here?' asked the psychiatrist.

'This is the only place she'd come to. It took me ages to get her to come here.'

'I'm calling an ambulance,' she said, reaching for the phone, 'she'll go to Jervis Street.'

'But ...'

'We don't have the facilities here. Now don't tell her – she'll only run off.'

I did as bid, later driving Nuala's seething, silent brother and nephew back to their caravan.

Nuala had her stomach pumped in Jervis Street and ended up back in her bed in St Ita's. I'd messed up. Agreeing to bring Nuala to St Ita's was a bad call and the psychiatrist had no choice but to send her where she would get appropriate medical treatment. On the other hand, Nuala would never have gone direct to Jervis Street so maybe the end result was inevitable and maybe saved her life. Poor Nuala. When I went to her bedside to apologize, she wouldn't talk to me and we never spoke again. I was so sad. I thought I could help her and I was wrong. Given the life she had, Nuala is probably dead by now. Me writing this is a tribute to her resilience, her inner beauty and her warmth.

I spent most of my time there talking with other patients, either sitting beside their beds or in the dayroom, seeming to have particular rapport with the alcoholics. I didn't yet consider myself a fully-fledged alcoholic although some part of me knew I had the problem. Sometimes I'd have a hangover so toxic that it pulsated through my whole body while I sat talking with a bunch of people who remembered hangovers with nostalgia, who craved a hangover and would set about getting one the minute they had satisfied their carers that they were on the road to recovery and were let out.

It was with no sadness that I left St Ita's. Apart from Mrs Crowley, a couple of staff and some of the patients, I detested everything about the place. It was a horrendous example of first of all British, then Irish, attitudes to people with mental illness: if you hide them, you can forget them.

29

Again I joined the pit orchestra in the Gaiety and kept the Sunday jazz gigs going. With matinees in the Gaiety, I was playing fourteen gigs a week for the first four weeks of 1976, plus I'd have regular work as a session musician. Plus I had UCD lectures. Plus, and this is the biggest plus, Marian was pregnant. We had planned to have a baby and were thrilled when she got positive news. I struggled on with the Gaiety and UCD and began exams in May.

When Marian woke early on 25 May, we knew what to do. We got to the maternity hospital on Holles Street and, as men were not permitted in delivery rooms back then, I sat in a corridor and waited. After an hour or so I was told to go home, that there would be no baby for ages. I went to an early pub in the markets and was too edgy to relax so I drove to Churchtown and waited there with my mother-in-law, Mimi.

The phone call came later that morning: Alex was born.

Mimi and I drove in to see Marian and baby, she a grandmother in her mid-forties, I a new dad in my early thirties, both of us happy beyond words.

When I held her for the first time, it was a life-changing moment of the most pure happiness I ever felt, like being carried on a soft cloud of serenity where nothing else mattered. This little life gave me more than I could ever give it.

I passed my exams in late summer 1976. Although it was stressful, I had got some enjoyment out of UCD, classmates and teachers, especially Ann Lavan and Bill Somerville-Large, both of whom it's always good to see.

I also quit the pit. I missed all those guys and Thelma when I stopped playing in the Gaiety pit. They were a down-to-earth, funny crew that accepted me totally even though I was only passing through.

I had now studied, drunk and played my way through a total of six years in Trinity and UCD without anyone detecting my problems. I now had MA, Dip.Soc.Sc., DASS, CQSW after my name, which is an impressive amount of the alphabet for an alcoholic musician. None of it related to music either.

The postgrad year in UCD forced me to start talking in public. I had always had a problem addressing a crowd. Unless I had a sax hanging from my neck or a glass in my hand, I would run a fast mile from any kind of public speaking. A turning point came when I was at a case conference as a social work student in John of God's Hospital. I was sitting in a circle of professionals who were giving their opinions about a poor man who had a range of problems. I was thinking I should really be a patient here. Ironic or what, when the psychiatrist suddenly said, 'And you, Keith? You haven't said much. What do you think?'

Every pore in my body popped a bead of panic-driven sweat. I wanted to run, to vanish, but it wasn't possible and I stammered my way through an opinion.

Afterwards I realized it hadn't hurt me, that I had got through it and that, if I could stop thinking about my own inadequacies and just focus, really concentrate on the issues, then perhaps I would get through it better the next time.

I started 1976 as a full-time student and professional musician. While still at UCD, I set up a jazz group with my classmate Bill Somerville-Large on piano, Mick Nolan on trumpet and flugelhorn, Frank Hess on bass and John Wadham on drums. The Nolan-Donald Quintet played a few gigs, mostly in theatres like the Focus and the Project Arts before Bill headed back to work in London and we recruited Noel Kelehan on piano and changed the band name to his. Towards the end of 1976 we started a residency in the Killiney Court Hotel that ran every Sunday night for four years. We had great gigs there and many guests including American greats like Zoot Sims and Barney Kessell. Mick and I often hit the booze heavily after a gig and on several occasions when the barman wouldn't serve us any more, we'd go round the tables drinking what the audience hadn't finished: the dregs – a bit like ourselves at that stage of the night.

I was also playing jazz-rock with Sleepless Knights and Jump, big-band jazz with the St Lawrence Band and had gigs with Jim Doherty's Spon, with pit orchestras in the Gaiety and Olympia theatres and recording sessions with Jolyon Jackson, Noel Kelehan, Bill Whelan, John Keogh and Shaun Davey and hired-hand gigs on *The Danny Cummins TV Show, The Sonny Knowles TV Show* and with the Stylistics from the USA. The 1976 totals, 75 jazz gigs, 220 pit gigs plus recording sessions meant I didn't spend as much time as I should have with Marian and baby Alex. An outside observer would have seen an energetic young man who had everything – wife, child, music, rewarding day job – but drank too much. Life was indeed good but the lethal combination of insecurity, drink and Keith were about to ruin everything.

30

Contact advertised a post for a social worker with the CQSW qualification. I was interviewed by some nuns and subsequently employed by the Irish Sisters of Charity as a psychiatric social worker, working in the Contact offices in Westmoreland Street. Six of us worked there: four nuns and two recent UCD graduates, Eileen Fitzgerald and me. I liked them all and got on well with them, being accepted as the only man, the only Northerner and the only Protestant without comment and with mutual respect.

Contact had an open-door policy: anyone with any problem was welcome to come and talk with us, so we developed good links to specialist organizations and their staff, often referring people to them when it was appropriate. We met many people with problems relating to unemployment and homelessness and did our best for them too.

The nuns preferred it if Eileen or I met with clients that had psychosexual problems and thus I met gay men, confused teenagers, women who had been raped by family members and a few people who had been abused by priests. I worked for four years in Contact but never met enough people who had been raped or abused to see a pattern or establish the horrendous numbers of tortured individuals that would later bravely accuse their abusers from the Catholic Church. The gay men's problems were not of their making: they had to cope with societal disapproval and illegality. Gay women never came to see us, their problems never being discussed back then I guess.

Working in Contact was never predictable or routine and I liked that edginess about the place. A couple of times it got a little too edgy: one morning one of our regulars, an eighteen-year-old from a troubled family, arrived almost in hysterics. When she felt calmer, she was able to explain that her father had been released from hospital for treatment for schizophrenia that day and was in pursuit. It was evident that she didn't trust him and that there was some very negative history between them. We thought it safer for her to not to go home until we knew more about her father and the threat that he might pose, so we organized a temporary place in a hostel for her. An hour or so later a grey-faced man with the build of a wrestler arrived and asked to speak with me. I brought him into my office on the second floor overlooking Westmoreland Street.

'You know who I am?' he said, coming straight to the point.

I said no, not having made the connection.

'You saw my girl this morning. You're going to tell me where she is.'

I tried to explain that I was bound to confidentiality, like a priest or a doctor, and couldn't reveal anyone's whereabouts.

'Mr Donald, I was going to come here with a can of petrol, pour it over myself and threaten to set it alight if you didn't tell me where she is. I decided against that.'

'Good, but ...'

'... what I have decided is that if you don't tell me how to find my daughter, you and I are going out that window.'

We sat in silence for a long moment while he stared at me, unblinking. The window in question was a tall Georgian sash window and, as my brain raced through my options, I had no doubt that he could manhandle me through it. The phrase 'strength of a madman' came to mind.

'OK, if I tell you where she is, what do you plan to do?'

'None of your business. She's my daughter, not yours.'

I told him the name of the hostel and he stormed out.

Sister Anne Marie and I rang the hostel, the gardai and the institution that he had been released from. A squad car would sit opposite the hostel. The girl was contacted and moved in another garda car to a different hostel. He didn't come back.

In early 1977 we were asked by the Department of Education if we would send a representative to a five-day conference on youth unemployment at the European Youth Centre in Strasbourg in north-eastern France. I was asked if I'd go and agreed to. To this day I wish I'd said no but I went, as much as anything to get a break for a few days from the daily barrage of other people's problems. Of course I did my best for them but it was exhausting, emotionally draining work.

I've always hated flying and used to take the edge off nerves with a few in the bar at Dublin airport. And a few on the plane. I got to Gare du Nord in Paris in time for the Friday evening exodus of people going home for the weekend. There wasn't a seat on the entire train so I sat on my luggage between compartments, swigging from a bottle of Bushmills.

We were around twenty-five delegates from different countries. On the first day, presumably as a bonding exercise, we were taken by coach up the hills around Strasbourg on a wine-tasting trip. About half of us got drunk. That night there was a sing-song in the centre with lots to drink and a pretty Danish delegate playing guitar and leading the singing. I fetched my clarinet and joined in. But the guitar was a quarter-tone flat and made the clarinet sound awful. I tried everything I knew to get in tune and couldn't.

'Call yourself a musician!' said somebody, joking.

My pride and my identity as a musician were battered. I put the clarinet back in its case and drank. Next day I slipped away from meetings on youth unemployment long enough to tune the guitar and that night was able to join in the music and redeem myself. My playing got applause and recognition and I drank for Ireland. As if forgetting that I had a lovely wife and darling daughter I went to bed with the Dane. It was the worst thing I ever did.

I think I had some kind of a breakdown on my last night in the European Youth Centre. Almost everyone had left. I was on my own in a huge conference room with a superb sound system. I fetched the clarinet, put the record of Keith Jarrett's Cologne concert on the turntable and began playing along. I never went to bed. The only things that stopped nine hours of playing were turning the record over and drying my tears.

I came home to Dublin and confessed. End of marriage. And I broke the trust of several people who were dear to me. I had become the kind of disloyal shit I used to despise.

At first drink removed tension, shyness, an unhappy childhood and social unease. Then it removed judgement.

31

My desperately bad judgement had made life unbearable for my little family. I woke up with guilt and felt it every minute of the day. Even drink couldn't subdue it. I felt like a traitor beneath my own contempt. I tried to make amends but most of the people I'd hurt wouldn't talk to me. Most of my male friends couldn't understand why I'd confessed and thought me naive and stupid. People took sides. A few wise people stayed friends with both of us. And I now had to earn enough to keep two households going.

I can't exaggerate the madness of my life in 1977. I can't exaggerate the madness of me. As well as trying to be a father to a child who wasn't living with me, I was trying to be a social worker and a musician to the best of my ability. My alcoholism was beginning to peak too. Typical was Sunday, 22 May, which started at 10 am in Trend Studios with a rehearsal of Spon, Jim Doherty's nonet that had great players like Des Moore, John Wadham, Brian Dunning, John Curran, Louis Stewart and Mick Nolan, continued at 2.30 in Release Studios with a session for Shaun Davey followed by a break when I took a bus to see Alex for a couple of hours, then a two-band show in the Gaiety with Spon and the Ronnie Scott Quintet, followed by the Noel Kelehan residency in Killiney. A rehearsal, three gigs and Alex. I got to bed drunk, well after midnight. I was at my desk in Contact at 9 am on Monday.

There are two diary entries that numerically sum up my year. One states: *TOTALS. 102 jazz and fusion gigs, 46 pit gigs in Cabaret, 22 recording sessions, 1 full-time day job*. The other records income and expenses. *OUT per month 42 mortgage, 25 credit union, 10 insurance, 3 TV rental, 7 phone, 17 ESB, 6 rates = 110 p.m. IN per week 57.40 from Contact. 25 to Marian, 29 to bank leaves £3.40 per week plus gigs.*

By unconscious design or by accident I had created a non-stop life of wildly varied activity and no real achievement or creativity. In addition my negative feelings about myself and what I had done tainted every thought and deed for a long time. I was a desperately long way from forgiving myself, or even considering it.

It's right and proper that I describe the madness of my life in the late 1970s. Here's the truth of a lost weekend:

It's Friday, end of the working week, start of the working weekend. Write up the last client I saw. Case notes into the right file, say goodbye to the nuns and I'm off to make music.

It takes ten minutes to walk from social work in Westmoreland Street to the musicians' bar in Chatham Street. Ten minutes to shake off everyone else's problems and start suppressing my own.

Into the bar. Musicians come and go for an hour, coming from orchestra jobs, teaching jobs or session work, all of us refuelling before heading out to pit jobs and dance bands. The craic is unfailingly good. I down a few pints of Guinness and a cheese sandwich before another brisk walk to my first of five gigs this weekend, the pit orchestra in the Olympia Theatre.

We are well into the run of *Cabaret* and us musicians know exactly how many breaks we have and of what length. We can have a drink or two every time we stop playing.

Theatregoers see a bunch of professional musicians playing their parts in calm perfection and never suspect the frantic, organized dedication to drink behind the scenes. We are like ducks gliding serenely on a lake of alcohol, every so often turning our tails skywards and paddling like crazy while we try to drain the lake. And my name is Donald ...

After that Friday night show and its eight or ten drinks, Mick Nolan and I stroll along Dame Street in our dress suits, instrument bags on our shoulders, into the Trinity College campus where the Trinity Ball is in full swing. We play two sets with the Jim Doherty Big Band, blowing jazz solos and tight ensemble parts for a couple of hours before finding ourselves alcoholically stranded at 2 am.

We wander through throngs of excited, chattering young people, the women in ballgowns and Chanel, the men in dress suits and lust, walking over Trinity's cobblestones from exam hall to dining hall to buttery.

'Didn't you used to live here?' asks Mick.

'Nineteen sixty-six I had a room over there in the GMB.'

'What was it you studied here?'

'Do you want the headlines or the whole story?'

'Give us the lot.'

'Greek, Latin, ancient history, archaeology, philosophy, Sanskrit and comparative philology.'

Mick gives me a long look of disbelief.

'Useful,' he says.

'Feels like two lifetimes ago.'

We trudge on, desperate and dry.

'Jesus, that was a roast,' says Mick. 'I could do with a drink.'

'I think the bars here are all closed.'

'And the early houses aren't open for another three hours.'

I am about to give up and call it a night when Mick says, 'Did you notice the punters dancing in the dining hall?'

'How do you mean?'

'When a young guy gets a young one up to dance, they don't bring their drinks onto the dance floor.'

'Let's go!'

So we spend a couple of hours stealing drinks from half-drunk students, trying to get fully drunk ourselves while counting the minutes until we can go to an early house.

Around dawn we're marching along the quays and up Capel Street, determined. Our focus may be on drink but we are still careful with the instrument bags on our shoulders.

'Will your chick not worry about you not coming home?'

'Don't forget she's an actress,' says Mick.

'So?'

'She sleeps late.'

'The first recorded case of the early worm eluding the bird.'

And we fall into the pub.

Mick and I leave Slattery's in Capel Street around 10 am to get some sleep before a matinee gig in the Olympia Theatre, he heading to his flat off Leeson Street, me heading back to the office to kip in the chair I'd worked in all week, with the difference that now I'm unshaven and wearing a tuxedo. I feel light-headed, woozy and exhilarated from Mick's mad good company.

An alarm call from the phone company wakes me at 2 pm. I'm totally wrecked after three hours' sleep but have to shake myself awake for the matinee. As I head down the stairs I'm thinking at least there'll be time for a quick one to sort me out before the gig. Suddenly I've a problem: the shop at street level closes at lunchtime on Saturdays and there is now a locked steel shutter between me and Westmoreland Street. Back upstairs. Deep breath, act sober and ring my boss and hope she's in the convent. Maybe she'll think I came into work on a Saturday to do some filing or report writing. Maybe she won't cop on to the Mr Hyde-me that can go madder than any of our clients at the weekend.

'Hello, Sister Anne Marie? Sorry to bother you on a Saturday but I'm locked in the office.'

'No worries, Keith,' comes her gentle reply. 'I know the shop's owner. We'll get you out.'

I wait. And wait, anxiety taking me over: What if nobody comes. I can't ring Sister again. If I miss the pit gig, I'll get sacked. Should I ring the Olympia? Could I get somebody else to play? No, too late. The keyholder for the shop arrives at five to three and lets me out. I run through shoppers, dodging and weaving like I'm playing rugby for Ireland, a quarter of a mile from Westmoreland Street to the Olympia, arriving into the pit with seconds to spare, assembling the sax and clarinet while my colleagues play the opening music and the conductor glares at me. I'm so out of breath a heart attack seems not out of the question. The mouthpiece sits in my mouth unblown for minutes while my knowing colleagues play fortissimo to cover for me.

Into Maureen's Bar at the first break for a liquid mid-afternoon breakfast. Better not start on the shorts yet – there's goodness in a Guinness, isn't there?

'What happened you? You look a mess!'

'Mick and I hit the early house. I only got three hours' kip,' I'm saying, like it's a badge of honour to the heavy drinkers quizzing me. Deep down I know it's not.

'Is that the same shirt you had on yesterday?'

'Everything's the same – I never made it home to change.'

'You've got stout on it now.'

'I can't stop my hands shaking.'

'Come on, time we were back in the pit.'

After a couple of drinks at breaks, I surprise myself by enjoying the music and start messing about, playing harmonies to the written parts or reading them up an octave so that my sax is in amongst the trumpets. The conductor glares. My colleagues giggle. At the interval I get a friendly warning from the conductor, 'Play the parts or you're sacked.'

After the matinee, I consider getting to a shop and buying a new shirt and underwear. Good idea. But not good enough. I'll hit the pub instead. I make a mental note to eat. Of course I then forget the mental note and continue the mental behaviour between shows.

I get through the evening show without missing a note and without missing a drink in a break. Two shows done today, I spend a couple of hours in Maureen's Bar and am the last to leave. Back in the dusty, never-cleaned dressing room, a huge wave of tiredness washes over me and I sit down to pack my instruments.

I wake up on the floor inhaling years of dirt from a filthy mat, hungover beyond imagination, in total darkness. Where the hell am I? Don't remember much. Better find a light switch.

Oh dear God, head staggers: the room is revolving. Take it slowly or you'll fall over and hit something. I must still be in the Olympia. Light on – who turned it off? Did I? Right, finish packing the sax and clarinet and get out of Dodge. OK, let's go.

Ten minutes later and I have established that every door to the outside has a chain and padlock on it and that I can't get into Maureen's Bar for the hair of the dog. It's six on a Sunday morning. There's no Sunday show and nobody will be here until Monday. I have no change for the phone. Deep breath. Act sober and ring the police because you don't need money for it.

'Hello officer. I'm locked into the Olympia Theatre.'

'In Dame Street?'

Resisting the temptation to say, 'Are there two?' I say, 'Yes, that's the one.'

'How did you get in there, sir?'

'I work here.'

'Now, sir, if you work there, don't you have keys?'

'I come and go through the stage door, officer.'

'You weren't robbing the place, were you?'

'Absolutely not. I work in the pit orchestra.'

'You're a musician?'

This guy has refined the art of stating the obvious. 'Yes, I'm a musician.'

'Can you prove who you are?'

'Not exactly, like I don't bring my passport to work.'

'Don't get smart with me. I'll get a keyholder but I'm telling you now, it's Sunday morning and I'm not going to disturb anyone's sleep for some musician with no manners.'

And the phone is a dead thing in my hand. Can't ring him back either – can't ring anybody in fact. Damn but I shouldn't have got smart about the passport. Now I'll be here all day. And maybe all night – bloody hell, I have a gig tonight. And work tomorrow. Oh God, I'm a complete idiot, maybe I'm mad. I sit resigned and stupid in the empty theatre.

A policeman and a keyholder arrive at noon, quiz me, joke to each other about the interesting shades of dust and dirt on my shirt and tux and finally let me go. My legs carry me unsteadily but automatically up to the musicians' hang-out and I stand uncommunicative on the pavement among the truly desperate, waiting for it to open.

Phil the barman says, 'Jesus, the state of you. Have you a gig today?'

'Tonight, a jazz gig with the Noel Kelehan Quintet.'

'OK, I'll give you one pink gin, on me, then you go home and clean yourself up.'

Before I finish the gin, in comes Mick Nolan, all fresh from his night's sleep and ready for chat and mischief. Phil shrugs his shoulders and lets me stay.

Mick drank with musicians and lived off Leeson Street and often talked about going home by rail. Anyone who knows the area knows there was no train within miles back then. 'Rail' was Mick's black humour: he'd often get so drunk that he'd weave his way home, hanging onto the railings around St Stephen's Green for support. Now we both go to his flat by rail.

I doze in an armchair there before borrowing a shirt and getting a lift out to Killiney and the gig with Mick, Noel Kelehan, John Wadham and Frank Hess. We play the music of Miles, Coltrane and originals by Noel and Mick. After the music is done, the barman won't serve us, probably because of the state I'm in. No bother – Mick and I cruise the empty tables and finish off whatever the audience has left behind. Sometime after midnight we cadge a lift back into the city.

I wake up in my flat on Duke Street off Grafton Street early on Monday, unsure how I got home. I check myself before I leave the bed: no shakes, just the unsettled nervy feeling of a hangover. One black coffee and I'm off to walk the mile to work, to try to help people with their problems.

Psychiatric social worker during the working week, psychiatric case at the working weekend.

32

Keeping two households going on a social worker's salary was impossible so I asked the nuns if I might use my holidays for gigging. Thus I went to Hamburg with a Eurovision song competitor, Cathal Dunne, for two weeks in early 1978. It was a great band with Don Harris on drums and Dick Farrelly on guitar. The band decided to drive to Hamburg. I'd have to fly. It was the one and only time I missed a flight, waking up in my flat in Duke Street off Grafton Street as the plane left Dublin. I managed to get standby to Brussels, another standby to Dusseldorf and a final one to Hamburg. I drank all the way and arrived at the enormous club with an hour to go before showtime. We played nine until ten, eleven until midnight and one until two. I thought that was the end of it and fell into a coma-like sleep at the side of the stage where I slept through the final set that ended at four in the morning.

There was a constant tension between the German club owner and the band. He was a strange guy who had paid artists to create a Sistine Chapel-like ceiling in the club. As you looked up from the stage, the nearest nymph had the club owner's bald head and dodgy smile atop a naked baby's body. Repulsive. While he wanted us to play pop covers, Cathal and the band had a much more interesting repertoire of originals. After a week of rows after every gig, he sacked us. We were living in rooms on the top floor of the building and didn't trust the club owner and his crew of tattooed, scarred heavies so we barricaded ourselves in for our last night. My room had been the party room and everyone's empties were stacked there. I deeply resented being sacked and took my frustration out on the glasses and bottles, throwing them one by one against the wall opposite my bed until there was a mound of broken glass. I felt better, went in search of mates and found Don Harris in his room, gouging lumps out of an antique coffee table with a Swiss army knife. Apparently he'd never been sacked before and also needed the therapy of destruction.

Next day I stood alone on a snowy Hamburg street corner and waved goodbye as the band drove off, realizing too late that my coat was in the bandwagon. I trudged through slush to the airline office to change my ticket and was told I couldn't. I would have to buy a new ticket that would cost as much as I had just earned or else wait a week. I rang a Frenchman that I'd met on the Dusseldorf–Hamburg flight and he very kindly put me up for a couple of days. When I left, his wife gave me a suitcase full of their daughter's cast-offs. The kindness of strangers: at least I'd have something to bring home, quality German kinder clothing. Then I took a train to Copenhagen to stay with friends for the rest of the week.

Two nights later I was drinking with Danish friends and asked about jazz clubs in Copenhagen.

Half an hour later a few of us were in a taxi that my friend Kenny Nitschke had called. Half an hour after that we were sipping drinks at a table in the Jazzhus Montmartre when my name was mentioned in an announcement from the stage.

'They just invited you to play,' said Kenny. 'I smuggled your sax in the boot of the taxi. You'll find it at the side of the stage.'

I played a few solos with a band of very fine Danish players and enjoyed the feeling of living on the musical edge, where all senses are heightened by uncertainty and adrenalin.

33

Back in Dublin, I needed a break. Through my own weakness and stupidity I'd created a life that meant working every day and evening, all year round, if I were to have any chance of meeting commitments and paying bills. Marian had said that we should never make Alex a pawn in our strained housing and financial arrangements. In return, I was determined to do my absolute utmost for them, perhaps hoping that I might repair some damage both inside and outside of me. Then I saw a notice in a social work journal that offered fellowships to the Council of International Programs, a US organization that brought social workers to the States for learning and experience. I asked the nuns and was encouraged to apply. I was interviewed in Dublin by an American and was offered one of their fellowships and soon headed off to study and work in Minnesota.

I spent the evening before I left with my best friend Eddie Campbell, a talented lead guitarist and singer whom I'd known and played music with since we were kids in Belfast. We were the same age, born a month apart in early 1945, and had lived near each other in East Belfast. Eddie was a sweet guy, always smiling, five feet three inches tall, a racing cyclist and footballer when he wasn't playing a Gibson guitar. He was also an orphan who lived with his sister. The first time I saw him was from the inside of a bandwagon we pulled up in front of a corrugated Nissen hut, a left-over from the war. I thought we were stopping to collect equipment but Eddie emerged from the hut immaculate and smiling. He wore his wide smile almost constantly and never complained, despite losing his father when he was eight, his mother when he was sixteen and the family house when he was seventeen. He'd get a bit glum when his beloved Liverpool FC lost a match but otherwise he was the most positive, sensitive guy you could meet. I never heard him speak badly of anyone. I had moved to Dublin in 1963, played with Eddie in the Federals in Belfast before joining the Greenbeats in 1965 and when a job came up in the band, I recommended Eddie and he moved to Dublin. We became close friends, at one stage living in a caravan in Monkstown, at another stage sharing a two-bed ward in hospital after a fatal car crash.

So, on the night before I headed to Minnesota for four months' work, Eddie and his new Canadian wife, Sherri, and I moved from pub to restaurant to pub around Grafton Street. A great night we had, bumping into loads of pals and fellow musicians, finishing well after midnight with hugs and promises to write.

Next day I flew to New York and four days' orientation regarding the Council for International Programs. Then we had four days free so I decided to take the bus to Boston where my jazz flautist pal Brian Dunning was studying at Berklee.

I drank Bushmills all the way to Boston. The bus driver was Irish American and wanted to talk. He turned a blind eye to my bottle while asking all sorts of questions about the old country. I got there at midnight and Brian and I drank until four. He woke me a few hours later:

'Come on, bring your sax – I've a class in Berklee. You'll get a blow.' And, exhausted and hungover, I did spend a morning blowing in Berklee with Brian and his classmates.

Four days later I flew to Minneapolis and was met by a young guy holding a placard with my name on it. He was twenty-five, the son of the people I was to spend the first month with, my 'host family', Marylou and George. As he drove me into Minneapolis, I was quite taken aback by him: he said he didn't like it when I said 'God Almighty!' and he had sharp creases in his spotless blue jeans, always a bit of a giveaway.

He asked me to a party that evening 'for friends who just got engaged. Ain't that real neat?'

The party was a revelation, an insight into the social mores of white middle America. I watched him mix the punch – crushed ice, fruit juice, slices of exotic fruits, no alcohol – and I was standing with him when the guests started arriving. They were the kind of clean-cut American youth that look as if servants polished them before they left home. During the first part of the evening's fun I fell in with two of them, a young woman who was arguing that the Bible said women should be subservient to men and a young seminarian who argued the contrary position. Weird it was and it got weirder when the host said, 'It's time to eat folks. Let's bow our heads in prayer,' and every eye closed and every head went down bar this Irishman's. After they gorged like starving animals – I was glad to see a vice at long last – the host announced, 'Now it's time for the party game. Bring out the prizes, Joleen.' A hostess trolley that was piled high with beautifully wrapped boxes was pushed into view and I wondered what kind of a game we were about to engage with. The only games I'd played as an adult were drinking challenge games that were often funny and usually dangerous. This party game turned out to be Spot the Biblical Quotation and at first I thought they were joking. An hour later I got the booby prize, which was a bottle of oh-so-carefully wrapped shampoo. The party broke up around the time that parties in Ireland start and the host gave me a lift to his parents' house where I was introduced to Marylou who was extraordinarily welcoming and to her husband George who seemed world-weary, waited for his son to leave and then looked at me knowingly.

'Keith, if you're a drinking man, feel free to take whatever you want from that liquor cabinet, even a bottle. You can take it to your room if you want to drink in peace,' he said, 'and my liquor cabinet is never locked, OK?'

He winked before returning to his newspaper. I took him at his word and spent hours trying to find something to watch on the TV in my bedroom while finishing a bottle. I hoped that other Minnesotans were more like father than son. Drinking alone that night was perfect – I could let my guard down, no fear of getting caught out.

In fact, drink rarely caught me out now. I'd developed some sort of mental dipstick that warned me when I needed to top up or slow down. Ideally I could reach a pleasant plateau and stay there, neither getting higher nor falling off the surrounding cliffs. Life through whiskey-coloured glasses. The downside was the disengagement. I wasn't a fully functioning person emotionally or creatively. And the two are related of course: I wasn't creative because I didn't allow myself take the risk of experiencing emotions. If I risked deep feelings, I'd be exposing myself to the unresolved anger and fear that abuse had engendered, and grief for those I loved who had died. And I didn't have the tools to cope with any of that. So I drank. In a way, drink caught me out all the time.

34

Minnesota was way outside of my experience and very tough going for a recently qualified social worker from Ireland. I was to work for the Department of Corrections in its Serious Juvenile Offender Program, which aimed to rehabilitate teenage murderers, rapists, arsonists, armed robbers and kidnappers through the intervention of a team of psychologists, counsellors and social workers like me. It was an experimental project with a decent budget boosted by President Carter's government. It was divided into three phases: in phase one, the teenager was in lock-up and would stay there until he or she had written and signed a contract with the program, the judge, the probation service and any parents or guardians that might still be interested. The contract would have measurable goals and no time frame. There could be practical goals like 'I will get my grades' or 'I will pass my driving test' and psychological goals like 'I will learn to live with myself and others' and 'I will do something about the chip on my shoulder' and atonement goals like 'I will figure out how to make amends to those that I've hurt.' Achievement of these goals in phase two could take years in an open prison before they were able to move to phase three when they would be back in society. They might then be at home if it were deemed suitable, or placed in a halfway house or a hostel. Wherever they were, they would be in daily contact with their mentor, a person who was paid by the program to keep an eye on them, work with them and furnish regular reports. One example that I came across was a boy who had been a heroin addict and persistent car thief and had beaten up two old farmers for their car keys. In phase three, his mentor was a sober alcoholic who had raced cars and owned a service station and car repair business. He was thus able to relate to the boy's problems of car theft and addiction. The two old farmers recovered from their injuries and I was present at a highly charged meeting when the two old brothers, dressed in their best Osh Kosh B'gosh denim overalls, were introduced by the mentor to the young man who had beaten them nearly to death. The kid cried. The old men were hardy and gracious.

I found it all new and difficult – the teenagers were challenging, my colleagues were all much more qualified and experienced than I, the study programme in the University of Minnesota was demanding and I was drinking or gigging every evening.

My supervisor was Willa Mae Dixon, a forty-year-old Black woman who had been born in Birmingham, Alabama. Willa Mae had grown up with awful racism there, had seen her father wounded by a white policeman's gun and had taken part in every civil rights protest she could get to. Despite Willa Mae's illness, cancer, she and I drove all over Minnesota to rural courthouses to talk with judges, probation officers, parents and guardians about the Serious Juvenile Offender Program. Usually I drove while Willa Mae spat blood into a metal dish. She kept apologizing for being sick. We met the most interesting characters imaginable, often finding ourselves in bizarre situations. We spent many days in little country courthouses and were once asked by the judge to go for lunch in his country club. The prosecutor and several defence lawyers also came along.

Willa Mae pointed to the defence lawyers.

'See the difference, Keith?' she whispered.

'Sorry, I don't get it,' I said.

'Look at their shoes. The guy with the Gucci loafers is defending the rich kid. The others have cheap shoes. Bet the judge listens to Mister Loafers more than the rest.'

She was right. Over a leisurely lunch the case was discussed and sorted, the court proceedings choreographed to everyone's satisfaction. The kids would be sentenced according to Mr Loafers' suggestions and they would be sent to our program.

One Friday the boss of the program, Jay Lindgren, invited me to a party in his house.

'Bring your instrument and you can play something for us,' he said.

It was quite a sedate evening with Jay's wife, their kids, some neighbours and his coworkers. I was asked to play and said to the forty or so guests that I would play them some music that came about in the southern states because Africans and Europeans had all met there in the New Orleans melting pot. I would play the blues. I was into my third or fourth chorus of a simple twelve-bar when a voice sang out and joined me, 'Oh Lord, I'm gonna see you soon,' a voice pure and true and filled with emotion, Willa Mae's voice.

That evening we discovered a common love of jazz and blues and I was amazed to find that my social work boss sang in a choir with George Foreman.

Despite being a non-smoker all her life, Willa Mae's lung cancer was terminal. Frequently she had to ask me to drive when we headed out of Minneapolis to the little courthouses of rural Minnesota where she would drag herself up the steps to make a case for a Caucasian, African American, Hispanic or Native American teenager to come onto the Serious Juvenile Offender Program. Despite everything she'd seen and suffered, Willa Mae carried out her rehabilitation work in a colour-blind way.

One sunny day we were in a single lane bounded by the traffic cones of massive roadworks near Duluth, Willa Mae driving at the speed limit of forty miles per hour, when a huge truck roared up behind us and began flexing its muscles, bullying us with airhorns and a battery of lights, trying to get us to go faster.

'There's no place to pull in. What'll I do?' asked Willa Mae, her voice rough from constant coughing, full of anxiety.

'You're at the speed limit. Ignore him – he's just ignorant,' I said.

Mile after mile the lights and horns were incessant as the giant truck came to within a couple of feet of our back bumper. Willa Mae pulled in to the kerb in the next little town for me to get ice cream to cool her throat. The enormous truck skimmed past and came to an abrupt halt in front, all hissing of airbrakes and clanging clunks of towbars. A fat white trucker dismounted from his cab and came waddling back to our car.

'Lady,' he bellowed at Willa Mae, 'if you can't go over forty, you shouldn't be on the road.'

Something snapped inside me and I yelled back at the top of my lungs.

'If you can't keep your truck below forty, you shouldn't be on the road, you ignorant fuckin' bully.'

Whether it was my accent, my language or my colour I don't know, but it did the trick: he backed away, surprised, and waddled off up the street. For a moment I was worried that my cursing would upset Willa Mae. I was wrong: she threw her arms around me.

'Oh my. That was just magnificent. A white boy standin' up for this lil old Black girl.'

The rest of that day was punctuated by her chuckles and remarks. 'Are all Irishmen like you?' and 'Did you see the bastard's face when you roared at him?'

For once I was proud of myself.

Jay set it up for me to spend a day at the state penitentiary, so one hot summer's day I got up really early and headed for the nearest bus. As we travelled into downtown Minneapolis in silence, I took in all the other men and women in short sleeves, their suit jackets off in the heat. All heading to desk jobs. For a moment I experienced their lives and felt as if I was one of them. For all they knew, I was. They'd never have guessed that I was an alcoholic Irish jazz musician turned social worker on his way to a state penitentiary.

I was shown around by Robert, the senior social worker. The first cell we came to was covered in sheets.

'Sorry this is the first thing you see, Keith. Young guy came in yesterday. Couldn't make it so he hung himself. It's a crime scene now.'

Another cell housed a thirty-year-old who didn't look up as we passed.

'Guy has his own computer terminal in there, whatever that is. He's some kind of genius. He's making so much money he won't apply for parole.'

While their guards patrolled the periphery of the canteen I met several Native Americans and some white and Black prisoners who would have talked all day with me about jazz and blues. We talked about cars, American and European. Some of them were knowledgeable about Ireland. Some had Irish names and blood and asked loads of questions, perhaps saving up my answers for their dreams of freedom. Robert showed me where some of the inmates had kidnapped the prison governor's wife the previous year and explained how it was resolved without loss of life. An extraordinary day and a rare glimpse into another world.

Minnesota was remarkable, a mix of Lutheran religion, clashing right and left-wing politics and damaged child clients that had perpetrated horrendous crimes, so remarkable that every day was memorable in a different way and I began to get into it and lose touch with Ireland. Phone calls were hugely expensive so that my only reminder of home was a letter from Eddie every week.

I had good times too, managing to sit in as a visiting jazz musician with several US musicians, spending interesting weekends in rural Wisconsin and Minnesota, camping once on a reservation where the Native Americans were welcoming and kind.

I learned a lot too, both at work and in the classrooms on the University of Minnesota's spacious campus on the banks of the Mississippi. One particular lecturer, Professor Brantner, a tall man with long white hair, an academic, a practising psychologist and a published poet, affected my outlook on life's big issues through his incisive thinking and clarity. Brantner took us on a journey through a child's life and the conditioning processes it was likely to find in different societies and in different classes in society, all delivered in a clear, non-judgmental way. I signed up for a psychology module he was delivering in evening classes, at my own expense.

One evening he conducted an experiment and asked another psychologist to sit in with our class. They conducted a kind of blindfold test where one would outline the results of the Minnesota Multi-Phasic Personality Inventory (MMPI) for two people and the other would predict the likelihood of the couple's compatibility. The MMPI is a set of psychological measurements for the determination of an individual's character traits and it seemed like the two psychologists couldn't fail, getting real cases right every time.

'With that information, I'd say their break-up is a given.'

'Yes, they divorced after two years.'

As a recently separated person, I did wonder why people weren't given the option of such character profiling before choosing a life partner.

There was also a Black lecturer, a handsome guy in a sharp suit and gold jewellery who taught us about poverty in the USA. After a morning of lectures he set the class a challenge: each of us had to visit the down-at-heel bars in downtown Minneapolis and St Paul, observe poverty and report back.

This isn't research. This is my life back in Dublin, day in, day out.

On my pub crawl in the cause of social research, I came across two winos sitting on the pavement against the low wall of a surface car park, a man and a woman, whose weather-beaten skin bore the deep lines and scars of a hard life. I asked if I could join them and spent a sunny afternoon sitting on the sidewalk slugging wine, buying bottles and swapping life stories. One custom of theirs stood out: when each new bottle was uncapped, the man would fill the cheap metal cap and spill the contents on the tarmac and solemnly toast absent friends.

Then a coincidence of place: our lecturer drove past with the prettiest women in the class in his six-seater convertible. Which made me wonder who understood more about life in the gutter.

My second host family had two adopted children, a six-year-old boy and a little girl from Vietnam who was the same age as Alex. I used to borrow a bicycle with a child seat and take her sightseeing in St Paul. The family also lent me their second car, a VW Beetle, to go to gigs in the evening. I'd head off on a musical adventure to a bar or a club and ask the band or singer-songwriter if I could sit in. Occasionally they showed some reluctance but, once I got on stage, they all wanted me to stay, most of them asking me to come back the following week. Through this musical living-on-the-edge, I could gig as often as I wanted to. I'd accept the free drinks I was offered but always turned down their offers of dollars: for once, music wasn't about money.

One Friday my third host family, decent wealthy people, loyal Americans, invited me for a weekend of sailing on their racing yacht on Lake Superior. Although I'd been there with them before and enjoyed it, I felt uneasy for no obvious reason and declined the offer. The next morning I was alone in their mansion on Summit Avenue when the phone rang. Marian's sad voice from Ireland told me that Eddie had died suddenly from a brain tumour. Soon I was sitting in the kitchen, numb, catatonic, unable to think, dead inside but still breathing, drinking steadily like it was medicine. With a sense of panic I suddenly remembered that Eddie had written to me the previous week and I had torn up his letter before posting my reply.

That's the last letter he'll write to me.

I headed carefully down the stairs to the basement and its storage area for household rubbish. I had to work my way through four big plastic sacks and sift through a congealing mound of rotting, smelly garbage before I finally held sixteen precious pieces of paper. I brought them upstairs with reverence, cleaned them carefully and painstakingly stuck the pieces together with transparent tape. Then I had Eddie's last four pages intact. I brought them up to my bedroom and laid them side by side on a desk to make sure they got dry.

Back downstairs I hit the bottle in a 'don't care if I live or die' way.

Some hours later, I recognized that I shouldn't be alone and rang Guri Tveit, a Norwegian friend, also in Minnesota as a social worker. She arrived half an hour later and I finally let go and began a marathon of tears, drink and memories of Eddie. My own pathetic version of a wake maybe. My recollection of events after that is hazy but I do have a clear picture of waking up on top of my bed, with Guri sitting patiently on the floor waiting for me to come to, anxious to care for me.

Then I saw Eddie's letter and had a moment of extreme clarity, like a lightning flash at night that cuts through black clouds to reveal everything for a second. I knew with absolute certainty that I had to leave Minnesota and the Council of International Programs and the work and friends like Willa Mae early, now in fact, and go home to Ireland. It was a definite instruction from Eddie's letter.

Guri was hugely helpful, sorting the logistics of an air ticket that wasn't valid for six weeks, packing, getting me transport to the airport, being with me.

I went standby from Minneapolis to Detroit and standby again to New York. In the beautiful Kevin Roche architecture of the TWA building at JFK I was told that I would have to queue until 4 am on Monday and even then I wouldn't be guaranteed a seat to London. I joined a line of about twenty people and waited. By six on Sunday afternoon, I was dehydrated, hungover and dizzy, having spent the last of my dollars on drink in Detroit airport. I was very, very hungry, not sure when I'd last eaten and began to feel faint. I didn't know if I could get through another night of no sleep. Asking a stranger to mind my baggage and sax case, I went back to the ticket desk.

'I have to get home to Ireland. Is there any other way than staying in that queue, I mean line, all night?'

'I'm afraid not,' said the TWA woman, gravely.

'Don't you have some leeway for emergencies?'

She looked at me, long and hard, eyes to eyes.

'Is it a family death, sir?'

'No. My best friend just died. His wife, I mean widow, is Canadian and doesn't have any close friends in Ireland yet.'

Another long look.

'Wait over by that pillar, sir. I'll be over in a few minutes.'

I did as she asked, keeping one eye on my sax case forty feet away. She came over.

'Now, sir, tell me your story.'

As matter-of-fact as possible, I told her about Eddie and Sherri. I explained I had no money, was at the mercy of TWA, and was not physically able for another night without sleep or food.

'I don't know why, but I do believe you. Now listen: I'm risking my job for you so this is between us, right?'

I nodded.

'I'm going to give you a boarding pass for a flight that leaves in half an hour. It'll get you to London. You have to act as if you are part of an English tour group, can you do that?'

An hour later I was sitting on a plane at altitude over the Atlantic, silent lest my accent betray my TWA angel, even when the stewardess offered me the first of many free drinks and a menu. As I sat amazed at technically being a stowaway, I wondered at this miracle, not sure if Eddie's honesty and goodness had shone through me and connected with the TWA woman, or if there was some other magic at work.

I was too late to get to Eddie's funeral service in Dublin but I did make it with minutes to spare to Roselawn cemetery outside Belfast in time for Eddie's cremation, standing beside Sherri, feeling her grip on my arm become vice-like when Eddie's coffin began to slide out of view.

Eddie and I were thirty-three when he died. He had done a lot in his short life: racing cyclist, great footballer, professional guitarist and singer in Ireland, the UK and Canada, served his time as an apprentice in Mackie's Engineering works, survived his parents' early deaths without bitterness or self-pity and married a beautiful, funny, kind woman from Canada. And he did it all with an ever-present smile.

He was my best friend, never criticizing my numerous weaknesses, always there for me with his wide smile and good sense. In getting me home, he enabled Sherri and me to support each other in grief. Then he passed the baton of friendship to Philip Kinane, a lovely man who has become my lifelong friend.

35

When Eddie died, I became temporarily insane: like a survivor in a failed suicide pact, things couldn't be worse and now I had no shoulder to cry on. The nuns in Contact must have seen how upset I was and told me not to come back to work until I felt alright. I had sublet my flat in Duke Street to a barman pal and it wasn't due to be vacated yet, so for three weeks I didn't plan where to spend the night, sometimes walking up O'Connell Street to Contact's offices in Hardwicke Street, letting myself in at midnight and sleeping on the chair in my office for a few hours before going to an early house, sometimes staying with a pal or with Sherri in her and Eddie's house in Dundrum. I drank all day and every day, crying a lot, laughing like a maniac, craving distraction, averaging two bottles of spirits and many, many pints of Guinness.

At the beginning of the third week I was heading to a pub for company and more of the same when I heard a voice in my head.

'Keep this up and you will end up in the gutter.'

It was so clear that I did not dismiss it as a thought. Shocked at hearing voices I walked slowly around the block three times and did not enter the pub. Later I bumped into Roy Esmonde, an old pal, got talking and was asked if I'd like to house-sit while he and his wife were out of town for a week. I made a couple of phone calls and, for the first time, bought some marijuana and cut myself off from everyone for a week while I came down from the two-week grief-binge. If I'm to be ruthlessly accurate, I should say 'binge' because it's not right to blame the binge on grief. All drink ever did was let me shed a few superficial tears while 'protecting' me from the emotional uncertainties of grieving. 'Fear-binge' would be more accurate.

That week gave me time to think about the mess I was and the wild ride of my adult years. Since leaving home aged eighteen in 1963, I'd had the no-floorboards injuries, I'd graduated from Trinity in 1967 and two months later been injured again while Paul died beside me. Trauma had removed ten years of study from my consciousness. My mother had died the next year. We'd started a new band and had number one hits. Then I bought a couple of houses, changed bands a couple of times, restarted in jazz and had another crash, spent nine months recovering and lost all my money and the second house. My father had died. I'd got married. We'd had Alex. The marriage ended. I'd graduated from UCD and was employed as a social worker. Now my best pal was gone. While I was trying to help others, I was a crumbling fool surrounded by wreckage, much of it of my own making. Social worker, heal thyself.

By the end of a week holed up in the Esmondes' I felt I might manage for a while without a drink, the first time I'd ever thought about it and the first time I had decided to try life dry. In a way, I have Eddie's death to thank for starting me on the long road to eventual sobriety.

I was thirty-three when I quit drink that first time. It was a big transition that I didn't manage well: I kept going to the pub to hang out with the same bunch of heavy and problem drinkers. I should have sought out some sober alcoholics for help but didn't, not yet regarding myself as fully fledged. I smoked a little dope for relief. It was a start and I didn't drink for seven months.

There are people who drink vast quantities, realize it's not good for them and just stop. I know people like that. Although they were problem drinkers, they aren't addicts. I thought I was like that. Though I stopped after Eddie's death I couldn't stay stopped. I was edgy, ill at ease around people, panicky about things that others would regard as routine, utterly without self-confidence, lacking the tools I'd need to accept myself and get on with a dry life.

Addiction is the only disease that tells the sufferer they don't have the disease. So after seven months dry I began to rationalize. I could drink less. I could be sensible. Maybe just a few at weekends.

I fell off the wagon and was soon back at square minus one.

36

In early September I got a letter from Jay Lindgren to say that Willa Mae Dixon had died on 21 August. She was only forty. He sent me press clippings of her huge funeral: apparently she was a real hero to the Black community in Minnesota. When Jay had visited her as she was dying in Mount Sinai Hospital, she asked to be remembered to me. It was a huge privilege to know and work with her. I wished I had spent more time with her and had been able to say goodbye.

Then I read that the Irish Department of Justice was planning to open Loughan House as a prison for young people. I wrote a letter to *The Irish Times* outlining the alternative treatment of young offenders that I'd seen in Minnesota. It was published and I was contacted by the Irish Council for Civil Liberties, recently set up by Mary Robinson, the future president, and was then co-opted to its Anti-Loughan House Committee, chaired by Professor Mary McAleese, the future president.

Through 1979 and 1980 I worked in Contact and played jazz-fusion with Metropolis and jazz with the Noel Kelehan Quintet. Plus a lot of recording work with such groundbreakers as Midnight Well and Andy Irvine. Also lots of commercial work – I could hear myself eight or ten times an evening if I watched the ad breaks on Irish TV, disliking them so much I used to mute all ads. Once I was asked to appear in a TV ad for Guinness, filmed in the bar at Comhaltas in Monkstown. In the ad I'm part of a traditional Irish band, playing wooden flute. We filmed all morning and broke for lunch, a good meal with as much wine as you wanted. I was still trying to stay off drink and abstained. Then they asked if any of us did actually drink Guinness and I put my hand up. All afternoon they filmed, forty or fifty takes and each time I had to leave off flute playing to reach for the most perfect pint, hold it so that you could see the harp on the glass and drink about two inches of it. The really scary part is that I drove home.

In 1979 the Noel Kelehan Quintet made an album of Noel's and Mike's originals, recording and mixing it in two days in Trend Studios off Lad Lane. We called it Ozone. Then we were invited to play for two weeks at the 1980 Sense of Ireland arts festival in London. We would be playing in Ronnie Scott's Club as support to Johnny Griffin and staying in the Tara Hotel in Kensington. Ever since I had been refused admission to Ronnie's when I was a teenager, I had wanted to play there and this would be a jazz ambition achieved. We went by ferry and train to London and checked into the Tara. That's when it all began to unravel. Mick Nolan turned up for the first night so drunk he could barely speak. When he came onstage I had to keep an eye on him so closely that at one point I was playing a solo on tenor sax and had to fumble on with one hand while my other one was stopping Mick from falling into John Wadham's drum kit. His playing was pathetic and was the same every night and no amount of talk from Noel or me changed anything. Ronnie Scott's partner, Peter King, asked us if we could find a way of sorting the problem but, short of barring Mick from the stage, which Noel was reluctant to do, there was nothing. I felt both pity and anger: I loved Mick, had been his pal for years and used to subsidize him from time to time, lending him money that I knew I'd never get back, paying some of his dental and medical bills, even breaking into the house of his justifiably angry, bitter ex to retrieve his flugelhorn. I was both fellow sufferer and enabler. Scuttling my long-held ambition didn't seem to be fair.

After one of the gigs in Ronnie's I was in my bed in the Tara when the phone rang and an unfamiliar voice said, 'Hi there. You don't know me but I was at your gig in Ronnie's tonight and was wondering if you'd like to hook up?'

I said maybe and where was she?

'Downstairs,' came the answer and I took a chance.

Minutes later a lovely woman came into the room. I spent some time with her over the ensuing ten days and was introduced to cocaine by her pals after a Don Weller gig in the Half Moon in Putney. I'd always been wary of drugs other than marijuana, even refusing painkillers and antibiotics unless absolutely necessary. I baulked at the sight of lines of cocaine, then thought, If all these well-off, very together people like it, why not try it? On 10 February 1980 I had my first few lines and liked it. The next day I had a chat with myself: this coke thing is not a good idea. It was so pleasant I could see myself ending up a drug addict. I'll be wary of that in the future.

I spent all the money I'd earned for the two-week stint in Ronnie Scott's on a bass clarinet.

It was hard to adjust to social work after the highs and lows of being a full-time jazz musician for two weeks in London. And it rattled me when all the other staff in Contact decided to have a gentle chat with me about my drinking. They were confronting me about something I hadn't really confronted myself with. I didn't like it at the time, rationalizing that I did my job as well as any of them, sometimes seeing clients out of office hours too. I was annoyed at them for imposing their values on me. Now I view it as a stage in a tortuous process of recovery.

Social work really was beginning to unhinge me. Maybe it was a combination of listening to other people's problems five days a week, gigging six or seven nights, working through my holidays and trying to have time to see Alex that did it. I'd become that rare thing, a workaholic alcoholic, a restless, driven addict.

Even though the nuns had promoted me to senior social worker status in recognition of the fact that I was jointly running the agency with

Sister Anne Marie, even though I was getting reasonably well paid, I gave Contact three months' notice. I thought I'd try living off jazz and pit gigs.

Jazz is cyclical, sometimes in fashion, sometimes not. When I stopped being a social worker in 1980, there were gigs in Conway's in Parnell Square, in the Gresham Hotel, the Shelbourne Hotel, Sachs, Killiney Court Hotel, the Parliament Inn, Slattery's in Capel Street, the Harp Bar and the South County Hotel as well as one-offs in the Project Arts Theatre, Focus Theatre, Peacock Theatre and the Abbey Theatre. Although I didn't consider myself a great sax player, I was getting a lot of work with star players like Louis Stewart, Jim Doherty and Noel Kelehan. Maybe there was nobody else available or perhaps I hadn't been found out yet. The irony is that I was a good jazz clarinet player with all the technique of a classical player thanks to John Johnston and six years of tuition and practice. But the clarinet was irrevocably associated with the commercial trad jazz of straw boaters and striped waistcoats and nobody wanted to hear clarinet anymore so I didn't even own a decent one.

Between Noel's band, the Allegro Jazz Band on Sundays at lunchtime, Metropolis and other jazz-fusion gigs, recording sessions and other music work, I reckoned I might be able to make a living again as a musician. Plus I wanted to spend more time with four-year-old Alex. So I left on 20 September 1980, four years to the day after I had started.

How did I feel about being a social worker? I don't think I was trained enough for what I encountered. That's not the fault of my teachers in UCD but it is to some extent mine in that I was too preoccupied with making a living. For the work in Contact I should have taken courses in counselling and studied more psychology. And drunk less. How do I feel about social work itself? I think social workers have two responsibilities and the systems are designed so that they can manage only one of them: while they are concentrating energy, time and resources on their clients, which is right and proper, they don't have anything left to effect social change, which is necessary. Thus a lot of social work is society's bandage when it should have the opportunity to contribute to society's overall health.

Alex came to live with me that same month, starting school in Dundrum. I was a basket case and didn't know it: each morning I'd leave Alex to school and come home and light the fire. I'd sit, maybe reading but more likely staring at the fire for the few hours until it was time to collect her. I was drained. Then the hotel that hosted three of my gigs closed for renovation and I was broke too.

After a month or so, my girlfriend, Betty, took me on holiday. Alex's maternal granny, Mimi, was happy to take her while Betty and I went to Greece. I drank in Dublin airport, in Heathrow, on the flight to Athens and all night in Piraeus. We fell asleep on a ferry next day and woke up in darkness as the ferry docked in the middle of a raging storm. It was nearly midnight and we had no idea where we were. A crowd of people and animals trudged along the pier. We joined them, getting soaked as we tried to find a place to sleep.

After a night on camp beds in the open, in rain and in utter darkness on some kind woman's roof, we got a nice, bare white room and went exploring in bright sunshine. The island was Icaros, near the coast of Turkey, and had no tourist facilities because that's the way the locals wanted it. Apparently, during the military junta's rule from 1967 until 1973 all the activists and lefties had been banished there without national funding or support. They had had to do it all themselves, building roads and schools and other infrastructure and were happy enough to do without a tourist industry and all that it might have brought. A dedication to drink had accidentally brought us two Irish leftie activists to Icaros to join them.

It seemed that the only other non-Greeks on the island that week were half a dozen students from Queen's University Belfast who had also got drunk on a ferry and ended up there accidentally. They were musicians and played Irish traditional music every evening outside a taverna. One evening I was inside the taverna buying drinks and had to wait for a while. I listened to the Greek music coming from a record player behind the bar, becoming aware of its decorations and what appeared to be delicate improvisation. With a tray of drinks, deep in thought, I went outside to hear more Irish traditional music and began to think about these two examples of indigenous music and the similarities they had with American jazz. I spoke excitedly with Betty about this and she said I should talk with someone who might know about these things when we got home.

'Didn't you work with Donal Lunny once? Maybe you could talk to him?'

I did and it changed the rest of my life.

37

I tracked Donal Lunny to a gig he was doing in the Baggot Inn, with Christy Moore, Declan Sinnott, Eoghan O'Neill and Brian Calnan. I talked about my moment of revelation on Icaros. He told me they wanted to expand the band and had considered asking me to join but hadn't because I was gigging with other bands. A couple of weeks later I brought an alto sax to their rehearsal room above the Baggot and played along with Christy's singing, nothing madly inventive, merely the kind of cautious, sparse playing that jazzers have always done to support singers. When we finished the first song and Christy suggested a second one, I said, 'What do you want me to do?'

'Exactly what you just did,' said Christy.

Generous man.

A week later, Davy Spillane came to rehearsals. To find an instrument that would work with his uilleann pipes, I brought everything I owned: straight soprano, alto, tenor and baritone saxes, all the clarinet family and all the recorder family, around a dozen instruments. I also owned a very rare instrument, a curved soprano sax that had been in my father's band in the late 1920s. Dad had rescued it from my mother's cousin Drew Alexander's attic for me in the early seventies. Davy and I worked away all day, trying the sound of different instruments with his pipes. We discovered that his pipes and the soprano sax have almost identical ranges, which meant we could play in unison. But the combination of straight soprano and pipes was too reedy, too cutting and razor-like. Then

I remembered that I had also brought the curved soprano, which sounds less like an oboe and more like a sax. It was the last combination we tried.

'That's the one,' everyone agreed.

By pure fluke, on 15 January 1981, in a scruffy attic room over the Baggot Inn, we had created a new sound. If my dad hadn't gone to the trouble of getting that instrument for me Moving Hearts, and fourteen years later Riverdance, might have had a different sound.

The first recording I did with Moving Hearts was on 3 February in Windmill Lane. I was in agony that week, at home with a slipped disc. Christy called to see me and said, 'You don't have to come to the studio but if you can, I'll get somebody to drive you in a van and you can lie flat.' I played the session with the help of strong painkillers, recording the sax and pipes riffs with Davy for 'Hiroshima, Nagasaki' that morning. The first full gig I did with the band was on my 36th birthday, Sunday, 8 February 1981, in the Embankment Inn and I got home drunk at 7 am.

The four years with Noel Kelehan's jazz quintet had been great: we'd made an album, played in Ronnie Scott's Club and played nearly four hundred gigs. The two years with Metropolis were also a great experience: we'd made an album and played over two hundred gigs. Now, Moving Hearts looked like it might monopolize my musical life and I had to say goodbye to mates like Noel Kelehan, Mick Nolan, John Wadham and Frank Hess, plus Paul Barrett, Garvan Gallaher and Don Harris. The music business and the film business have that in common: you work closely and intensely with people until suddenly they're out of your life and you're getting to know a new bunch.

Moving Hearts was unlike any band I'd played with before in many ways: first of all, it was a co-op and a crew member got the same wages as a musician. I liked the idealism of this and happily signed up to it. It took a couple of years for me to find out why it doesn't work in practice. Secondly, the music was an amalgam of Irish traditional music, folk, rock, funk and jazz, all creatively arranged by Donal Lunny and Declan Sinnott, with input from others, especially Eoghan O'Neill. Up to 1981

I had played trad jazz, 50s jazz, jazz-fusion, classical music, pop music, rock and pit music. I'd never listened much to Irish trad and it felt like there was no drawer in my mental filing cabinet of musical experience to put this new music into, so it took some time to understand its subtleties. There were also huge technical problems: playing unison with Davy's pipes meant playing in his keys of D and G which put me into E and A, keys that are ergonomically difficult for your fingers to play fast. I joked to myself about my new life in A & E. And a piper doesn't have to breathe, the air that vibrates the reed being created by bellows that are controlled by the player's elbow (the Irish for 'elbow' being 'uileann'), whereas every wind instrument player has to find logical, musical places to breathe. I identified with Ginger Rogers in her dance partnership with Fred Astaire: when somebody remarked to her what a great dancer Fred was, she retorted that she had to do the same moves, but backwards and in high heels. Struggling with all this, I bought some albums and learned a lot, particularly from the approach to the taking of breath in the middle of a traditional tune that the flautist, Matt Molloy, uses.

The band took stances on the political issues of the time, everyone having the power of veto over song lyrics. The second wave of hunger strikes in the Maze prison outside Belfast started around the same time as Moving Hearts. Some of the song lyrics were perceived as being in support of the hunger strikers, particularly 'No Time for Love', 'Irish Ways and Irish Laws' and 'On the Blanket'. I'm proud to have been a member of a band that sang about nuclear war, religious hypocrisy, environmental plunder, apartheid, slum landlords, and 800 years of colonialism in Ireland, all on our first album, as well as three original instrumentals, 'McBrides', 'Category' and 'Lake of Shadows'. But some listeners and pundits latched on to a few specific lyrics and labelled us IRA fellow travellers. Personally, I think I understand the reasons for the 'armed struggle', both in Ireland and in South Africa. I knew that the current struggle had started as a reaction to the UVF shooting dead three innocent Catholic barmen in Malvern Street in 1966 and to police collusion in the ambush of peaceful marchers including unarmed students at Burntollet, and to the RUC running amok in Derry. Peaceful protest seemed to be gaining nothing from Stormont and Westminster.

I asked myself: what would be my reaction if some well-conditioned thugs burned me, my brother and my mum and dad out of our house and the authorities did nothing? How would I feel? What would I do? I couldn't answer that because it's unimaginable. On the one hand I abhor bullying and injustice; on the other, I don't think violence is a useful response. So I did what little I could: I contributed to songs that might help people to see things differently. I was always careful to read the lyrics to see if violence was advocated.

It seemed that many Irish people liked our approach: our eponymous first album was the very first Irish album to go straight to number one in the Irish charts.

Touring Ireland in 1981 was unsettling. There were black flags attached to telegraph poles in every county in sympathy with the hunger strikers. Bernadette McAliskey was shot by the UDA and survived. Sir Norman Stronge was shot by the IRA and died. Two days before our first gig Paisley brought journalists to see hundreds of his followers in military formation. Our crew had to examine the underside of our truck and bus every morning after a gig in the north. Abuse was heaped on us by a few journalists. We got threats over the phone. There was a constant, uneasy feeling of *what next*?

We were rehearsing for a week in Merrion Cricket Club when Christy came into the room.

'Norman has too much to do. If he's not sorting out transport, he's building PA speakers. He doesn't have time for all the financial stuff too. So who's up for it?'

Nobody volunteered. Eventually, Eoghan O'Neill, Declan Sinnott and I were given all the responsibilities for finances, legal stuff and negotiations with the record company. Next day Eoghan resigned from this, saying that he'd had to do it for years in his mother's shop and he didn't like the déjà vu he was suffering. I understood that and kept at it. Declan stuck it for a few weeks, sitting beside me in the bus on the way to gigs to sort out finances before he bailed too, explaining that bookkeeping was diverting his energy from music arrangement. Fair point, I thought and struggled on, basically because I had to. There were aspects to it that I hated, for instance frequently having to tell a virtuoso fellow musician, 'No, you've already got more than everyone else in advances, there's no money left.'

But I did have some fun too. Like the time I had to set up the band's two companies and went to a solicitor's office in Upper Fitzwilliam Street with my best black suede ankle boots and black jeans tucked into them, a shirt with abstract musical motifs emblazoned on it, a black denim jacket with buttons like skulls and my hair halfway down my back. The young solicitor was in neat pinstripes, plain black shoes, white shirt and careful tie. Although he'd inherited his fashion sense from his grandfather, I quite liked the cut of his uniform. I don't think he appreciated mine much. All went well until he started talking about the company seal and asked if it was alright for it to remain in his office.

'Just be sure to feed it regularly.'

He looked at me blankly. Maybe he'd heard it before.

What makes a virtuoso musician? The facile answer is 'a lot of practice' but that doesn't address the real question: what kind of character is driven to do the hard work, put in the long hours and study every day in order to become good? I always thought that it was either someone who was trying to lose themselves or find an escape from the outside world – like me – or someone that is obsessive and perfectionist and feels compelled to be as good as they can. When you have a band that is a hand-picked collection of virtuosi, you will probably have a group of strong personalities who may not make a cohesive group. Certainly, in all the bands I worked with, I never came across such a bunch of extraordinary people who happened to be world-class players.

I always knew where I stood with Christy; he knew what he wanted and where he wanted to get to. He was and is scrupulously honest, both with himself and others. He is deeply affected by injustice and strives to do as much as he can to alleviate it or draw people's attention to it. He has a great sense of fun and appreciation of the absurdities of life and I have cried with helpless laughter in his company. He works hard at writing, singing and song selection. Sometimes we travelled together and he excused himself while he practised a song, often trying out different phrasing for one single line mile after mile.

Quite recently I said to him, 'Isn't it strange that we never had a drink together, being the same age, being in music and even in the same band for a couple of years?'

'But we did, Keith. After I left the Hearts, I snuck into the Baggot one night to hear you all with Mick Hanly. You and I hit the clubs in Leeson Street after.'

'Are you sure?'

'Absolutely. We didn't get up to anything more than getting poured into taxis at dawn.'

I had to confess that, as far as my sodden memory was concerned, this hadn't registered. Damn the blackout – I'd like to have a memory of having a drink with Christy.

Eoghan O'Neill is an utter perfectionist with a deep understanding and appreciation of music. He has a good heart and would be the most supportive guy you'd need if things were going against you. And what a brilliant bass player. He's also one of the funniest people you can travel with. I was sitting with him and a couple of crew members, young technicians who hadn't gigged abroad much, on a flight to London. When the flight captain had addressed us for the last time, it was Eoghan's turn: doing a perfect impression of the captain, he said, 'Thank you for flying Aer Lingus. Please fasten your seat belts for our final descent. In the final seconds we will plummet to the tarmac at Heathrow where the temperature will be a thousand degrees centigrade ...' – our crew members were now forcing laughter while turning pale – 'leather body bags will be provided for those in first class while the rest of you will have to make do with plastic. Please keep your mouths closed as you assume the crash position as your dental records may be used for identification purposes ...'

Davy Spillane was and is a genius. He was the youngest in the band and roomed with me, the oldest. We never fell out. In his early teens, he had left a middle-class home in Blackrock, County Dublin, to apprentice himself to a family of pipers. He had already starred in an acclaimed film, Joe Comerford's *Travellers*, before he joined Moving Hearts at twenty-one. Davy was anxious to learn, frequently quizzing me about tuning and phrasing as well as mortgages and banks. Davy is very, very funny and could have done stand-up if the pipes hadn't worked out. He and I have maintained a great friendship for forty-four years.

Donal Lunny is one of the best rhythm players I ever worked with, his bouzouki chords neither behind nor ahead of the beat but played so exactly and intricately that they drive a whole band. He is also a talented arranger, composer and record producer. He is music to his core.

Declan Sinnott was a fine guitarist and arranger with an interest in and collection of all kinds of music. He and I managed to have a mild row that lasted weeks but it was about a particular musical arrangement so that was alright. He had and has my total respect.

Brian Calnan was a lovely guy and a fine drummer. Once he was driving Davy and me to a gig in Donegal and we got stuck in a stationary snarl of traffic in the centre of Galway in the early afternoon. We had miles to go and looked like being late. Lying in the back of the car, a bit hungover, I thought I had a solution to the problem and assembled the soprano sax.

'Wind down your window, Brian, I'm going to make this sound like an ambulance.'

'I will not – you must be joking.'

So I wound down my own window and played an alternating couple of notes as raucously as I could. The traffic parted like the Red Sea for Moses and Brian slowed down as if there was an ambulance behind us.

'Go for it Brian,' yelled Davy. 'We're the friggin' ambulance.'

We gathered speed, a cacophony of irate car horns in our wake.

I went on and off drink throughout the few years of full-time Moving Hearts. Smoked a bit too.

Because so many US and English jazzmen had died from heroin addiction, I was nervous of powders and after a brief flirtation with coke and a single experiment with speed, I mostly steered clear. I once saw a friend hand over the keys of his car to settle a debt with a coke dealer and learned from that too. Maybe having one major addiction was enough for me.

Each year from 1978 I stopped drinking. I never knew when I'd start again and sobriety would last from six weeks to six months. Those in the know call it 'white-knuckle sobriety' because it's like clinging to your chair on the edge of a precipice. I was thoroughly conflicted because I wanted to stop permanently but didn't seem to have the wherewithal to do it. I thought I could do it on my own and all that I lacked was sufficient willpower with the result that each time I began drinking again I felt like an utter failure. When I'd start again, I'd make myself promises: 'I won't drink before 7 pm' or 'I'll drink just Guinness' or 'I'll be careful not to get into trouble this time,' but I never kept them and I'd find myself back in the same bad place again. In moments of honesty, I knew the life I'd signed up to would kill me if I didn't slow down. So I'd stop and smoke a little dope for a while.

38

In 1981 I was commissioned to write the music for Neil Jordan's first feature film, *Angel*. It's about a showband sax player who witnesses an act of violence and goes off the rails. The first thing I was asked to do was to work with Stephen Rea to help him take on the role of a sax player. He had already been sent to sax lessons in London. I asked him to play for me in his room in Buswell's Hotel and he tried.

'Stephen, the first time you make that sound on a film set all your credibility is gone. Why don't we aim to make you the best mimer in the world?'

'You don't know how relieved that makes me feel,' he said in his lovely Belfast accent, grinning.

We spent ten sessions in his room in Buswells devising and practising a miming system for Stephen's hands and breathing. When I was recording the music in Windmill Lane, I asked Neil if Stephen's hands would be in shot before I recorded each piece of music. If not, I could play freely; if they were going to be in shot, I restricted the music to the miming system that Stephen had learned. Stephen came to a few Moving Hearts gigs to watch his mime teacher playing and I went to all the location filming and gave Stephen miming reminders. When all the filming was complete, I went to Ardmore Film Studios to compose the backing track to film and took the opportunity to repair some small pieces of music that didn't fit Stephen's hands. Neil Jordan had been a sax player in jazz-rock bands in his youth and he understood and facilitated the desire that

Stephen and I had that his miming should be note perfect. And it is, one hundred per cent.

When we were taking a break one day, Neil asked me if I knew where he'd got the inspiration for the script. When I said no, he said, 'It was a couple of years back. Some friends brought me to a jazz gig and there was this tenor sax player. When he wasn't blowing manic modern jazz solos on stage, he was at the bar drinking doubles. It occurred to me that he was like a man possessed, maybe a man that had a dark secret. Can you guess who the sax player was?'

'I've no idea.'

'You.'

So it seems that Stephen Rea became an aspect of me through his brilliant acting and then I became a version of him through spontaneously composed music.

I went to the H Block rally in the Mansion House on 22 May with Betty. The atmosphere was tense and angry. Bobby Sands had died on 5 May, other hunger strikers were approaching what seemed to be their inevitable death and many decent Irish people blamed the intransigence of Thatcher's government. All year long it felt like Ireland was on the very edge of disaster.

Being full-time with Moving Hearts meant I had to turn down almost all pit work. I did manage to record with Jolyon Jackson, Freddie White, Metropolis, Shaun Davey and others. I played 110 gigs with Moving Hearts in venues like the Baggot Inn, the Meeting Place, the Embankment in Tallaght, Theatre L in UCD, Carlow, Kilkenny and on *The Late Late Show*. I also played jazz with Louis Stewart, Noel Kelehan and Metropolis, and rock with Full Circle.

1981: 1 daughter, 1 girlfriend, weeks of rehearsal, 130 gigs, 23 recording sessions.

39

Despite having worked ninety-hour weeks, paid my taxes and saved hard to buy my little cottage, the blunt instrument that was the Marriage Home Protection Act meant that Marian owned half of it from the day we got married. Blunt instrument? Of course: if one spouse buys the home, the other spouse's ownership should increase on a sliding scale, not go to fifty per cent on day one. I had to obey the law so, in 1982, thanks to an amateur musician friend who was also a banker, I was able to borrow a large amount of money from a small bank and give Marian half the value of the cottage. Having already borrowed from the EBS to do up the place for Marian to move into when we got married, I now effectively had three mortgages and a level of financial anxiety that drove me to work harder and harder. As well as being full-time with Moving Hearts, I also played recording sessions with the Virgin Prunes, Auto da Fe with Philip Lynott producing, John Keogh, Eamon Gibney and others.

I wrote and recorded the music for Brian Friel's farce *Communication Cord*. Temporarily I became a member of the Field Day Theatre Company. And very proud to be so. It was my first experience of writing for theatre and I wanted to get it right so I read and re-read the script many times to get inside it. I also rang Brian Friel in Donegal and checked in with him often. He kindly held my hand, guiding me through what he envisioned for the music. Maybe all those years playing in pit orchestras for pantomimes and for *Annie*, *West Side Story*, Gypsy and *Cabaret* helped my subconscious too.

When Christy told us that he was going to go solo and would be leaving in September 1982, we had a band meeting to discuss what to do. Initially I was devastated and knew I was going to miss him as a friend, a singer and a guiding force within the band. We thought we should make another record and do one final tour with Christy. In May Moving Hearts went to Ridge Farm Studios in Surrey to record a second album, *Dark End of the Street*. We had to break off from recording twice to drive to Ireland and play festivals. It was a messy way to record but we needed the money. While the rhythm tracks were being laid down, I headed up to London and spent a morning in a tiny room in Bill Lewington's shop at Cambridge Circus with a selection of curved soprano saxes. Heaven! I finally settled for a Yanigisawa. While the little Lafleur sax that my father had rescued from his old band had enabled us to discover the new sound of curved soprano sax and uilleann pipes in unison, for me it was like driving a 1920s Bentley: you knew it had been great in its day but it wasn't equipped for modern traffic. The Yanigisawa's ergonomics made it like driving a modern Ferrari.

We divided out responsibility for sorting out the last tour with Christy and then broke for a month's holidays in July. At least, some of us did: Christy and Donal toured the UK with Planxty. I rang everyone to check what progress they had made regarding dates for the tour and found that nobody had done anything. What co-op? I cut my holidays to one week and spent the other three weeks on the phone, talking with every venue owner, promoter and contact I could think of. The final tour with Christy that resulted from my work made enough money to pay him what he had lent the band, pay everyone's wages and get the banks up to date. Christy generously gave back some of what we had paid him and we then had enough to rehearse with our new singer, Mick Hanly, for a few weeks. My utter panic and everyone else's irresponsibility had turned me into a band manager, working pro bono. This is the exact point at which all the idealism of the co-operative took flight, never to return.

That July Planxty had hired our personnel bus for their UK tour and had crossed the Irish Sea twice for Irish festivals during their tour. When we got the bus back, Peter Clarke, our driver, cleaned it out and found my old briefcase under the rear seats. When Peter and I opened it there was a small bundle of banknotes and a bag of grass in it. It appeared that I had nearly ended Planxty's UK career and given them police records. Oops!

When people ask me about drugs, my standard reply is, 'Well, we were young and it was the eighties.' If pushed, I'll then say, 'I have seen a mirror in a hotel room with *happy birthday keith* written in coke. All lower case of course, never capitals.'

I can't talk about anyone else except to say that the twenty-six musicians and umpteen technicians that have been Moving Hearts at one time or another include cigarette smokers, dope-smokers, speed-freaks, cocaine-sniffers and alcohol-abusers as well as those who did none of the above. I was at the end of the spectrum that did them all.

I was recording once in London as a session musician with a band that used so much coke there were ashtrays of it lying around. On the second day, fuelled by coffee, coke, little sleep and no breakfast, I was making a mess of a sax riff. Trying it over and over, on my own in a glass-enclosed iso-booth, I couldn't seem to get the damn music under my fingers and I made a different mistake on every take. After loads of fruitless attempts, I did something that I had never done before, unstrapping the sax and flinging it to the floor. My beloved Conn alto that my mother and I had jointly bought when I was sixteen. I began to choke up with tears and walked out of the iso-booth, out of the performance area, out of the studio and into a corridor where the French record producer caught up with me and said, 'It's the coke, Keith. Take the rest of the morning off. Go for a walk, have a drink, eat, whatever you need. Come back when you're calm.' I did all of those things, ending up in a pub where I thought about my treatment of the poor sax, coming to the conclusion that coke is insidious, creeps up on you and drains you of appropriate emotions when you're not looking. I decided to give it a miss from then on and mostly adhered to that.

There was one other drug I tried once. Four of us went to Cork to do an awareness-raising gig about Nicky Kelly's wrongful imprisonment in

Portlaoise Prison for the Sallins train robbery, a crime he didn't commit. We were to be joined by two Cork musicians. The gig was late at night in a theatre and ten minutes before we were due on stage somebody came into the band room with a recently boiled kettle, a bottle of Jameson and a big jar that contained honey impregnated with magic mushrooms. While we were discussing what repertoire we had in common to fill an hour, he made the most delicious punch. I remember walking on stage, nothing more. The following day I was walking along MacCurtain Street when I bumped into someone who had been at the gig.

'That was the funniest gig I've ever been to,' he said.

'Actually it's all a bit hazy to me,' I said, 'fancy a drink?'

When we were sitting down, he continued:

'I was with my girlfriend and we couldn't understand when you all came trooping on stage and in amongst your instruments you had a kettle.'

'I know what that was for. Go on.'

'You played great for about half an hour and then you formed a circle beside the drums.'

'Did we say anything to the audience?'

'Not a word. The kettle was plugged in and some of you were down on the floor behind an amp. Then steam came up behind the amp. It was surreal and there was a fair bit of muttering in the audience. Then you started again.'

'Was that it?'

'Are you kidding me? That was just the start of it. It got so that you were having little huddles every few songs. You were all making announcements, speeches more like, rabbiting on about Nicky Kelly at first but then anything that crossed your mind.'

'Like what?'

'The government. A big long rambling chat about how wonderful Cork is. The Metropole Hotel and how nice they all are there. The whole thing went on for over two hours. For about the last hour, the music was just about OK, the announcements were mad and the audience were in hysterics. Finally some theatre manager guy came on stage and apologized.

He said he hadn't been able to get you to stop. Then somebody in the crowd shouted back, "Don't be saying sorry – I wouldn't have missed it for the world," and everybody applauded in agreement.'

That total blackout took magic mushrooms off my list of possible future escapes.

I tried speed once and found it affected me like two dozen cups of coffee. Yes, I was alert. Yes, I could keep going. No, I couldn't sleep at all and the comedown was awful, so never again. Dope and drink were different. I had a rule that I didn't drink before a gig and I did stick to that. I couldn't smoke before a gig because I became too easy-going: no edge, no fire, no passion in the playing. One of the crew, a lovely guy called Cid Isaacson was responsible, amongst other things, for supplying our on-stage drinks. Most of the band needed water on stage. I had an arrangement with Cid that he would put vodka and tonic in an innocent-looking litre water bottle. Once I asked him, 'How much do I get through on stage?'

'I buy a bottle of vodka before every gig and mostly there's some left. Once or twice I've had to go and get more,' he said.

That's up to and sometimes over a bottle of spirits, which equals twenty vodkas in less than two hours. And after gigs I'd go drinking, several nights a week. I drank vodka like people drink water – it's a wonder I'm alive. It's possible that the only thing that protected me was giving everything up for months at a time, from the time of Eddie's death in 1978. I used to call it 'sending my liver and lungs on holiday' but I never knew when the holidays would end.

40

In 1983 and 84 an Italian promoter brought us to Milan, Turin, Bologna, Rome and Naples a few times. We were voted third-best live act after the Police and Ricki Lee Jones in an Italian music journal and got to play festivals and some larger concert halls. Once we played a sold-out gig in Turin and the promoter brought us to an expensive restaurant afterwards. I was at a low point in my addiction so I said no to food, sat on my own at the bar reading a book and drinking neat vodka. The first vodka arrived in a gorgeous little frosted shot glass. When I finished it, I stowed the glass in my sax case.

Fast forward two hours: I've had many, many neat vodkas, when the restaurant owner sidles up beside me: 'Meester Moving Art, I know you like our glasses, because you now have all twenty. You keep one, but I need the rest.' And I had to give him nineteen gorgeous glasses.

The following morning I woke up in my hotel room with no memory of getting there. I checked everything: yes, all the band's money was intact; yes, my soprano sax was present; no, there was nobody else in my bed. I needed a drink and lurched across the room to investigate the minibar. The first bottle I saw was champagne and I remembered that I had a six-pack of Guinness in my suitcase. Ah-ha! Black Velvet for breakfast. That'll fix me. After a couple of glasses I was feeling no pain and thought I'd risk opening the shutters in my room. You always know you have a bad hangover when you'd prefer surgery to sunlight. When my eyes got used to the Italian brightness, I saw that my room looked down on a courtyard three floors below. There were buildings all around, quite close and I wondered what the acoustics would be like. So it's eleven in the morning and I'm playing the soprano sax out my window. The sound bouncing off the other buildings was wonderful. Even more wonderful was the audience that gathered on the other balconies within minutes: beautiful Italian women clapping and shouting requests. 'Volare'? You want 'Volare'. No problem, I'd give you more than 'Volare' if I could.

Some of the crew used to slag my drinking. Fair enough but I wished they would also give me credit for doing all the business side of the tour without misplacing a single lira, never missing so much as one demisemiquaver of complex music and doing most of the driving in the personnel car without incident. Sure I was a lush most nights but I never let anyone down until after show time. Including myself.

One night we finished a packed gig in the Astoria, Bundoran, County Donegal and were in the band room beside the stage changing out of sweat-soaked clothes when the promoter dashed in, ashen-faced.

'You never played the national anthem,' he said.

'We've never played any anthem, anywhere.'

'Well you better start now because nobody's going home until you do.'

Somebody looked out into the hall and reported back: 'He's right. There's over a thousand still out there. In angry little knots. We'd better play it.'

'We can't,' said Cid, 'the gear's down. Most of it's in the truck already.'

'I have my sax here,' I said.

'I could play a snare drum,' said Noel Eccles.

The two of us walked out on the bare stage, waited for silence and solemnly played the Irish national anthem. The crowd stood rigidly to attention and headed for home. Probably the only time two Belfast Protestants silenced a thousand angry nationalists and republicans with a sax and snare.

There were no cheap flights then and there were up to fourteen of us, band and crew, so we drove everywhere in Europe. We would set off from Dublin, play a few gigs in the UK, then Italy, Austria, Brittany, the UK again and home. It was also before mobile phones, the internet, emails and the common currency of the euro so managing the band while on the road was an almost impossible challenge for me. Sometimes we'd have to stop for ages in a services area beside a foreign motorway so that I could get the right change in the right currency, find a phone box and make calls to hotels, agents, venues, publicists and record companies in several countries. Where were my bandmates? What co-op?

I loved the couple of hours on stage as they were my escape from logistics.

We were booked to play a gig in North Wales that was to be televised live on Welsh TV. The day went well. Our picturesque, small hotel was within walking distance of the venue and that's always good. The afternoon soundcheck and two hours of camera rehearsals went smoothly. And then the gig.

As we gathered at a door that opened onto the side of the stage, the stage manager was bellowing into his walkie-talkie in rapid Welsh. It sounded like he was cursing a lot and mentioning 'smoke machine' a lot. In fact it sounded like a steady stream of curses interrupted by 'smoke machine'.

'What's happening?' asked Davy.

'Fucking smoke machine's gone berserk,' he said.

'How berserk?'

'Very fuckin' berserk. Look you, we can't hold back the broadcast. You'll just have to go on and make the best of it. Probably best if you go on now.'

'When do you start broadcasting?' asked Donal.

'Exactly two minutes' time.'

'Won't that sort of an entrance take away from the audience reaction?' I asked.

'What do you mean?'

'If we go on now, we'll get their applause and then have to stand around like spare pricks waiting for a signal from you to start playing.'

'The audience won't be able to see you.'

‘What? How much smoke are we talking about?’ asked Eoghan.

‘A lot. You’d better go on,’ he said, opening the door to reveal … nothing.

‘Holy fuck,’ said someone near the front, ‘this is wild.’

We trooped through the door in silence. We could hear that there was an audience but we couldn’t see them and presumably they didn’t know we’d taken the stage.

‘Ah fuck,’ yelled someone nearby.

The audience began to giggle.

‘What’s wrong?’ I asked.

‘I stubbed my fucking toe.’

‘Lads,’ said Donal with urgency, ‘start “McBrides”. We’re live now.’

‘I haven’t found the friggin’ drum kit yet.’

‘Is anyone able to start? This is going out all over Wales.’

‘Don’t worry. They won’t know it’s us.’

‘Very funny. Somebody play.’

The audience sounded as if they were in hysterics. Maybe the whole Welsh nation was. Or perhaps they thought they’d tuned in to some avant-garde comedy programme. After some more minutes of Q&A and curses, we got going. We needn’t have bothered with camera rehearsals in the afternoon because the fog didn’t even begin to disperse until we had finished ‘McBrides’ and ‘The Category’. I imagined people for hundreds of miles adjusting their TV sets fruitlessly. Normal service resumed about fifteen minutes into the gig.

In 1983 we were booked to play in Paris with Rory Gallagher before heading to the UK and a tour of the Dingwalls circuit of venues all across Britain. The day before we were due to take the ferry to France, Dingwalls went bust and all the venues closed their doors. We decided to go to Paris anyway and duly played to 5,000 Gallagher fans who gave us a good reception. Rory and band played for nearly three hours, an unbelievably strong set that had the French audience with them from the start. Rory had that ability to transform himself the second he hit a stage: backstage, he was quiet and unassuming but became almost feral the moment he hit the stage, striding back and forth, guitar solo peaking, excitement personified. After his gig, I waited a while before going to Rory's dressing room to chat and collect our fee. 'There's a bit extra there,' said Donal Gallagher, 'we heard about Dingwalls.' I counted the money later and discovered that Rory and his brother Donal had doubled the agreed fee. What extraordinary decency!

In May 83 we flew to New York for our first gig there, a concert in the Savoy Theatre promoted by Una Johnson and Phelim Lunny. We stayed in the Iroquois Hotel, right beside the Algonquin – I had to go in there and see where Dorothy Parker and her pals used to hang out. We had a busy week of radio and press interviews. I had meetings with our record company execs as well.

The second night we were there Una introduced me to Maggie Smith in her bar, Tin Pan Alley on West 49th Street, opposite the side of the famous Brill Building where Carole King, Gerry Goffin, Neil Diamond and dozens of others composed the charts for a decade. Maggie and I began talking before midnight and were still talking when the sun rose. By then we were sitting on a pier beside the Hudson river. She took me to breakfast in her favourite diner and we began a year-long relationship.

We had a great gig that got several standing ovations and a brilliant review in the New York Times. U2's manager, Paul McGuinness came into the dressing room after the gig, hung out for a while and made us a present of a bottle of Bushmills. I was the last to leave the dressing room and the bottle was sitting unopened. I took it with me and, as I was leaving the theatre, I heard voices in the orchestra pit. I found my way there and got a great welcome from the Savoy crew so I shared the bottle with them. When I was finally leaving an hour later, one of the crew said, 'Hey buddy, you shouldn't be walking the streets at this hour with your instrument case. Where are you heading?'

'West 49th.'

'I'll walk you.'

As we walked and talked I heard a busker playing 'St Thomas' on flute, a great tune by Sonny Rollins.

So I said to the busker, 'Do you mind if I join in? You keep the money. I just want to play.'

So we played and were soon joined by an old Black tap-dancer. We got quite a crowd and played for half an hour. The flute player was well pleased and gave some dollars to the tap-dancer. Little did the crowd know that my sax case was sitting open and had all Moving Hearts' money from the Savoy gig tucked away in it, thousands of dollars. Then the Savoy crew man walked the tap dancer and me to Maggie's bar, Tin Pan Alley and stayed for a drink.

'Your newfound friend is a homeless person,' said Maggie, nodding towards the tap dancer.

'Are you sure?'

'Absolutely. Tell him we'll get him a place for tonight.'

I did and at 4 am, Maggie locked up and we booked the tap-dancer into a small hotel, which Maggie paid for.

And the band played on. And on and on. We had to keep playing because our overheads were colossal and our record company had no sway with its sister companies abroad. I had spent much time with the Dublin CEO Clive Hudson, and had gone with him to Hamburg to meet the boss of WEA for Europe. I'd visited their offices in Toronto and New York several times but kept hearing the same explanation for their refusal to back us: 'We don't know where you fit. You're not folk like the Dubliners, you're not a rock band like U2, you're not trad like the Chieftains but you've got elements of all those different aspects of Irish music in your band. So what box do we put you into in the record shops? Besides, you're too political.'

So nobody bothered, nobody took the chance. Here's an example of how much of an opportunity was missed: we turned up one sunny afternoon to set up for an open-air gig in Milan, during an Italian tour. Around a hundred teenagers were waiting for us with autograph books and posters from previous gigs to be signed. We noticed some technicians busying themselves during our soundcheck and assumed they were connected with the promoter. The gig was good and we had to come back on stage several times for standing ovations and encores. Afterwards it felt like the entire Italian press had turned up to plead for interviews and photos. When we finally made it into the dressing room, the local WEA man introduced himself to me. After compliments about the gig and our music, he assured me that Clive had indeed been in touch and all was well. I asked how our new record was selling and he told me, 'I think it get on sale in shops here in a month or so.' I was raging inside but had to keep it to myself, knowing that people who had just enjoyed our gig would be trying to buy our records immediately, not in a couple of months. Even worse is that an Italian friend of mine, Serena Ferrari, was in Milan in 1990, seven years after the concert, and was able to buy a bootleg of our gig in a record shop. She mailed it to me: the recording quality was as appalling as the record company's efficiency.

So we weren't selling records but we owed money for the PA and the trucks to a bank, Lombard and Ulster Finance, and Allied Irish Finance. They had to be paid every month, come rain or come shine, come work or come holidays, come recording or come writing, come festivals or come January.

Band members complained about the constant gigging and I didn't blame them. Behind the scenes I tried to wangle money from WEA. I rang the banks and explained why they'd get their money late or next month. I put a spin on our prospects and kept them from taking us to court and I had great support and advice from our accountant, Pearse Farrell, and our lawyer, Carroll O'Dalaigh.

Donal Lunny wrote in my diary: *Dance, dance, dance – Moving Hearts World Tour 1983. Three nights only – Paris, New York and the Baggot. "We'll lose money, but never lose touch."*

Was his noirish humour suggesting that our musical accomplishments, our art if you like, had to find a way of continuing while losing money? How could it?

Then Christy's replacement, Mick Hanly, said he would have to leave for family reasons. Mick is a lovely man and his reasons were utterly genuine but it was a blow. The task of finding a new vocalist was assigned to Donal and Eoghan O'Neill. While they were doing that, I went on another round of meetings with finance houses, the bank and our advisers. I was getting exhausted by this and I'm sure all the men in suits were equally fed up with me but I had to try because I still believed Moving Hearts had something unique and special and I couldn't do otherwise.

Van Morrison rang me in 1983. I'd met him often, in Belfast and in London when our paths crossed on the road. He liked Moving Hearts' music and wondered if we would be interested in trying to work together. I asked my bandmates. They were up for it and I rang Van back to say yes. He asked me over to London for a chat and we met in his house in Holland Park. I'd always got on well with him, maybe because we are the same age and lived near each other in Belfast. This time was no different and, after talking about a possible collaboration, we headed out for the evening, taking in a private party and Ronnie Scott's. A couple of months later he flew to Dublin and we played together for a day. He seemed to gravitate towards Davy Spillane and me and we looked after him for the evening, warding off drunks, intervening when people's pestering got too much, having the craic. He and Davy stayed in my cottage up the hills that night, Van heading to bed with a book on Plato's philosophy that he borrowed from my bookshelves. The next day we rehearsed in the Baggot Inn.

We met up with him again in London in the middle of a UK tour and spent two days recording with him in Odyssey Studios. Of course, it being the music business, I didn't see him again for ages.

For the almost four years that Moving Hearts was a full-time band, I had no time to think, to write music or to practise my instruments. I hadn't asked to become the band's manager and was doing it by default – nobody else inside or outside the band wanted to take it on – so my life was governed by lists in my diary, of phone calls to make, letters to write, meetings to attend, banks to placate, recording sessions, interviews, gigs, tours and travel to organize. For 1983 I managed to organize 133 gigs including English and Welsh TV, New York, an Italian tour, Paris, the main stage at Glastonbury, the Ace in Brixton, the Trinity Ball, live recording at the Dominion Theatre in London, Brittany and the UK. Plus lots of rehearsals in Dublin and the two days recording in London with Van.

Throughout I went on and off the drink. Giving it up was increasingly difficult, a little bit tougher every time.

41

In January 1984 we played in Milan, Cassano, Turin, Bergamo, Rome, and Naples. We had a break down near Bologna but still made it to the gig, triumphantly entering the city sitting in a Peugeot 504 estate car that was perched atop a breakdown truck. We had to go to Vienna by train the next day.

The day after the Vienna gig, my diary records: *up at 8 am, leave Stuttgart at 9.20 am, drive Strasbourg, Reims, Calais and ferry, Dover, to London arr. 2.15 am*. Sure, we were only in it for the glamour.

That same year I was phoned by a company called Rock People's Movies. RPM made TV programmes for Channel 4 in London. They were making an interesting series that allowed bands to choose an issue and make a programme about it. We chose Nicky Kelly. It was commonly accepted that there was a 'heavy gang' within the police and that they took exception to left-wing political activity. Nicky Kelly and other peaceful activists had been framed for the robbery of a mail train at Sallins, County Kildare. After several planning meetings, the RPM crew arrived to film us. Band members interviewed various protagonists and I did the introduction to the programme leaning against the doorway of the Baggot Inn. I also got to interview Vincent Browne as well as the apolitical doctor who had examined Nicky in prison and concluded very definitely to camera that his injuries could not have been self-inflicted. We played a gig in the SFX to raise awareness and Special Branch cruised the street outside, harassing our fans. RPM filmed that too. A few weeks later RPM flew me to London to do the voice-over for the hour-long documentary. I made the mistake of spending the evening with a German actress I knew, Konni, and was still awake and drinking gin in her bed in Lewisham when the taxi arrived to take me to a little studio off Oxford Street. RPM's director Don Coutts told me later that I deserved some kind of special award for arriving drunk at 6 am, continuing to drink and pulling myself together before each segment, never stammering, never slurring. Channel 4 was available on the east coast of Ireland and, to my delight and pride, a TD raised the issue in Dail Eireann, complaining that a bunch of musicians dared comment on affairs of importance. Sure isn't that one of our roles? I thought.

We wished Mick Hanly well and Flo MacSweeney joined Moving Hearts as lead singer in early 1984. This particular band played on but not for long. We released a couple of singles and toured Ireland relentlessly. In the summer of 1984, we played the Montreux Jazz Festival and some gigs and festivals in Italy. Because of our numbers and the expense of flying we drove to Switzerland for Montreux, gigging in London en route. As usual, we stayed in the Irish Club in Eaton Square in London's Belgravia, which offered good deals to large parties. One morning one of the crew, Cid, needed to take a leak and when he had finished, turned round to see John Hume MEP slumbering in a bath.

No wonder, I thought, feeling empathy with the great man, sure hasn't he been on a tour of Brussels, London, Belfast and Derry for the last five years!

In Montreux we stayed in luxury in the Hotel Suisse overlooking Lake Geneva. We were part of a three-band show and were apprehensive as to how a jazz audience would take to us. The first band on stage was the All Stars, with Joe Henderson on tenor sax. The third band was Van Morrison with Richie Buckley on sax. I had introduced Richie and Van and was now quite envious of Richie, comparing his life with Van – great music, very well paid, no organizational responsibilities – to my life as a musician who had to manage the band while resenting every minute of it, bar the two hours on stage.

The tour was to end with concerts in the Bottom Line in New York, a festival in Quebec and the Lorient festival in Brittany. I had explained in advance that there was no easy way of playing Quebec on a Friday and Brittany on a Sunday: unless we spent huge money hiring a plane, we would have to suffer and, since the best paying gigs of the whole tour were these last two, it made economic sense for us to suffer a bit and travel the hard way between New York, Quebec and Brittany.

I had visited New York several times in 1983 and 84, to gig and to meet with our record company and promoters. It was also great to see Maggie Smith and spend time in her bar and hook up with her friends. I stayed in her apartment in midtown, gigged in the bar a couple of times and often drank there. The bar, called Tin Pan Alley was many things: neighbourhood bar for all those who worked in the porn industry in Times Square, and people from all the nearby shops and offices, performance space at weekends, gallery for new art from all the women artists who worked behind the bar, including photographer Nan Goldin, and Kiki Smith and Cara Perlman the acclaimed artists, and meeting place for the likes of Wim Wenders and Joe Strummer. Maggie wouldn't allow me to pay for drinks – 'Make sure you tip well, that's all, honey' – and I had to ask her how much I was drinking. 'Bottle a day, minimum,' came the answer, 'but you're never drunk. In fact, most of the time, I don't know whether you're on your first or your twenty-first drink.'

It was Maggie that encouraged me to play solo gigs. After I'd played a small jazz gig one night in 1983, she brought me to a late-night cabaret in an old cinema. Of course I'd had a few drinks after the jazz and was up for anything. Maggie squared it with the cabaret producer, Houie Montaug, and I found myself on stage. I told the audience about Nicky Kelly and his innocence and his current hunger strike. Then I played a slow 'Blues for Nicky', composing while playing, passionate, living on the edge. I didn't realize I was being filmed and was surprised when someone saw the footage and asked me to play a solo gig whenever I was back in New York. So that July I rehearsed by walking New York streets talking to myself, trying to get it right. The gig was on the roof of the famous nightclub called Danceteria, seven floors up. It was a hot and humid night and the atmosphere on the roof was pure New York with skyscrapers all around, a small stage, sound and lighting rigs and a bar in one corner. There were 300 hip young fans digging the act before me, a solo dancer, part-ballet, part-jazz and her colleague, a follow-spot operator who seemed to know her every move. She finished off with a high leap near the parapet and her colleague timed the darkness so well it was as if she had sailed off the edge. A hard act to follow.

Some minutes later, close to midnight, I took the stage and told the audience about the Twelfth of July celebrations in Belfast, describing the history, background, the marchers, the banners and the Field before playing and singing 'The Sash'. I finished off with an avant garde version of 'The Sash' on soprano sax that was distorted, raucous and rough but still recognizable. My last words, 'It's as if a quarter of a million Ku Klux Klan were to march through Harlem in praise of slavery' got sustained applause. I left the stage and went for my first drink of the evening with Maggie, Phelim Lunny and Una Johnson at the bar on the roof. There I was accosted by two guys in their twenties with Belfast accents and great distaste for my act. They got heavier and more threatening and we all thought I was likely to get thrown over the edge until Maggie said, 'Time to go, Keith. Come on now or we'll be late' and we all scurried off.

We played two sets in the Bottom Line. My old pal Bill Whelan, who went on to compose *Riverdance*, was living in New York that summer with his wife, Denise. They came to the first show and we chatted in the street outside between shows. The day after the Bottom Line gigs we were driven from New York to Canada by a New York hippie who chain-smoked joints and stopped fifty yards from the border to empty all the ashtrays out the driver's window. Of course the border guards saw this and were waiting for us. Before our driver stopped the engine, we were hustled out and lined up against a wall while a team of guards went through every piece of luggage, leafing through diaries, squeezing toothpaste tubes, feeling the lining of jackets until the chief guard said, 'We have a dog. Before the dog is brought to sniff you, I want to warn you that if any of you is carrying any weapons, drugs or ammunition, the dog will find it and I cannot be responsible for how the dog will react.'

'I have a bag of grass in my underpants,' said the driver.

As he was hustled away, a dog-handler was towed into view by the biggest Alsatian we ever saw. Definitely some Irish wolfhound in its DNA. After two hours and nothing found because there was nothing to find, we were allowed to go, soon passing a sign that said *Bienvenue au Canade. Welcome to Canada.*

The Quebec gigs were set in a natural amphitheatre where we played on a floating stage on a lake to a huge audience looking down at us from grassy slopes. We had two great gigs there at a festival that purported to celebrate 450 years of Canada but in reality was marking the discovery of Canada by a Frenchman who kidnapped two of the locals and brought them back to France to prove he'd been somewhere. Quebec is a beautiful city and I got plenty of time to walk around, seeing the old town and the island in the St Lawrence where any Irish that had survived the forced emigration of the Famine were processed.

After the second Quebec concert, we were driven to a hotel in Montreal where we stayed for four hours before getting on an Amtrak train that trundled slowly all day Saturday to New York where we were driven to JFK and a Virgin Atlantic flight to Heathrow where we stayed in a bare transit lounge for a few hours until we got on a tiny plane to Brittany in time for the soundcheck on Sunday afternoon. We travelled for forty hours and spent four in a bed. The gig was good as we all knew it was the last of the tour. It was also strange as it felt like there was a disconnect between us, as if each of us was enclosed within a wall of plate glass. After we played, I asked someone backstage where I'd find something interesting to smoke and was directed to a young woman who was a lighting engineer. As she worked, I sat at her feet rolling joints, smoking and passing them up to her. She was great fun and we parted at breakfast.

Back in New York for a few days, Maggie and I spent some time in galleries and at gigs in places like CBGB's. We called into Cara Perlman's studio on Ludlow Street where she was working on a series called 'Fingerprint Portraits' to be published in a book with Keith Haring's work. Maggie also brought me to political events and educated me regarding women's issues in the USA and the situation in Central America, particularly Guatemala. Her friends asked if we would come to a 'Goodbye Keith' evening in somebody's apartment. I commissioned a dress for Maggie from her artist friend Kiki Smith and presented her with it. Kiki Smith gave me a painting and Nan Goldin showed us her new series about human sexuality in all its forms with slides and a projector. I could easily have lived in New York and become a small part of an incredibly vibrant scene but I never considered it because of love for Alex, a vulnerable little person with whom I had an unbreakable bond.

Back home we played some freebies, mostly awareness-raising gigs like the Anti-Criminal Justice Bill concert, the Anti-Reagan in Nicaragua gig with Christy and Philip King guesting, and a Campaign for Nuclear Disarmament gig in St Anne's Park.

After some more gigs in Ireland, we had a band meeting in the Queens Hotel in Ennis and reluctantly decided to call it quits as nobody was enjoying the endless gigging and the constant travel any more. How did I feel? Confused, angry and exhausted: no matter how hard I worked, something had been wrong from the outset and no amount of work could put it right. I had no personal plan and suddenly had plenty of time to think, coming to the conclusion that Moving Hearts had a structural fault: while Christy was a natural and gifted leader who had an innate ability to bring others with him, without him the band became an unstructured co-op committee with too many decision-makers and not enough executive to follow through. In effect I had let myself become the civil service for a rowdy parliament.

The break-up left two outstanding issues: a mountain of debts and an unfulfilled record contract. We owed money and wages to a host of suppliers and people who had worked for us. On the plus side, we did own two large trucks and the best PA system in Ireland. With great assistance and support from Matt Kelleghan, we moved the PA into my cottage where it filled an entire room, and began meeting potential buyers. While everyone else got on with their lives, Matt and I began a process of negotiation with the three lenders and the people we owed money to. First, being the decent people we are, we paid all the individuals and small companies what they were owed. This took months and many meetings at the end of which we'd sold the trucks and the PA and the only debt remaining was to the bank. We had run out of things to sell and could promise them only our royalties. So we met with a senior manager every couple of months, sometimes with a royalty cheque, more often with nothing more than a smile and a promise.

The other issue was that we owed an album to Tara Records who had been very supportive when we were in the musical doldrums. We hired Andrew Boland and the Eyrie mobile studio and cleared the cobwebs, dust and furniture from a couple of rooms in Ringsend. With the recording truck parked on the pavement outside, we worked for three weeks and recorded an album of instrumentals, which was released as *The Storm*, a tribute to Christy whose nickname was 'Storm in a T-shirt'.

That was the end of Moving Hearts as a full-time professional band. In that last half year, we played 55 gigs in Ireland, 21 in the UK, 6 in Italy, 1 in Switzerland, 1 in Austria, 3 in France, 3 in the USA and 2 in Canada. In addition, I played 10 jazz gigs and 6 in the Gaiety panto. 108 gigs in 8 countries plus a score of recording sessions and I was broke, demoralized and exhausted.

42

Back in 1981 Alex's mother had written an impassioned letter to me outlining the reasons why Alex should move to County Cavan and live with her and her partner, the fine musician Terry Woods. Five-year-old Alex and I talked about it. It was hard on both of us and unfair to Alex to expect her to be part of such life-shaping decisions. She was then and still is a brave person and the upshot of our discussions was that she said she would give it a try. On the morning of the day that I drove her to her new home, I asked her if she'd like to bring one of our cats with her and she duly chose the most affectionate, stunning black one. We drove the 62 miles mostly in silence, with heavy hearts. When I left her at Marian and Terry's picturesque cottage beside a lake in Cavan, Alex took my hand and walked me to the car to say goodbye. As I drove uphill on the deserted country road and looked in the rear-view mirror, I could see her little arm waving and waving until we couldn't see each other. Blinded with tears, I had to pull the car off the road. It was ages before I was able to drive. I hadn't realized that being parted from her would affect me so much.

The journey back to Dublin took time because I had to stop more than once. But in the ensuing days, I came to a big realization: I had for as long as I could remember felt that there was some emotional gap at the core of me, frequently comparing myself to one of those Henry Moore sculptures of a fluid human form with a hollow centre. I thought that I couldn't sustain a relationship and maybe would never find within me a real capacity to love someone. I knew that it was in some way related to my experiences at the hands of Miss Hucker and suspected it might have something to do with an inability to trust people. Now this torrent of tears proved something to me: I could love someone and it was a complete and unconditional love, for here was a little somebody for whom I would die. No debate, no conditions. In the midst of missing Alex, I found something in me that I had given up hope of ever finding.

Two months later I was at home when one of my neighbours tapped the kitchen window and said, 'There's a cat been run over down the road. Sorry but I think it's one of yours.'

I walked down the hill and there was the half-Persian that Alex had taken with her to Cavan. Very recognizable and very dead. I brought it back home and rang Cavan. Yes, the cat had gone missing three days previously. As I dug its grave I thought, There's something tragic about this. The cat managed the 62 miles and successfully found her way through Dublin only to die a hundred yards from home. What a tragic little feline odyssey. It evidently didn't like Cavan. I hope Alex is getting on better. Paranoia kicked in.

I made regular visits to Alex in Cavan while I was in Moving Hearts and she came to stay with me in Dublin whenever I had a break. She also stayed with her maternal grandparents quite often, finally moving to Dublin to live with them in 1984. One of the benefits I derived from the band's demise was time, time for Alex, time for jazz, time to think. Time for drink too.

Towards the end of that year, Shay Healy asked me to take part in an RTÉ radio programme about the 1960s called *Strawberry Fields Forever*. We talked about my memories of jazz groups, university, showbands, hit records and car accidents in great detail. Like all great interviewers, Shay makes the process enjoyable and we had lots of smiles and easy conversation while the tape recorder preserved it for RTÉ. Then:

'Keith, one final question. What's the best time you had in a showband?'

It flashed across my mind that I had wasted nine years playing other people's music, up and down the same roads for half a million miles, in and out of hospital ...

'The best time? In a showband? Maybe the two minutes and ten seconds I was technically dead after the Real McCoy crash.'

We had to stop recording the programme for a long time because we were both incapacitated with laughter.

43

Did I mention I keep a diary and I've kept all my old diaries? I'm going to give you a series of snapshots from two years' worth of diaries to show you the variety and fun, but also the precarious nature of a freelancer's life.

1985 started badly: I played a jazz gig with Honor Heffernan on 25 January and was driving home sober when three medical students from Qatar drove through a stop sign on Rathgar Avenue and wrote off my car. For a split second I thought, Whiplash? Could stay here and act – might make a packet, but then I said aloud, 'No, just be thankful you're OK.' I got out of the car to see if they were alright. The insurance didn't give me enough to buy anything better than a second-hand bike so I was without a car.

Struggling to keep up with effectively three mortgages, I took every bit of work I was offered in 1985. Some of it was interesting like recording with Mary Coughlan for her first album, recording with Charlie McGettigan, De Danaan, Tommy Sands and others but most of it was routine like sixty-six shows in the Gaiety pit, commercial recording for jingles and working in sax sections on different projects. I recruited Donal Lunny and together we wrote the music for a Channel 4/RTÉ co-production, a film called *Summer Lightning* based on a Turgenev novel, *First Love*, rehearsing in Luke Kelly's house, recording in Nicky Ryan's studio.

Coming near Christmas, I headed down to Henry Street to stand outside Dunnes Stores with the Dunnes Stores strikers. I busked, they collected. I played a few festive tunes and, when I took a break, the strikers' union rep, Brendan Archbold, and I decided I wouldn't play 'I'm Dreaming of a White Christmas' again lest it be misinterpreted. I was amazed at how much money was given by generous, supportive Irish people who seemed to grasp the importance of the strikers' refusal to handle fruit that was the product of virtual slavery in the apartheid regime of South Africa. The only gainsayers were a few of the junior management of Dunnes Stores who seemed to think it was hilarious when they urinated from the windows over our heads. The strikers were always quick with umbrellas and they never let juvenile ignorance stop them.

Soon after that I was asked by the Irish multinational Smurfit's to organize two evenings of music, one in the Royal Hospital Kilmainham and one in Sneem, County Kerry, to entertain an international group of paper manufacturers. They had a considerable budget, hiring planes and multilingual tour guides. I booked Noel Kelehan, Mary Black, Declan Masterson, the Diceman, Louis Stewart, Nollaig Casey and others and paid them and myself well. Driving a hired Mercedes 190 back from Sneem, I had Noel, Nollaig and Mary fall asleep; Noel must have been sleeping very deeply because he suddenly yelled, 'Don't give me any more of your James Last!' Such are the nightmares of great musicians.

Alex and I went to London for ten days in May, the first of our many holidays on three continents. I used the Smurfit's wages to have fun with eight-year-old Alex, visiting Hamleys toy shop on Regent Street, Pollock's Toy Museum, the Planetarium and Madame Tussaud's, cruising on an open-top bus, walking the King's Road, Oxford Street and Soho and taking in a screening of the film Donal and I had worked on in the BAFTA screening rooms. Ten days when I was a very happy dad. Ten days when I could forget that Moving Hearts' bankers were putting weekly pressure on me, when I didn't have to worry about the three accursed mortgages, replacing the wrecked car or finding work. Bliss!

From the outside you'd have thought I was successful: in one week in May I put saxes on Mary Coughlan's first album and Charlie McGettigan's first album, and two films that I'd written music for were on Channel 4.

The reality was a hand-to-mouth struggle. A week in October was typical: Matt and I went for tough, confrontational meetings with Moving Hearts' lenders, two finance houses and a bank. I spent the afternoons with Alex, buying her a decent winter coat and bringing her to the Carnegie Library three times. I had meetings with two record companies, a promoter and a publicist for Moving Hearts. I gave four people sax or clarinet lessons, including Steve Norman from Spandau Ballet and Eleanor McEvoy. I took the train to Cork to play three jazz gigs. I know it sounds like I had a busy, rewarding career, but, like a lot of freelancers, I was only as good as my last gig. If I fucked up, word would go round and my subsistence life would be over. Freelance often equals waiting for the phone to ring.

On 30 December I flew to Iceland with the Johnny Logan Band for a week of gigs in Reykjavik as one half of a double bill with the Tremeloes. We got into our hotel at 9 pm and spent the first evening drinking with them – a great bunch of guys who had been together since the early 60s and since then had twenty-one singles in the UK charts. The following night I went up on the roof of the hotel with two Tremeloes and watched a twenty-minute, 360-degree firework display as the Icelanders welcomed the new year. It was as if every household in Reykjavik had spent a hundred dollars on fireworks. I never saw a display like it before or since. The first night we played, Miss World, Miss Iceland, the Mayoress of Reykjavik and the woman prime minister of Iceland were seated in front of the stage and Johnny sang to them for a while, the crowd loving it. Johnny Logan is an amazing performer and had the crowd of two thousand on his side immediately.

The club's management had explained to us when we arrived that we were allowed two free drinks each night we played. But there were eight bars in the huge club and pretty soon a couple of Tremeloes and a couple of us were moving from bar to bar. We got away with it for three nights until the management called us for a meeting and stopped us having sixteen free drinks each. One night I walked into a bedroom and took in a sight that was at once hilarious and revolting: a musician was naked and performing a handstand on his bed, against a wall. In amongst his bits and pubic hair he had a pair of glasses and a cigar and was shouting, 'Look lads, Groucho Marx!' And indeed it was.

We left Iceland on Sunday, 5 January 1986 and smoked the last of our dope huddled in a big circle in the airport concourse with assorted Logan Band, Tremeloes and new Icelandic friends saying farewell. We spent the night boozing in London and it was on the Aer Lingus flight the following morning that I got chatting to a stewardess who told me Philip Lynott had died. I burst into tears for the gentleman, friend and sometime colleague. RIP.

1986 started hectic. On 15 January, I played four gigs: a rehearsal in the Peacock Theatre from 10.30 until 2.30, a pit job in the Gaiety Theatre from 3 until 5.30, a gig in the Peacock Theatre from 8 until 10 and a late gig with Christy, Donal, Mary Black and Declan Sinnott in Liberty Hall to protest against Section 31, which had been enacted to prevent Sinn Fein spokespeople speaking on radio and TV. And I had plenty to drink that day.

In February Alex and I took the Enterprise train to Belfast where I recorded with Christy and Liam og O'Flynn, playing 'Ride On', 'Before the Deluge', 'Viva la Quinta Brigada', 'Back Home in Derry' and 'Raggle Taggle Gypsy' for television.

Moving Hearts had one of our rare post-break-up gigs in the Royal Festival Hall in London on St Patrick's Day. It took dozens of phone calls to organize people, trucking, ferries, a hotel, a BBC recording and cash for musicians and technicians. Not one person said thanks and I was resentful at the lack of reward and gratitude. After playing to a packed house in London, I got back next day in time to do a gig in a nightclub – no organization, no hours on the phone, no grief, no resentment, just music, fun and payment.

On Friday 16 May I rehearsed during the day with Moving Hearts and played the Trinity Ball in the evening with a jazz big band, drinking with the horn players afterwards. On Saturday 17th, Moving Hearts played an open-air gig called Self Aid in the RDS in Dublin that was filmed. I met some guys backstage, not musicians, not technicians, guys who had got backstage because of a desire to leave no turn unstoned. I broke a rule, sharing a few joints with them. I realized I had the confusion of stonedness at lunch time and thought I was fortunate when I bumped into a musician who said, 'Fancy a line?' We went on stage at 9.15 pm. Night was beginning to fall and we played at dusk with the moon and stars as backdrop. RTÉ's film crew captured the atmosphere perfectly. People told me afterwards that they loved that piece of film but I could watch it just once. Every note I played was slightly out, either infinitesimally ahead of the beat due to the coke, or infinitesimally behind it due to the dope.

Next day I did a recording session for a jingle in Windmill Lane in the afternoon and a gig in the Olympia at night and got drunk in the green room. Typical weekend of five very different music events, three drugs, a lot of self-loathing and not much job satisfaction.

Moving Hearts also went on a wild trip to Wales the weekend of 23–24 August. Handwritten instructions were posted to me that read *Blaenffos near Boncath, Dyffyd, Morfa (a farm), half hour from Fishguard, A487 towards Cardigan, A478 towards Tenby, 6 mile Blaenffos. On stage 9.30 pm*. I shrugged my shoulders, gave the piece of paper to a driver and let somebody else interpret it. We were to receive £2,500, a good fee in 1986. Here's the split: £250 to an Irish agent, £250 to a UK agent, £220 for two days' per diems, £90 for a rehearsal space in the Warehouse, £250 for a truck and driver for four days (we had sold ours), £80 to a lightsman, £40 for diesel. Every ten minutes somebody would come up to me and say, 'I need a fiver for a taxi' or 'Can I get a score in advance to leave for the missus before we head off?' or 'I have to get strings. Give us a tenner and we'll sort it out.' All of which had to be written down. When you total it, there's not a lot for a dozen or so very talented musicians and technicians. During the festival in Wales it rained torrentially and constantly, bringing the mud up to the level of the audience's knees. Small children had to be hoisted on to their parents' shoulders. We went on stage late and afterwards Donal Lunny,

Noel Eccles and I were driven at high speed to catch the Fishguard ferry at 3.15 am as we had to be in Dublin by lunchtime the next day. Everyone else stayed over and had an extremely rough crossing the next morning. That's when the weekend began to get wild because Hurricane Charlie reached Ireland at the same time as our colleagues. With trees blown down behind them and the road flooded in front of them, they eventually gave up somewhere near Wicklow town, opened their duty-free cigarettes and booze and had a twenty-four hour lockdown in the hired truck while the weather raged outside. While they were there, I did a recording session in the afternoon for a TV jingle and played in Gypsy in the Gaiety Theatre in the evening. When I finally headed home at midnight, a full day ahead of my stranded colleagues, I only just made it as the Owendore river near the cottage had burst its banks and flooded the road home.

When I was off drink, I was strict with myself and would stay teetotal for months at a time. Here's an example of when I was back on it: on the morning of Friday 19 September, I wrote an article for *Hot Press* magazine on wind instruments and delivered it. Then a liquid lunch before heading to RTÉ for the *Late Late Show* rehearsal at 4 pm. Then I hit Long's in Donnybrook at 7 pm for drinks and a sandwich. After the *Late Late* I got a taxi to the Speakeasy Club where I played from midnight until 3 am. On Saturday morning I was collected at 10 am by Kevin Ward and driven to Tallaght. Two double vodkas at 10.30 am before giving a talk on jazz to some music students. A few drinks at lunchtime before the matinee in the Gaiety Theatre. Then a few drinks before, during and after the evening show. Sunday, all day rehearsals of some new music with Moving Hearts for a recording session and some drinks every time we took a break. I could quietly drink more than anyone I knew. My secret badge of dishonour.

Rehearsals with Mary Coughlan started in autumn 1986 and soon we were on the road, touring Ireland, the UK and Germany, playing interesting venues like the Hammersmith Palais and Ronnie Scott's. Mary had recruited good players like Dave McHale, Robbie Brennan, John Kearns and Greg Boland. We were all sober on stage but afterwards depended on who among us was trying to stay sober and who had given up, and who walked into the dressing room and what drugs they brought. After one gig in London we were back in the hotel bar when a pleasant guy sitting beside me produced a ball of coke the size of a tennis ball. Nobody got much sleep that night.

I liked working with Mary: she has a lot in common with Christy – straight-talking, very talented, good fun and concerned about injustice. We were on stage in Ronnie Scott's once, playing to an audience of male Japanese businessmen who chattered loudly throughout. I was in the middle of a subtle sax solo when I heard Mary's delicious Galway accent bellowing at the businessmen over the speakers, 'Will ye for fuck's sake shut up?'

Good woman, Mary.

I think I was still getting away with the crazy drinking because I wasn't a troublemaker: early in my drinking life I had trained myself not to stagger or fall, and never to pick arguments or fights. So I didn't stand out in the drinking crowd. Plus, I had so many things going on in so many different places that no one person was aware of the totality of my drinking. I could have a few here, a few there, a quick one before, one at the interval, a couple after the show, and nobody was counting. Besides, the music business provides camouflage: in most bands and pit orchestras, and on tour, I could always find someone who drank way too much.

44

I turned forty-two in 1987. It was to be my last year as a professional musician for over a decade but I didn't know it at the beginning of the year as I played over fourteen gigs a week, twelve in the Gaiety Theatre pit orchestra, two jazz gigs on Sundays and whatever recording sessions came in.

During the year Moving Hearts played eleven gigs, in Ireland, the UK and Denmark. Mary Coughlan played gigs all over the UK, Germany and Ireland, so much so that I was beginning to recognize villages and buildings as we sped past them on the autobahns and motorways on our way to venues like the Palladium in London, the Quasimodo in Berlin and the Markethalle in Hamburg. At the soundcheck in the Palladium I played the theme from the old ITV show *Sunday Night at the London Palladium*. Nobody got it. That night I stuck it into a solo in the middle of one of Mary's songs and one old man applauded vigorously, puzzling his neighbours. He and I exchanged a knowing nod.

I also played folk with Mick Hanly, country rock with the Fleadh Cowboys, punk rock with the Radiators and in *West Side Story* again. Plus, I had eleven sax or clarinet students that I tried to see regularly.

In June a new word entered my vocabulary: Somafco, short for the Solomon Mahlangu Freedom College. I'd been spending time with my ex Sherry McLean's new man, Marius Schoon, a South African exile. Marius had grown up hating the apartheid system of repression that his fellow Boers inflicted on South Africans. He had been found guilty in his twenties of sabotaging some infrastructure and had served fourteen hard years in prison. Soon after his release he met and fell in love with Jeanette, a young activist with whom he had two children. But the authorities made them 'banned' people and they were not allowed to be in each other's company. So they moved abroad and continued their important, subversive work until the South African secret police sent them a letter bomb, which killed Jeanette and their daughter, Katryn. Marius took his two-year-old, Fritz, and fled Africa. Garrett FitzGerald's government was progressive enough to give them residence status in Ireland and Marius met Sherry at a party in John Mulcahy's house in Ranelagh.

Marius liked a drink and a laugh and we liked each other from the off. We were drinking together when he told me that Somafco, a college in Tanzania for hundreds of children whose parents were exiled or dead as a result of apartheid, had no musical instruments. If he was planting a seed, it fell on fertile ground for I thought I knew the value that music could have – therapy and a possible career – and resolved to do something.

In the summer the Arts Council advertised in the national newspapers for someone to fill a new post, Popular Music Officer, to be jointly funded by the music industry and the Arts Council. I wasn't interested until I was phoned by a significant industry figure.

'Have you by any chance applied for the post in the Arts Council?' he said.

'No. Why do you ask?'

'There's a new organization, the Popular Music Industry Association – it's all the record labels, recording studios, promoters, royalty collection, everyone is there – and some of them have been saying you would be ideal for the post.'

'Are you serious?'

'Absolutely. You know the industry. You have a good reputation with all the main players. You have a couple of degrees too – very acceptable to the Arts Council. You should apply.'

'OK, I will. Thanks.'

'No guarantees you'll get it! A lot of applications in already.'

The more I thought about it, the more interested I became. It would be a new challenge and might enable me to make a difference. On a personal level, I was fed up with the road, the motorway and the autobahn, and I wanted to spend more time in Dublin, especially with Alex. Plus, I might get a wee jazz band together. I applied just before the closing date, with referees from Trinity, UCD and Sister Anne Marie from Contact. I was asked to write a submission on the music industry and worked on it, drafting and re-drafting until Christmas. I was called for interview in early January.

On 17 December I went to Alex's school to see the kids perform *The Sound of Music*. She was the lead and I had a quality of nervousness that was new to me. Unlike a gig of my own where nerves would vanish once I got into it, I was nervous throughout her gig. But I needn't have worried as she was brilliant, cool and calm, making her dad walk tall with pride.

The year 1987 was my last as a fully professional musician until 1997. I played 207 gigs and sessions with great people like Moving Hearts, Mary Coughlan, Christy Moore, Mick Hanly and Don Baker. I'd given around 120 lessons and played a score of freebies for several good causes. I'd managed to spend a lot of time with Alex whenever I wasn't abroad and to take her on holiday twice, to Cushendall and to the Canary Islands.

I'd been off drink a number of times for a total of ten months but found it hard work and was always relieved as well as disappointed when I'd have a few days' binge. It was almost ten years since Eddie had died and I'd gone on the bender that scared me into my first attempt at sobriety. The voice in my head had said, 'Keep this up and you will end up in the gutter.' A decade later, the non-drinking days far outnumbered the binges. Progress? Yes, as regards amount consumed but no as regards my attitude, thinking and spirit.

Childhood is fascinating: two children can have an identical experience and react in very different ways. So the product of our little personality and our experience can influence the rest of our lives. That's what psychoanalysis is about: undoing our conditioning so that we can re-condition ourselves in a more positive, less painful way. If asked, I could describe the abuse I suffered in a matter-of-fact, emotionless way. So I did remember it. But I didn't want to remember it or spend time thinking about it because I was afraid of it, afraid of the emotional chasm that I might fall into. So the safest thing to do was drink like a madman. It was the behaviour of a madman that I clung to because it was preferable to the risks I'd have to take if I were to examine my childhood on my own.

Alcoholism is the only disease that tries to convince you that you haven't got it. I'll find a way of sorting myself out. Not today though. Sure I can quit whenever I want. Think I've a few more drinks in me yet. I'm not an alco – alcos are down-and-outs. I'm not like them!

When I was drinking, how much was I drinking? I had friends who owned a restaurant and kindly let me eat and drink at staff prices. On a day off when I couldn't see Alex, I'd go there at lunchtime and order a decent meal and a bottle of wine. I'd finish the *Irish Times* and a second bottle soon after 3 pm. By 4.30 I'd have finished a cryptic crossword while sipping a third bottle. Then I'd order another large meal and a fourth bottle. Before 7 pm I'd be drinking with intent in a pub, the theory being that the four bottles of wine didn't count and the two meals would somehow keep me healthy.

Never healthy, ever delusional.

When I was drinking, it was the self-medication of the truly desperate. I wanted to stop for good but didn't know how. I was scared to find out how. Often in the mid-to-late eighties I'd leave a gig feeling the warmth between audience and band and drive home to a freezing cold cottage, turn on the electric blanket and sit reading and sipping a half bottle of gin or vodka in the little galley kitchen in front of the open oven for warmth. Many times I looked up the Samaritans' helpline number and left the phone book open. I never rang them. I'll do that another time. Then I'd race through the house to get under the covers and hope that I had drunk enough to get to sleep without engaging my stupid brain. I was afraid to lie awake analysing my drinking because logic would say stop, stop now. I was afraid to stop permanently because I didn't have the emotional experience and strength to deal with a life without a drink, or the prospect of one. My emotional development had stopped somewhere in my mid-teens, arrested by alcohol. I was afraid to think about what 'normal' people thought of me. I felt shunned by some family and friends and could see their embarrassment when they saw the stupid amounts I'd feel compelled to drink in order to make an attempt at being sociable. I felt defeated by fear.

45

The Arts Council interviewed me twice more before giving me the job. I started on 1 February 1988. A week later, on my forty-third birthday, the Arts Council gave me a present of an assistant, Sharon Monaghan, and I started planning what a Popular Music Officer might do. But on Thursday 11, the council invited the press to their offices at 70 Merrion Square to launch the new post before we had time to strategize. These press launches were usually sparsely attended but such a crowd arrived that some of the staff wondered if the upstairs floors of the old building would support the throng. Before I had time to discuss anything with my new colleagues, I was on RTÉ's *Borderline* programme, its Sunday Show, *The Ronan Collins Show*, BBC Northern Ireland, French television and in every major newspaper on the island. Everyone seemed to have a notion as to what the job should focus on and I got phone calls in week one from County Arts Officers, Donal Gallagher, Bill Whelan, Paul McGuinness, Brian Molloy, several musicians, a couple of promoters, a college and several journalists. Once again, my diary became filled with appointments, meetings, travel and lists of people to phone. I got stuck in because I wanted to.

I wasn't long in the job when I got a call from David Hanly, brother of Mick, inviting me to be interviewed for half an hour on his RTÉ TV programme, *Hanly's People*. As the appointed day loomed closer, I decided I needed to prepare. The interview was to take place at 11 am in RTÉ and I'm not the most articulate in the morning so I needed to replicate late evening: I got up at 7 am, lined up four double vodkas, a couple of bananas and an eggnog and downed them methodically between showering and dressing. The theory was that the bananas and the eggs would give me energy without the lethargy that might follow a big breakfast while the vodkas would calm my nerves enough to make me chatty. Mad or what? It went OK though.

Irish tax provisions included Section Two of the 1969 Finance Act, which stipulated that any work of art, in music, theatre, literature or visual art could benefit from zero tax on royalties, providing it was 'of artistic or cultural merit' and was 'original and creative'. Charles Haughey had initiated it and it was the envy of many artists abroad. One morning I was in U2's manager Paul McGuinness's stunning office overlooking the River Liffey talking with Paul and Adrian Munnelly, CEO of the Arts Council. Paul posed a question, 'How come my clients, U2, can benefit from Section Two and other songwriters like the Hothouse Flowers can't?' Adrian explained how the system worked and how various Arts Council officers would decide whether to grant the tax exemption or not. He said the problem was that the council had no way of knowing if a song was 'original and creative' or not. I said, 'If the writer or writers are members of a royalty collection society, wouldn't that prove originality? The society couldn't accept work that was not original.' There was a beat of silence before Paul said, 'Where are all the applications for exemption at the moment?' Adrian admitted there was a stack of them in his office. Later that day I managed to change something important, trawling through dozens of applications and recommending that every single one got tax-free status.

In July the Arts Council decided I should go to the New Music Seminar in New York, a four-day convention that 5,000 music business people attended every year. I wrote to its founders, Tom Silverman and Mark Josephson, suggesting that we meet to consider running a version of it in Ireland and they replied that they would be interested and I should contact their CEO, Una Johnson – the same Una that had brought Moving Hearts to New York for its first show in the Savoy Theatre. So I set up the meeting and went to New York a couple of days before the seminar. Maggie Smith was out of town and lent me her flat on West 49th Street. When I got through the sauna of New York's July, I rang Una and found that the meeting had been deferred. What to do?

Paul McGuinness was set to make the keynote speech that year. I thought I'd write some notes for him regarding popular music and the Arts Council and Ireland, thinking that it might be of use to him and might also help my cause with the New Music Seminar and an Irish version of it. I spent the morning writing and walked for half an hour to deliver my notes to U2's office near Columbus Circle. Utterly soaked with sweat, I walked back to West 49th and opened a bottle of duty-free Bushmills. By late afternoon I was sitting stark naked in the un-air-conditioned flat, reading, half way through the bottle when the phone rang and Paul McGuinness asked if I'd like to come to dinner. I got into a cold bath with a pot of black coffee and tried to smarten myself up. At 7 pm I was in the bar of the Ritz Carlton having drinks with Paul, his wife, Kathy Gilfillan, and Sheila Roche, who managed his office in New York. I didn't mention that I had a serious head start on them. Then a limo delivered us to a very upmarket restaurant where we were joined by Tom and Mark and their partners. Each course was accompanied by an appropriate bottle or two and soon I was feeling no pain. We finished off with brandies before Paul, Kathy, Sheila and I went clubbing. With over 5,000 music business people in town, the clubs were jammed with people that wanted to talk to Paul so it got hectic. By 3 am we'd had enough and took a taxi back to the Ritz Carlton, where Paul and Kathy had a suite of rooms overlooking Central Park. After a couple of hours of drinks and chat, Kathy and Sheila had fallen asleep on a couch. Paul and I were deep into a conversation about the arts in Ireland when I suddenly felt everything assault my system. The day's heat, the walking, the half bottle of Bush and different wines and brandy in the restaurant and vodkas in the clubs all combined to make me hit a wall. I didn't know what would happen next but something told me it shouldn't happen in company. I had to interrupt Paul and go.

'Paul, it's been a great evening. Thank you so much. I think the jetlag is affecting me so I should head off.'

Paul was very gracious, standing to shake my hand, thanking me for coming. I opened the door to head off as quickly as I could before fainting or vomiting or worse and found myself not in a corridor but in a confined, dark space. It filtered through the fuzz in my head that I'd walked into a wardrobe or cloakroom and I couldn't find a light switch. It took a while to find the handle to the door I'd come in through and, when I finally made it back into their sitting room, Paul was so helpless with laughter he could only point at the correct door. I waved goodbye and fell out into the corridor. The worst exit of my life. I had held a good lead throughout a social drinking marathon only to run into the wrong stadium at the finish.

A couple of days later Paul and Kathy invited me to a bash in their hotel. I was talking with the Irish consul general to the UN, Daithi O'Ceallaigh, when his wife, Antoinette, joined us.

'Do you by any chance know Mary Coughlan?' she asked.

'Indeed I do. I've huge time for Mary. I toured several countries with her.'

'Well I love her voice. Daithi, give me one of your business cards please.'

And she wrote, *Dear Mary, you've got to come over here to the US. We have to let them know we have great women singers as well as all the men. Sincerely, Antoinette.*

'Now Keith, pass that on to Mary when you see her, please.'

When I got back to Dublin, I photocopied the card, sent the original to Mary and a copy to her manager, Denis Desmond. A year or so later I bumped into Mary.

'Keith, I never thanked you for sending me the card and message from Daithi and Antoinette. You'll never guess what happened.'

'Go on.'

'My sister was on the run from a difficult partner in the US and got as far as JFK where she discovered the papers for her and her wee boy weren't in order. Long story short: she rang me. I remembered the card and rang Daithi. He sent a car to JFK, collected my sister and her boy, brought them into New York, fed them, sorted the paperwork and ferried them back to JFK!'

Taking the example of New York's New Music Seminar, I started a series of seminars around the country, hiring professional musicians and managers who explained copyright, music publishing and all the other intricacies of the music business. There seemed to be a hunger for knowledge like this and all the seminars were filled to capacity.

I owned a nice car for six weeks, a metallic green Volkswagen Scirocco GTI that was comfortable, fast and economical. It was left-hand drive and Alex and I had fun as we pretended she was driving me to school. One night there was a farewell party in the Arts Council's offices for a staff member and I was offered a blast of poteen. Too good to miss. Ages since I had poteen. Wonder if it's good. I can always go back on the wagon tomorrow. So I had a good drink of it. A while later I was driving home and came around a bend to discover a big old car doing a U-turn, blocking the road. I swerved, managed to miss hitting him broadside on, clipped the back of his car and hit a lamp post. My thanks for saving the guy was to get breathalyzed. The Scirocco was a write-off too.

In 1988 Alex came to live with me again. She had been living with her maternal grandparents in Churchtown and, when they retired and moved to the country, twelve-year-old Alex elected to live with me. We both had a lot of adjusting to do, Alex to living with an alcoholic in his mid-forties, me to the total responsibility of doing my best for her. I had quit Mary Coughlan's band when I got the Arts Council job so at least I was off the road and able to spend time at home. When I had jazz gigs, Alex had friends come and stay for the evening. When I had gigs abroad, I usually managed to bring her with me.

One evening we talked about power in relationships and agreed that we had to respect each other in our new domestic arrangement and that I shouldn't exercise parental power unless it was justified. The only thing I remember us falling out over was the division of responsibility at meal times: I was to cook, she to clear up and wash dishes. After the umpteenth time the dishes stayed unwashed, I lost it and roared at her. Later she emerged from her room, tears in her eyes and, with quiet determination, reminded me of my agreement not to abuse my authority. I apologized and never raised my voice again. When she left the room, I cried, partly through shame, partly because I was so proud of her courage. I realized that it's hard to stand up for yourself in a single-parent family because there's no one else to turn to.

Ciaran Bourke died in May. I knew him as a member of the Dubliners and as a neighbour. Both Dubliners that I had spent many nights drinking with, Ciaran and Luke Kelly, had now died much too young. The Dubs were hugely kind to Ciaran in his last years, both with money and care. He was a talented, warm-hearted funny man. RIP.

Shay Healy's RTÉ show *Nighthawks* contacted me and asked if I would review Clint Eastwood's film about Charlie Parker, *Bird*. On the morning of 23 November I went to a press screening of the film. I was deeply affected by its depiction of Parker's descent into the madness of addiction while playing some of the greatest jazz ever and contributing to the reinvention of an artform. His addiction and the inability of those around him to help him got to me at a profound level and I had to walk around the city centre for a couple of hours to settle down.

That evening I brought my clarinet to RTÉ where Shay outlined the plan.

'Right, Keith. Top of the show you'll be over there at the piano. You'll get a hand cue for you and the pianist to start playing. Keep an eye on the far corner of the set and you'll see me coming in there. You stop playing and walk up that side of the set as I walk up this side. Then we'll coincide at the bar and have a chat about the film. OK?'

'OK, Shay. Do we get to try it?'

'Yep, we'll get a run-through presently. By the way, did you like the film?'

'It was excellent.'

'Good. You can tell me and the viewers later.'

When the show went live that evening, I was by the piano. There's the hand cue, time to start playing. Concentrate on the music until I see Shay ... Going well ... Good pianist ... Ah there's Shay, stop playing, leave clarinet on top of piano, start walking and try to time my arrival at the bar with Shay's ... Oh fuck! Some punter has him by the arm, wants to talk to him, fucker must think he's in any old bar, not one that's live on TV ... Shay can't get away from him. I'm going to arrive at the bar much too early and the camera is on me, not Shay. What to do? I can't stop so walk slow. If I walk any slower I'll be going backwards. I'm at the bar, camera's little red light on, standing ... Sweating ... Steal a glance – punter still gripping Shay's arm ... Maybe I should act exasperated like Shay is always late, so drum my fingers on the bar … he's away from the punter, here he comes and we're off.

Shay finally arrives beside me and says, 'Well, well, it's Keith Donald. How are you?'

As the camera comes to me for my reply, Shay rolls his eyes and nods back to the punter. I giggle inappropriately and keep going.

At the end of the year, Alex wrote in my diary: *To dad: Happy Christmas. How zit goin? Do you mind if I fail some exams? Cos I think I failed commerce, maths and Irish. I think I got honours in English and French. I still love you. Happy Christmas, Love, Alex.*

When Alex started living with me again, I knew the games of addiction I played and lost would soon have to end. I didn't know how and was scared of finding out. So I postponed hard decisions and practised the deviousness and self-deception of the alco: when I had finished Arts Council work, I'd get home, help Alex with homework, sort our laundry and cook, before walking fast to the pub a hundred yards away, ordering a treble or two double vodkas and a half bottle to go. While the barman fetched the carry-out, I would down the vodka like medicine. I was never out of the house for more than ten minutes and had myself convinced that it was justified.

That Christmas Alex went to stay with her mother and I went on a bender. On Christmas Eve I was sitting on a bar stool when it hit me that the shops would be closed in a couple of hours and I'd forgotten to finish buying presents. I headed down Grafton Street, newly pedestrianized for the Dublin Millennium and got most of what I needed in the narrow streets near Grafton Street. One more thing to get and half an hour until the shops close and I have to get back to the top of Grafton Street. The street was now so jammed up with last minute shoppers that I got stuck behind two slow old women with half a dozen bags in each hand – they were yards wide. Suddenly a gap appeared and I accelerated alongside them. I hit a bollard at full tilt and fell to the ground, shrieking in pain as the bollard was bollix high. I rolled around in agony while middle-class shoppers avoided me with studied care. All thoughts of Christmas left my head.

46

Early in the new year I met with Marius Schoon and another South African exile, Victor Modise, as well as anti-apartheid representatives from London and Amsterdam. We talked about Somafco in Tanzania and how we might help the children there. Then Marius, Sherry, our pal Sheena McCambley and I started planning some gigs to raise money to buy musical instruments to send to Somafco.

We started running weekly gigs to raise money for Somafco on 15 February in the Baggot Inn. Marius and Sheena ran the box office, I ran the stage, Sherry ran messages. Thanks to the generosity of the public and the performers – Christy Moore, Mick Hanly, the Benzini Brothers, Davy Spillane, Red Peters, Ton Ton Macoute (with Sinead O'Connor), Princes Street, Ellamental and Mary Coughlan – we raised enough to purchase dozens of guitars, drums, keyboards, basses and amps. Some kind person in the Department of Foreign Affairs got to hear of our efforts and provided free transport for all the gear.

By Easter 1989 I had been working for the Arts Council as their Popular Music Officer for fourteen months. Alex was thirteen and had been living with me for a year. Life was a balancing act that involved a demanding day job, occasional jazz gigs and recording sessions, travel in Ireland and abroad, single parenthood and, if I am to be truly honest, alcoholism, though I hadn't yet owned the word.

On the 27 March, Easter Monday, I kept an appointment to meet an Arts Council client in Doheny and Nesbitt's pub at lunchtime despite it being a bank holiday. I had four pints of Guinness and a couple of Jamesons. In the afternoon, I collected Alex and drove to meet up with Marian and Terry Woods. My plan was to deliver Alex to them for the holidays and drive on to the artists' retreat Annaghmakerrig where I would spend three days writing a report on popular music and the Arts Council's relationship with it. We met in a pub in a quiet village at 4 pm. The years spent perfecting my drinking meant that I never slurred my words, lurched, fell, fought or otherwise gave away my madness. I had a horror of being an obvious drunk, the stupid pride of the self-deluding. I guess Terry thought I was having my first drink of the day when he bought a round. I left the pub at 7 pm, declining Terry's kind offer to stay the night at their house.

As I drove away, I suddenly felt the effects of the day's drinking on an empty stomach and felt some concern. Right, you're probably reeking of drink so better not stop to ask directions. By 9 pm I suspected that I was driving in circles and had worked myself into a lather of confusion like a panic attack. Logic would have said stop, park the car, find a hotel! if I had been listening, but I drove on and on, determined to find Annaghmakerrig in time for a nightcap.

Shortly after nine, I came to a crossroads and was under the impression that I had been bumped mildly by another car. In my determination not to stop, not to be seen as a drunk, I waved what I thought was forgiveness at the other driver and took off. The police were waiting for me in the next town, Bailieborough.

I arrived at the police station in a squad car, confused and hurt by this turn of events. Hurt? Yes indeed: after all I was only doing my best for everyone – the Arts Council, the lunchtime client on a day off, Alex, her mother, the other driver whom I'd let go on. A policeman kindly explained that I had driven through a *Yield* sign, hit the other car and waved pleasantly to a driver who then couldn't get out of his car because of the damage I had done. I have nothing but praise for the Bailieborough gardai: they did their job courteously, talked about Moving Hearts for a while and then actually drove me in the squad car to Annaghmakerrig where I arrived and was welcomed by a bemused Bernard Loughlin at 2 am.

The next morning I woke late, feeling demoralized, ill and disorientated. I had no idea where my car was. All the papers I needed to write the report were in it. So were my clothes, washbag and a sax. It was a clear, sunny day outside but I couldn't see it. An outside observer who didn't know me might have envied me: after all, I had a wonderful daughter with whom I shared a home, a great girl I could be with as she blossomed; I had a job that 290 other people had applied for; I played jazz with the best players around; I had loyal friends and a good social life. But the view from inside was different: I needed a drink before I could socialize, being quite terrified at my own inadequacies; I knew that drink impaired my playing but I still had to have it; I hated the crazy risks I took when drink-driving; I detested being unable to control my drinking, despite attempts to stop for good several times a year for eleven years.

No papers, no car, no washbag, no clothes, no sax. No dignity, no self-respect, no confidence. Now I had two drink-driving charges to face up to and I felt horrible. The usual solution came to mind: have a drink to get rid of the rattling, then you can start to sort the rest of the mess. I began walking in the warmth of sparkling sunshine and clear blue skies with my own private thunderstorm raging in my head, like a little black cloud of scorn hovering above. The nearest town was called Newbliss and the irony was not wasted. I went into the first pub I saw. It was like a scene from a Samuel Beckett play: everyone seemed to be waiting for something. I ordered a pint of Guinness and a Jameson. There were three customers already in place as well as a teenage girl behind the bar. I sat near the door and took them in: a very old, painfully thin woman sat with her coat on by the fire with a bottle of Guinness and a small whiskey on the round table beside her, a cigarette between brown fingers – I guessed what she was waiting for. At one end of the bar, a fat farmer in rubber boots and worn tweeds was reading a newspaper and finishing each pint in two great gulps while at the other end, a middle-aged man in suit and tie was engaged in a quiet, rapid, neurotic conversation with himself. The teenage girl was bored, reading a book. I sat thinking about the previous evening, drunk-driving, the usual mess ... My shaking nerves began to settle with my third pint and Jameson.

Then the teenage girl turned the TV on. It was the *Oprah* show. The subject was alcoholism. That 28 March 1989 was a crossroads alright and I began to know it as I watched the programme, identifying in some way with all of Oprah's studio guests, hearing American life histories that could have been mine, feeling for the very first time that I wasn't alone with this problem. I listened to people telling stories of self-sacrifice on the altar of addiction. Stories of madness, hilarity, hopelessness and hurt. Then the stories began to be about recovery, seeking and finding help, hope and redemption. I walked back to Annaghmakerrig enjoying the sunshine, feeling a glimmer of hope for the first time after twenty-seven years of drinking troubles.

The next day I rang Derek, a musician friend who had seen the quantities I was drinking about a year earlier and had said, 'Here's my phone number. If you ever feel you need help with quitting, don't hesitate to ring me.' Two days later, Derek met me at the Arts Council and walked with me to a room in Trinity College and my first meeting with people who were similarly sick. I've been meeting with people like them for thirty-seven years now, and always learn something. I hope my experience, strength and hope has maybe been of use too.

47

After five years of business meetings with men in suits, five long years of selling assets, lodgements, promises, hassle and worry, Moving Hearts' sole remaining debt finally caught up with me in 1989. A contact in banking rang me to say, 'Keith, you didn't hear this from me, right?'

'You have my word.'

'The band's account has gone to a different department in the bank – not nice guys over there. As yours is the only band member's house that isn't covered by the Marriage Home Protection Act, they're coming after you. You haven't got long before you hear from them.'

'Oh fuck ... thanks.'

What to do? My strategy of taking out a second mortgage to buy my ex out seemed to have backfired. What was the point of keeping up with two mortgages throughout the 80s if a bloody bank was poised to take the house?

I called a band meeting. Fair play to everyone: their immediate reaction was support and an offer to try to raise money via a gig. I arranged to meet the bankers.

Midway through the meeting where I felt they were bullying me, I lost it and interrupted the chief bully.

'So what's the total of what we owe now?' I said.

There was scrabbling amongst a pile of files. Then the announcement of a fantastic sum.

'What? You're joking!'

'No, Mr Donald, that's what your band owes the bank.'

'That's at least three times what I thought we owed.'

'I guess you forgot there'd be interest.'

'That's outrageous. We could never raise that amount. You have to take the interest off it.'

'We can't do that.'

'Right,' I said, getting to my feet, 'listen carefully. You're going to have to take the house off me by force. I'm telling you now and I mean this: I will barricade myself and my daughter into the house with a load of food. I will inform every newspaper in the country – I know loads of journalists and press photographers and you will lose more in PR and goodwill than you'll ever get from the sale of a wee cottage. Good luck.'

'Hang on there, Mr Donald. Please. Sit down for a minute and I'll come back to you.'

I sat, livid, my determination to fight increasing until he came back.

'Mr Donald, I'm pleased to tell you that the bank is willing to forego the interest if you furnish us with a plan to repay the amount of capital outstanding,' he said.

'Thank you. While we're in furnishing mode, can you furnish me with a letter to that effect that I can show my colleagues? In other words, we get our personal guarantees back when you get repaid the capital.'

I rang around to tell people the target figure and was bowled over to hear that Christy had heard of our predicament and had volunteered to rejoin the band for one night. This meant we could play the Point Depot, which held five thousand. I rang Aiken Promotions and booked rehearsal rooms.

The gig was mighty. We hadn't played in Dublin for years and it seemed like every man and woman who had come to hear us in the Baggot Inn three nights a week throughout 1981 and 1982 had come from near and far to relive it. There was a frenzied scream like a Welcome Home from five thousand throats when we went on stage. Goosebumps for all of us as we shared grins and nods that said this is going to be special. There are gigs, rare gigs, when musicians and audience are as one, when there's a collective determination to have a good time. This was one of those rare moments and it felt like nothing could go wrong. If I could have smiled while playing soprano sax, I'd have smiled from the beginning of

McBride's Reels all the way to the encore. When Christy came on stage, you could have heard the roar across the Liffey.

At one point a couple of people left their seats and came up in front of us to dance. Some bouncers hurried over to remonstrate and get them back to their seats. What we could see and the bouncers couldn't was a tidal wave of hundreds of people surging up front to dance. The bouncers shrugged their shoulders and gave up.

Aiken Promotions told me it was the fastest-selling ticket all year and reckoned we could have played three nights. When I did the accounts with the Aikens later, I had enough to pay all the gig production costs, plus give every musician a small thank-you present and still have the agreed settlement for the bank.

I rang the bank.

'I have your money. Can I have an appointment and will you bring our personal guarantees?'

So, one fine day in December I went to an office where they kept the rottweilers I was dealing with. The senior rottweiler, a young pup in pinstripes and no smile sat down opposite me. No how-are-you, no how-was-the-gig?

'Right, Mr Donald, I believe you have a bank draft for us.'

'Yes,' I said, proudly pulling the piece of paper from my wallet, placing it on the table, 'and I believe you are to give me our personal guarantees back.'

'Oh, they're in a vault somewhere,' he said reaching for the draft. 'I'll write something to say the guarantees are rescinded.'

'Actually,' I said, grabbing the draft just before his hand got to it, 'you won't. The deal was the draft in exchange for the personal guarantees. You promised the original document and that's what I want. Tell you what: I'll go across the road for a coffee while you get the guarantees from your vault. If you can't get them here by the time I come back in an hour, you can bring them up the mountains to the house you were going to steal from me.'

I walked out, leaving him silent and enraged, and went for coffee. For an hour I couldn't read, do a crossword or anything except shake slightly and revel in the fact that after five years of getting a hard time from the bank, I was within sight of ending it.

When I went back an hour later, it was like something out of a Marcel Marceau mime show. I walked into an empty room and stood waiting. The pup came in another door and stood for a second before putting a piece of paper on the table between us. I picked it up, looked and took in all the signatures – Christy Moore, Donal Lunny, Davy Spillane, Declan Sinnott, Brian Calnan, Eoghan O'Neill, Keith Donald, Cid Isaacson, Matt Kelleghan, Norman Verso – and put the draft on the table. He picked it up, looked at it and left. I still have that very precious piece of paper that meant that Alex and I could continue to live in our home.

48

When I started the serious job of staying sober, it wasn't easy. For a while I had to stop going to pubs. Many times every week I went to meetings with other recovering alcoholics and learned from them. I thought I should play more music, that maybe it could be part of the therapy I needed.

So I got to play seventy-eight interesting gigs with bands in different genres of music, like the Davy Spillane Band, Scullion, Don Baker and his band, Francie Conway (in Kerry and Switzerland), and with Jimi Hendrix's bass player, Noel Redding in Clonakilty (for Friends of the Earth). I played with Mick Hanly in the National Concert Hall at an awards ceremony. BB King was there too, accepting an award for U2. When I got to the green room, he called me. 'Hey Mister Saxman, you a fine player,' so I went over to him.

'Man, you have the real sound of an alto sax going on there, not the sound of razor blades the kids get these days!'

I got to spend a couple of hours in his good company. We were joined by BB's manager and Aonghus McAnally, the musician and TV presenter. Aonghus and I fell around laughing at the double act that BB and his manager had developed: every time someone came up to them, BB would wink at us while he and his manager went through a routine of searching in each other's pockets for the little Lucille guitar badges he was giving out.

'You have them, man.'

'No, you put them in this pocket, man.'

The craic was good.

I played with Tom Robinson in the Olympia at an Aids Awareness freebie.

'Do you remember the sax riff from "War Baby", Keith? No? OK, I'll scribble it out for you. B flat, right?'

Once again I went on stage trying to remember something that was written on the back of an envelope.

In the year after I got sober I managed not to drink for 363 days and gave myself a talking to after the two separate days I did drink. Actually it was more of a question-and-answer session. What was that about? Why did I make a totally spur of the moment decision to have a drink? What weakened me? It wasn't boredom. It wasn't other people and pressure. I'm learning to cope with that. I wasn't lonely, never am really. I think I was already feeling rattled by something. In one case it was being in Berlin on my own a few days after the wall came down. I was there for a conference and couldn't find anyone until I realized there's two of everything, East Berlin's and West Berlin's equivalent, and I was in the wrong one. The other time was after being driven at speed by that young guy on snow and ice for 50 miles. Given my history with accidents and injuries it's no wonder I was rattled. I had to find a better way of calming rattled nerves.

Being free from drink for 363 days meant I did everything better. I hope I was a better father. I brought Alex with me whenever a music gig or an Arts Council job permitted. Thus we travelled to Denmark where I was gigging with a Danish band called Still B, to New York when I attended the New Music Seminar, to the stadium in Thurles when Moving Hearts played the first Trip to Tipp festival, and to the Point when Moving Hearts played a fundraiser for Romanian orphans, with guests Moya Brennan, the Hothouse Flowers, Ray Lynam, Mick Hanly, Flo and Christy Moore.

I took a week of holidays from the day job to go to Amsterdam, Switzerland and Paris with Francie Conway: one of the best fun tours ever.

I also got to play with Christy and Donal Lunny as a three-piece at an awareness raiser for the Birmingham Six, rehearsing in the afternoon in the Wexford Inn.

'Donal and I'll do around twenty minutes, then you come on,' said Christy.

'OK, what's my cue?'

Then Donal came up with a very musical idea. I was to time my arrival on stage so that it would coincide with an exciting change of key and I'd launch into a sax solo. It sounded great at rehearsal. That evening the Wexford Inn was packed solid with madly enthusiastic listeners. I arrived on stage to great applause, nodded to Christy and Donal and launched into my solo in the new key while they looked alarmed and stayed in the old key. The resulting chaos changed folk into modern jazz and stilled the audience. Thirty-two bars later we were all in the same key having changed back and forth separately, capos on and off and on again, brains whizzing, audience completely confused. After the song, Christy stopped laughing long enough to explain what had happened. The audience was in hysterics by the time he'd finished.

Moving Hearts played at the first of Vince Power's festivals in Finsbury Park. The huge London crowd seemed to love our gig. We hated it for a variety of reasons: the gig was a one-off, we hadn't rehearsed, we had all come from different parts of Europe and met at the side of the stage, mistakes from everyone, inability to hear each other, a sound in my monitor like someone was experimenting with a chemistry set and the constant uncertainty as to whether we might all make different mistakes that would grind the performance to a screeching halt. We always rehearsed before a reunion after that.

Nelson Mandela got out of prison after twenty-seven years and there was much hope and expectation in the worldwide anti-apartheid movement. Kader Asmal rang me and asked if I would help organize a gig to coincide with his visit to Ireland. We ran it in the Gaiety Theatre on 1 July with performances from Donal McCann, Olwen Fouere, De Danaan, the

Chieftains, Moving Hearts and Christy Moore. I got to chat with Winnie Mandela in the green room, her husband not able to attend through exhaustion. She was lovely, dignified and statuesque, and very interested in the arts in Ireland.

I suggested to Jerome Morrissey, principal at Senior College Ballyfermot, that he set up a course in music management. I ended up writing the curriculum, finding the people to teach it and interviewing prospective students. Around 450 people have since graduated from that course and are to be found working in every area of the industry in Ireland and abroad. I didn't make any money from it: I just didn't want people suffering from the same lack of knowledge I had when I was trying to manage Moving Hearts. I'm proud of that and of all the students.

49

In May 1991 I was still working for the Arts Council but I wasn't earning enough to cover Alex' and my living expenses plus pay off the loan I had taken out to pay the settlement with my ex when our marriage failed. So I took any job that paid well and used up my Arts Council leave to do it. I had had a call from Still B, the rock band in Denmark, asking me to play a festival in Esbjerg with them on a Saturday. After consulting my diary, I saw that I was due at an international conference in Lisbon the following Monday and asked the Danish band if they could guarantee that I would be back in Copenhagen on the Sunday. 'No problem,' they exaggerated.

I left home before dawn on Saturday, having made sure that a friend, Mark Gilligan, who had been a clarinet pupil briefly, would stay in our house for the week with his girlfriend and fourteen-year-old Alex.

A taxi, two planes, a train and a ferry later, I hooked up with the Danish band. The Danes and I played in the open air to a crowd of maybe five thousand at 9 pm and, since the event was running behind schedule, I was playing sax with one eye on my watch. I ran off the stage, was put into somebody's car and packed the sax as we drove dangerously fast to the nearest train station. I made it on to the train just before it began moving at 11 pm. As I settled down to what I thought was a four-hour journey, I realized the band had forgotten to pay me and I had very little money and no way of getting any more. When the ticket inspector visited my little compartment, I asked what time the dining car closed, my thoughts already on a decent supper. In perfect English, he told me that there was no dining car, that this was a mail train and we'd get to Copenhagen at 8 am.

'Nine hours!' I said, 'but it only took four yesterday.'

He gently explained that we had to stop for collections and deliveries. I thanked him and settled down to sleep, already hungry, with the knowledge that I was going to get a lot hungrier as there would be no time for breakfast in Copenhagen.

I had forgotten to tell SAS that I'm pescetarian so didn't eat the cooked breakfast on the flight. I got to Dublin via Manchester in the early afternoon and had my first food in twenty hours in the airport. Mark Gilligan knew that I had three hours at Dublin Airport and came to chat and collect my instruments. He drove me to Portmarnock where we looked at the sea and talked for an hour or so. The next flights took me to Heathrow and then Lisbon.

Alcoholics tell their fellow sufferers that sometimes they may need to HALT, an acronym for Hunger, Anger, Loneliness and Tiredness, four states of being that it is recommended that alcoholics avoid. I was up against all four when I arrived in Lisbon. Hunger: I had had one meal in twenty-four hours. Anger: I was fed up with so much work and no breaks. Loneliness: I felt very much on my own as I travelled day after day. Tiredness: without being aware of it, I was exhausted. When I got to my hotel room in Lisbon, I had been travelling for twenty-three hours straight: over Saturday and Sunday I had had six flights, two long train journeys, two ferries, four taxis and a hard gig. I was in a terrible state of mind, resenting the Danish band, the Arts Council, the lack of reward, practically everything and I threw away my sobriety in an instant, raiding the little mini-bar, grabbing the first miniature I saw and drinking it straight from the bottle. For alcoholics, one is too much but it's also never enough. By 2 am the mini-bar was empty and I was falling around the swanky room. In a drunken panic I told myself I'd be OK the next day and fell asleep.

I woke with a hangover so bad I couldn't face food. I got directions to the Gulbenkian Centre where the conference on European copyright was being held. It took ten minutes to walk there, ten minutes when I didn't take in the cloudless sky, the architecture, the well-dressed Lisbon folk, nothing bar the fact that I had a dose of the shakes and craved a drink. The Gulbenkian was where the deviousness of the alcoholic kicked in. As I registered for the conference, I was given a translation kit comprising earphones and a Sony Walkman-sized piece of equipment that turned out to be a remote receiver for the translations. It immediately hit my addled brain that it must rely on radio waves and that I wouldn't have to plug it in. I could be anywhere near the main hall. I found a cafeteria and tried out the system. I could hear the English translation like the translator woman was sitting beside me. And the cafeteria, in true continental fashion, sold little bottles of wine.

By the time the lunch break was announced into my ears, I was established in a pleasant corner of the cafeteria with a view of gardens below and a sculpture park beyond. I had scribbled some notes, drunk some wine and had stopped rattling.

Thus I continued, never once entering the conference hall for three days, never speaking to another delegate, taking increasingly indecipherable notes and drinking. Representing the Arts Council and the Department of the Taoiseach in my own pathetic way. Each evening I went to the same nearby restaurant and ate fish, washing it down with a sweet drink named Brandymel that tasted like fiery honey. Then I'd find a bar and drink until late before swaying back to the hotel. I vaguely remember meeting a man in a down-at-heel, spit-and-sawdust bar and drinking with him for hours while conversing in sign language and laughter. I found a piece of Lisbon pavement in my pocket one morning, a small square piece of shiny stone that remains a mystery to me. Nothing made sense. Memory let me down, becoming a series of blanks interrupted by vivid inexplicable scenes, like mental snapshots of mental behaviour.

On the Tuesday afternoon, the conference was engaged in deliberations on the legal niceties of copyright that would have necessitated a PhD to understand so I went walkabout.

I wanted to tell my civil-engineer brother that I'd seen the famous bridge on the outskirts of Lisbon and knew that if I walked south,

I'd find it. So I followed the sun, my journey taking me first through wide boulevards with stunning four- and five-storey buildings on each side. Apartments, I thought through a pleasant haze, nice places to live. On and on I trudged, taking in the architecture, the cars, the people, their style until I realized it was all getting a bit scruffy. Another half hour and I was in bandit territory and, although a bit drunk, my survival antennae were up. The buildings were now single storey, the cars were bangers. Rounding a corner, I came across two men drinking glasses of red wine. I couldn't see a bar so I asked them with sign language where to find a drink. They thumbed over their shoulders to a doorway. A second later I was in the queerest set-up: a shebeen of sorts, dark and full of smoke, plastic chairs on a stone floor. Groups of men were playing cards at plastic tables while a few stood talking at a counter behind which there were bottles and a barrel but no barman. The room fell silent as I entered, all eyes on me. I mimed drinking and they went back to their cards, bar one man who came over, still holding a hand of cards while mumbling to me in Portuguese. I pointed at a bottle of wine, meaning for him to pour me a tumbler full, like the men outside had. He wrote a number on a piece of paper and gave it to me. I gave him the right money and he gave me a tumbler and a bottle and went back to his card game. I had a glass of it at the bar on my own, trying to avoid eye contact with anyone. After a few minutes, one of the standing men pointed at me and said, 'Deutschland?'

I shook my head.

'England?' he asked.

'Ireland,' I said.

He replied, 'George Best!' and shook my hand.

A half-hour later and I was into a second bottle, sharing some wine with my new football-fanatic friend, chatting in sign language and nods and laughter about football, about which I know nothing.

I shook many hands and left, following the sun again.

I was walking through a deserted area on a path of dried mud, taking occasional swigs from a third bottle I'd taken from the shebeen when some movement made me look closer at the hillside to my right. Eyes. I was looking at lots of pairs of eyes and realized that these people are so dirt-poor, they're living in holes they've dug into the bare earth. Like cave-dwellers. This is awful, here am I, Paddy Foreigner, walking through their place, drinking like I owned it. I stopped, looked up at the eyes, took the money from my hip pocket and put it on the ground, setting the bottle on top to keep it in place. Guilt, pure guilt. Then I walked on.

An hour later I was looking at the magnificent bridge over the Tagus, the late afternoon sun glinting off it, traffic scooting over it like distant Dinky toys, the wide river flowing serenely hundreds of feet below. I stood for ages.

With no money, no bottle and no map, it took ages to walk back to the centre of Lisbon and my hotel. That night was the same as the previous: fish, Brandymel, a bar, conversations with strangers in sign language and basic French. Another night with no memory of it.

After a morning of note-taking in the Gulbenkian cafeteria, with wine for breakfast, it was time to check out of the hotel and go home. At reception I was presented with a bill and a huge list of extras for mini-bar drinks and phone calls.

'But I didn't make any phone calls!'

'Please wait for a moment, sir.'

I stood thinking, trying to remember, coming to the conclusion that the bill was a mistake, a 300-plus pounds error. You'd buy an OK car for less. She came back and waited patiently while her pathetic guest recognized all the numbers.

I took my bag and went to the nearest bar, utterly shocked that I could have made so many long phone calls and not remembered a single one. My last memory of Lisbon is hailing a taxi. I don't remember the journey to the airport, checking in, the flight to London, Heathrow, the flight to Dublin. My next clear memory is being in a car with Mark Gilligan. Three airports, two flights, ten hours and only one recollection: on one of the flights there was an empty seat between me and another passenger. Whatever I did or had just done, he shot me a glance, the kind of look a sane person might give to a pitiful madman. Was he ever right! I tried hard to retrieve memory but that's the only fleeting snapshot I could get.

Mark subsequently filled in the detail of the rest of that night. Apparently one of my many phone calls was to Alex and she could tell what condition I was in and had asked Mark to fetch me and look after me. She later told me that I scared her. If I thought about that for a minute, I could cry.

Mark started an argument with me in his car in the car park at Dublin airport, a strident debate about Irish politics. I was determined to find a bar that might serve me; Mark was determined to delay this in the hope that I'd fall asleep or get sick or that the pubs would be closed. No such luck: we left the airport around midnight and drove to the Four Seasons, a bar I had gigged in, where the manager was a pal, where I'd get served. We left there at 4 am and Mark drove me at speed around the Dublin mountains in an attempt to make me sick. Finally he left me home, putting me to bed in the survival position; that is, on my side with the upper knee further forward so that if I got sick, gravity would take it away rather than choke me.

They saved my stupid life, did wise young Alex and Mark, because when I woke, the pillow was covered in large lumps of undigested aeroplane food.

Next morning I went to work in the Arts Council, having to get off the bus in Rathmines to get sick. I wanted a drink. Really badly. I went for lunch but couldn't eat. I didn't drink, something deep inside me aware that this was the end of the road. I knew I had to talk to fellow sufferers and I did, ringing a good sober friend called Carole who encouraged me to go to a meeting as soon as I could and talk about my lapse. For three days I had a searing pain in my stomach that felt like a serrated blade was twisting deep inside me. For three days I couldn't hold down any food at all. I got sick so much it was like my body was rejecting my past.

With support from Alex, friends, the truth, counselling and other alcoholics, I began the life-changing project of staying off drink.

50

When you stop the active aspect of addiction, the slow suicide by glass and bottle, a physiological battle has been won but a psychological war still rages: you versus addiction. And addiction has precedent on its side: it won every previous battle.

Winning the physiological battle means that you'll get withdrawal symptoms. For most alcoholics, these awful side-effects are best dealt with in a medical setting. If you've been doing something to yourself for decades and you suddenly stop, your body is going to go haywire. In a hospital or rehab facility, they can make sure that this withdrawing of substance that your body has learned to process won't endanger you. So I'd advise it.

I never went to hospital or rehab, adopting a DIY approach to the physical withdrawal. I would not recommend it. Ever since my first attempt to stop drinking, after Eddie's death in 1978 and the ensuing three-week binge, I'd stopped every year. That's thirteen years of giving myself hell. Here's what hell felt like:

Identify a day when you don't have to leave home. Maybe in a week or two. Start building up your resolve to do it, every day reminding yourself that it's going to be hard but you might be able to get through it this time. The first sober day isn't much of a problem. Willpower should see you through. The first sober night is awful, waking up wet with sweat from head to toe, changing damp bedclothes, staring at the ceiling for hours, shaking mildly, the suffering body making the tortured mind turn somersaults – I could go to an early house and stop all this crap, No, I won't give in. All I have to do is last another couple of hours – mind games until it's a new day and a slight sense of accomplishment at getting through the night. The second night wouldn't exactly be fun but it would be an improvement.

The next day and night would be much easier and the fourth day would bring a sense of joyous achievement. Then being dry would feel good for a while, maybe weeks, maybe months, but edginess and unease would kick in and the internal tension would get stronger and stronger until it would overwhelm me and I'd succumb. The first drink would stop all the rattling and be a huge relief. It would also feel like a pathetic defeat born out of weakness.

The psychological aspects of addiction are another story. During those thirteen years of my 'on it – off it – back on it – back off it' nightmare, I never once addressed the underlying psychology of it. So this time my approach had to be different if the end result was to be different.

Soon after I stopped drinking in May 1991, an internal dialogue started. Other alcoholics have told me of similar battles raging in their thoughts. Mine was like bad music in my head: wild variations on the same theme, like an endless piece of rap music called *Go on, have a drink*. It went like this:

Maybe I could have just a couple, in the evening. Or only at weekends. Even one is too much. And you know from past experience it's never enough either. I can't do this. I'm used to having a drink when I really need it. Listen to yourself! 'Really need it' – it's the last thing you really need. What you need is to grow up. I'm forty-six, but only in years. I'm suffering the same crap I did at sixteen, but it's worse now. How am I so juvenile, so fucked up?

Stop beating yourself up. It's a disease. Like they say: it's not your fault. Drink arrested your development. You never did grow up. You never felt anything. You just got on with it. What was it that recovering alcoholic said to you recently? 'The good news about getting sober is that you get your feelings back. The bad news is that you get your feelings back.'

Suppose she was right. That means I've got emotional stuff to sort. Yes, stuff you didn't register, like all the pain: physical pain while your legs and back recovered from the no floorboards, trauma and physical pain for months in 1967 after Paul died beside you, trauma and physical pain every hour of every day and night for eight months from June 1973. Your mother's sudden death, your father's sudden death, Eddie's sudden death. Marriage breakdown. Losing all your money and a house. Losing good music. Losing your way.

That's right. I ran for the drink every time something like that happened. How am I ever going to cope with all of that? Gradually. And with help from other alcoholics. Remember what they told you: you are not alone. Help is there if you ask for it. Your part of the bargain is not taking a first drink. You now know your chance at life is gone if you do.

Bloody drink. It ambushed me when I was only a child and it seemed to take the hard edge off abuse. Then I used it to take away the unease and discomfort when I was with people. Then physical pain. It was like I was in the doc's surgery in a Western and could let anything be done to me provided I had a big bottle to hand. I was trying to be doctor and patient too. Self-prescribing idiot I was alright. Then the prescription stopped working. Not only did it stop working but it became the problem. Or another problem, like an additional layer that masks the underlying problem. That's it: drink creates its own problem while it stops you seeing the fundamental problems. Then you're driving blind and there's a dead end somewhere near that you won't see, you'll just hit it. What is the dead end, in reality? It's losing everything. If I keep going until I hit it, I will lose all that's precious, starting with Alex. She'd never live with an incomprehensible drunk for a father. And who'd blame her? I'll become unreliable, then unemployable and I'll lose music: nobody will work with me. My only friends will be other drunks and there's no depth there. No money. Can't pay the mortgage so no home. Pawning instruments. Drinking, not working. The gutter you were promised. That's the dead end for you. If you drink on, it's waiting somewhere. You mightn't see it until you hit it. Or it hits you. God, that scares me. I scare me. I'm scared. Only I can sort this out. I have to admit I'm in a mess. The mess that drink and I have created is my life now. How can I say otherwise? How long have I been trying to sort myself out? Thirteen years. Every year since Eddie died. Off it, on it, off it. Time I owned up: I cannot do it alone. I have to get help. But I don't have the strength. I don't have any confidence. I'm at the end of the line now: it's life or drink. Stark choice. If I drink I will almost inevitably lose everything. If I can stop, there may be a chance of a decent life.

The debate of the desperate. I had versions of that head-game every day, many times every day, every time I wasn't doing something. Maybe there was a wiser me inside, struggling to get out and be heard, struggling with the loser, alcoholic me for dominance. Fighting with an illness.

Reaching rock bottom was realizing how close I was to suffering loss upon loss that I might never recover from, a series of losses that would mean I would tumble down the tacit caste system until I was someone that people reluctantly chose to avoid. I'd be living in a homeless shelter talking about great gigs I'd played, to people who didn't believe me. Pulling frayed photographs out from a greasy pocket to prove where I'd been. Cadging from people who used to have time for me. Untouchable. I had a close musician friend who became exactly like that through drink. The prospect wasn't imaginary.

I realized I would have to take up where I left off at sixteen and race to catch up with maturity. Health, music, work, beliefs, responsibility, capacity for love: I had to start fixing me. Help me, please help me to like myself again.

That summer I went to a day-long party in Paul Barrett's big cottage in Wicklow with my then partner, Sarah. Loads of friends, music, other people drinking socially while I worked hard at drinking water. I got into conversation with a stranger and found myself breaking into a sweat, suddenly unable to concentrate on what he was saying, feeling a rush in my ears like I might faint, wanting to run away but rooted to the very spot in the kitchen where we were standing, feeling as if all eyes were covertly studying me, helpless.

This interminable state of sweaty fear went on until Paul interrupted us.

'Ah Keith, I've been trying to find you. We're going to play some music on the stage in the sitting room. Will you join us?'

All fear left me as soon as I left the kitchen. Doctor Stage once again cured my troubles temporarily. Later the same catatonic stupor happened with another stranger in a different room. This time, Sarah found me and said we should head back to Dublin. As she was driving, I felt the release of huge tension and couldn't hold back the tears. She parked the car and asked what was wrong. After a while I was able to describe the experience of feeling threatened, trapped, watched while I sweated and couldn't move.

'Sounds like you had a panic attack.'

'So that's what it's like. Strangest feeling, like total helplessness.'

'Must have been scary. Were you ever at a party before completely sober?'

'Don't recall. Maybe not.'

'It must be a massive adjustment for you. Give it time.'

I heard other recovering alcoholics talking about the benefits of counselling and knew I should try it. I found psychoanalysis very beneficial and spent an hour a week with Kay for four and a half years. She helped me with issues of self-esteem and confidence and enabled me to understand my panic attacks so well that they all but disappeared. I couldn't bring myself to talk about childhood abuse though. I had confidence in Kay alright, but not enough in myself yet. I thought about bringing the issue into our therapy sessions but fretted about being thrown back into active addiction if I did. I didn't have that kind of courage yet.

51

When I stopped drinking it was like I had to take up where I'd left off when I started regular drinking. It hadn't been normal to come home from a gig somewhat drunk in the early hours of the morning when I was a schoolboy. It was far from normal to go to school a few hours later with adult money in my pocket and a hangover. Counselling helped me realise that I had skipped adolescence and had gone directly from child to alcoholic.

When I'd been sober for a few months a feeling of desperation almost overwhelmed me: why did I waste so much time? All those hours and days spent in pubs, all those months in white-knuckle sobriety, like hanging on for dear life at the edge of an abyss, not knowing when I'd cave in and start drinking again. Three decades from my mid-teens to my mid-forties of life on a rollercoaster, up and down, up and down. Mostly down. When this awful realization settled deep in me, I had two alternatives: wallow in regret or make up for it. I chose the latter.

I thought about music and how much I wanted to play like I'd been able to before I stopped caring so I saved up and bought the best of instruments. I began a regime of regular practice. I thought about fitness and bought good running shoes and began jogging the Dublin mountains a couple of times a week. I thought about work and the things I wanted to do for the Arts Council and for musicians and writers, my wider family.

I wanted to become a better father.

Rebuilding takes time. I read books on addiction and alcoholism, went to a lot of meetings every week and saw Kay every Friday for psychotherapy. At long last I was a work in progress.

Of course the major thing about 1991 was finally quitting alcohol. Since this book is about music and addiction and I've stopped drinking, why write more? Because addiction doesn't suddenly leave your system when you manage to stop the thing you're addicted to. No, addiction is a lot more devious and psychologically insidious than that. So I'll write a little bit more, for two reasons: one is that I was still smoking marijuana in 1991, not huge amounts but enough to pause the well-disguised shyness and rattling tension I'd suffered since preparatory school as a result of the abuse there. Secondly, and this is important, life gets better. It may be slow sometimes, but better it is. People should know about that.

Music had come to my rescue as an escape from abuse when I was six and now music helped me stay sane.

I gigged at an AIDS benefit in the Olympia Theatre with Francie Conway and later the same night with Mary Coughlan. I recorded with Christy Moore, with the Furey Brothers, with Freddie White and in Switzerland with a French duo. I started a jazz gig and played weekly in the Four Seasons bar. I played festivals in Wales with Mojo and in Denmark with the Danish group Still B. I guested with Hothouse Flowers at a huge festival in Denmark.

All that in my first months dry. In the intervening thirty-two years, I've worked with the Pogues, Fiachra Trench and Carmel McCreagh, Full Circle, the RTÉ Concert Orchestra, Michael D. Higgins (as he read his poetry), Sharon Crosbie, Moving Hearts, Paul Ashford, Louis Stewart, Jim Doherty, Honor Heffernan, Metropolis, Anne Randolph, Moya Brennan, Vusi Mahlasela (in South Africa and Dublin), Maire Breatnach, Van Morrison, the Dubliners, Mary Black, Rory Gallagher, Jimmy Faulkner, Francie Conway, Jim O'Neill, Metropolis, Ozone and many more. Every single one of them respected and supported my sobriety.

Musicians are like that. We are a very loose-knit family, but strong when needs be.

I produced and played on an album for Ronnie Drew, with songs specially written for him by Bono and Simon Carmody, Shane MacGowan, Donal MacDonald, Elvis Costello and me.

Maire Breatnach helped me make my own first album in 1999, a classically-trained jazzman's take on Irish traditional slow airs. I called it *The Calm after the Storm*.

I realized I'd begun to play well again when I was asked to play a solo gig at the launch of a sculpture exhibition in the open air at Kilkenny Arts Festival. I found a place where I could prop myself against cool stones and began to play a traditional slow air, 'Donal Og'. There was nobody around yet and I closed my eyes and got into the music. What came out of me, came through me felt extraordinary. I played the same tune over and over with variations making it joyous like a piece by Mozart, then upbeat like a Dixieland tune, before becoming sparse like Miles Davis, then as Irish as I could, then like the arpeggios of Bach, all the time letting the music guide me and dictate the next change of genre, change of key, enjoying the unpredictability of adventure. When I stopped half an hour later and opened my eyes, there was a quiet crowd of a couple of hundred people around me. They seemed to like what I'd done. At first I wished it had been recorded and then thought that recording it might have made it different. I wish it had been secretly recorded.

I'd written bits and pieces of music and some songs when I was still drinking. I now treated composing much more seriously and wrote the music for a few plays and a score of documentaries for the BBC. I wrote songs with Paul Williams, the Oscar- and Grammy-winning American songwriter who has become a good friend, Shay Healy, Paul Brady, Ralph Murphy and Graham Henderson. Most of them have been recorded. I worked with Dubz, a talented young engineer, on the music for the documentaries, enjoying the collaboration and his creativeness.

In 1989 I had been phoned by Damian Gorman, a playwright and film maker from Newcastle, County Down, who lived in the Glens of Antrim.

He was making a film on alcoholism for the BBC and would I like to write the music for it? I met Damian and ended up being interviewed on film as a recently sober alcoholic. I asked Mick Nolan and Jim Doherty to record the music with me in Broadcasting House in Belfast and I'm proud to say that the film is still being shown in treatment centres in the UK and Ireland.

This led to many collaborations with Damian and Mickey MacGowan. Our most notable success came in 1998. It was *United*, a drama about a County Antrim teenager who forms a supporters' club for fans of Manchester United. It's an intimate, sensitive film that deals with the issues of bereavement, first love and the parades issue in Northern Ireland. It won BBCNI's first BAFTA.

52

One day in my early sixties, I was walking in Spain with a friend who told me of some horrific experiences in her teens. It started me thinking about Miss Hucker and her school that I had attended from I was five until I was eight. I rang the eminent psychiatrist Professor Ivor Browne and he kindly agreed to see me.

I told him that I hadn't suppressed the events and could still remember the abuse clearly but without emotion. He said he'd been able to help some victims of abuse by hypnotizing them and bringing them back to the abuse so that they could experience the emotions they should have had at the time. I said I was nervous. We talked about the process involved in hypnotism and he gave me lots of reassurance.

Then he hypnotized me. The muscles in my upper body began to flutter and tremble and jerk as I described my childhood and it felt like I was back in it. I was aware of the trembling but couldn't control it. We talked in the present tense as if back in 1950.

'So your family is moving to Belfast, Keith?'

'A rented bungalow in East Belfast.'

'Can you describe it?'

'It's on Ormiston Crescent. It's a dark little house with a huge monkey puzzle tree in the garden and a path to the front porch flanked by laburnum trees.'

The little bungalow is right there, in front of me, like I'm there now.

'Who lives there?'

'My parents and Philip. He's eight years older than me, already old enough for grammar school.'

'Just the four of you?'

'My grandfather, Thompson Donald is moving in with us.'

'How do you like that?'

'Not much. He walks me to school and I hate it.'

I'm walking alongside Grandpa, the silence broken only by his attempts to initiate conversation.

'Tell me about school.'

'I've been enrolled in a small private school for boys and girls on the Wandsworth Road. Miss Hucker runs it. My grandfather walks me there every morning.'

I was still conscious of the room in South Dublin and of Ivor but some part of me was aged five again, walking with my grandfather to the house-cum-school in East Belfast. Ivor seemed to be more and more distant as the school came closer and more present.

I can see the little desks, the scratches on them, wooden floorboards, a blackboard ...

'Tell me what is happening, Keith.'

'I'm in the classroom with Miss Hucker.'

'Describe her to me, if you like.'

'Miss Hucker is a big, scary old woman. I'm afraid of her. She wants to punish me for something.'

'Take your time, Keith.'

I'm crying in the past but not in the present.

'She punishes me all the time. I'm scared because I don't know what punishment is coming next. If I can't understand something, she's going to put me in a corner of the classroom, facing a wall, where I'll stand until the end of class. I think everyone is looking at me. I think they're all disgusted with me. I'm scared that there's wax coming out of my ears and they can all see it. When the room goes quiet, that's why: they are all pointing at the wax.'

'Take your time. If you like, you can tell me what's happening now?'

'She's trying to teach me something. Again and again. Now she's angry because she keeps telling me and I don't get it. I'm afraid. She grips me by the ear and drags me to the back of the school. She's putting me down the coal-hole. I have to descend through a trapdoor onto wooden steps. Down here it's just darkness and the smell of coal-dust. Now she's slamming the trapdoor. There is no light at all. I can hear her strutting away, ranting to herself.'

I am shaking violently, uncontrollably. I know it and can't do anything about it. It is scary but I know that Ivor walks with me through this dark memory, guiding and supporting, gentle but persistent.

'What's happening now, Keith? What are you seeing?'

'It's another day. Miss Hucker is angry because somebody has wet the classroom floor. She's feeling us to find out who did it.'

'Yes?'

'She likes to feel everyone's privates until she finds dampness and that's like a victory for her: "A-ha!" she says, "now get a cloth and wipe that up before I punish you," she says triumphantly before she marches you to the trap-door and the coal hole and the darkness.'

There's a silence. I'm shaking from neck to groin.

'And what's happening now?'

'I want to run again. I've started running away and hiding. Nobody ever asks why I keep running away. They just bring me back and apologize to Miss Hucker for my bad behaviour.'

'You're escaping?'

'Yes. Sometimes I get up before everyone, fill a hot water bottle and pretend I'm sick. When Mum takes my temperature, I put the thermometer to the hot rubber when she's not looking, just long enough to register a slight hike over normal: enough to miss school, not enough to call a doctor. Maybe Mum suspects something is wrong.'

After several sessions with Ivor, I would drive to his rooms with a mixture of nervousness and anticipation. During the last few sessions, he enabled me to re-experience abuse without stifling and burying the appropriate emotions. I'm shaking from my waist up, every muscle alive and uncontrollable. No suppression now. I can't control my own body.

'What do you see, Keith?'

'There is nobody else here. I think it's the afternoon and they've all gone home.'

'And who is there?'

'Just me and her.'

'Just you and Miss Hucker. What's happening?'

'I can't understand the concept of "profit" and she has kept me back after school to explain what it means. She has asked me to sit alongside her, on a wooden bench.'

'What is that like for you?'

'She is very big. I am scared. I want to get away but I can't.'

'And?'

'She is ... ... talking about profit and I can't think straight ...'

After some months seeing Ivor, I had experienced the emotions that I'd suppressed for fifty-five years. I felt more at ease with myself than I'd ever thought possible. Those sessions with Ivor were difficult but they were manageable in that I never felt under threat or worried about his ability to look after me, to reassure and support me throughout.

I realized that I had to try to forgive Miss Hucker or at least come to some conscious accommodation with her abuse of me. I imagined that something might have been done to her to make her into an abuser and that might be some explanation of why she was as she was. Might explain why she'd never married too. I said out loud that I was trying to forgive her and thanked her for forcing me to escape into music. I worked quite hard on myself, trying to undo hurt, trying to be less angry, trying not to flare up. The more I worked at it, the more at ease I felt. I'm much, much better now, but still a work in progress.

53

I kept up my friendship with Brian Bullick all the way from 1958 to 2023. In the early months of this new century, in the sitting room of her house in Cushendall, I had a chat with Brian's mother, Nora, then in her early nineties. I made her a promise: I'd always look out for Brian's best interests.

Nora died in January 2007, aged ninety-eight. I got the news in Glenties, County Donegal, during a Moving Hearts rehearsal in the Highland Hotel. On the day of the band's first gig in decades, I started driving while it was still dark, said the eulogy at Nora's funeral, played a tune for her in the tiny church and drove back, in time for the soundcheck. Although we weren't related, it felt like losing family.

Brian was now sixty-four, still with the mental age of about six, still playing the organ in church, still living in a wonderful care home in Templepatrick. I began renting half a house in Cushendall from my pals Carole and Paul McAlister, and was able to bring Brian there almost every month. We were a very odd couple, christened 'Rainman' by one of Brian's cousins. Our visits to his home village that he loved continued month by month, year by year until 2023, when he died of cancer on 29 April. I'd been able to bring him to Cushendall for the last time, on his eightieth birthday on 17 April. He wasn't able to move unaided by that stage but had demanded that I carry him to the car and drive him.

His funeral was beautiful. People came from Dublin, Belfast, Wales, County Down, County Tyrone and all over County Antrim to be there. All his friends in Cushendall village were there too. It's 200 yards from the funeral home to the church, and I walked behind the hearse, playing 'Just a Closer Walk with Thee' on soprano sax. During the service I told the congregation of Brian's unique greatness: never once, in sixty-five years of friendship, had I seen him get angry. And no matter how much I got frustrated with him or raised my voice to him did he show any resentment, often disarming me utterly by saying, 'I love you, Keith.'

I'm writing this with tears in my eyes for someone I loved.

54

I'm editing this for the last time in October 2024 and feel I should tell you I've had chemotherapy this year, from March to July. It wasn't pleasant – in fact it was rough sometimes – but I got through the side effects thanks to a lot of tablets and great support from Professor Elizabeth Vandenberghe and her team in St James' Hospital. My thanks to Nurse Grace Faulkner who'd ring me at home to check on me between chemo sessions in hospital, and to all the other doctors and nurses I met this year.

I love walking – always have, ever since my escapes from Miss Hucker around East Belfast when I was six. For a long time, when I'd walk in Dublin, I'd look at a building and say to myself, 'Used to drink there' or 'Was thrown out of that kip' or 'Was barred from that pub' or 'Got locked in there overnight' or 'How much time did I waste there?' I'd dwell on the negatives, the disappointments, the wasted life.

Now, when I walk in Dublin, Belfast, London and other cities, I keep saying to myself, 'Played there.' Then great memories rush to the surface: the Baggot Inn and Moving Hearts, the Gaiety and my pit mates, the Abbey Theatre and Jim Doherty's Spon, the top of Harcourt Street and the Monday nights in the TV Club, Windmill Lane where Moving Hearts recorded its number one album. When I'm abroad, it's the Dominion at the end of Oxford Street and 'recorded a live album there with the Rolling Stones mobile studio parked outside' or past a jazz club in Copenhagen or West 49th Street in New York or Ronnie Scott's in London and there's a smile on my face.

Recently I walked from Parnell Square to Stephen's Green and found myself saying 'Gigged there' over and over until I stopped on the pavement in the middle of O'Connell Street to count the gigs. In less than a mile it comes to twenty-four places where I gigged with eleven different bands, including the Gate Theatre with Christy Moore for the launch of *The Big Issue* magazine, the O'Connell Hall with the Greenbeats for our weekly radio show, on the back of a lorry with Sinead O'Connor and the Dubliners at the protest against the awful Warrington bombing, in the Metropole Ballroom with the Greenbeats the night Nelson's Column was blown up, Trinity the night Gerry Mulligan dropped in for a blow. I've been very lucky in music.

So very lucky. I'm grateful. First of all, there's the people I've met. I've been in countless bands and there's not a musician I don't like. I have friendships through music that have lasted many decades. I've played gigs tiny and huge in a score of countries. I've played in many genres. I'm still playing. So fortunate.

The ultimate challenge for me was to appear on stage on my own. Talking to people had freaked me out as a child. I'd got better at it with drink and, when I got sober, I had to retrain myself and seek help with panic attacks. I'd worked hard at it when I was chair of the IMRO board, finally able to make a speech without notes. But could I perform a show on my own? Over six months in 2015, I wrote twelve songs, several pieces of music, 950 lines of verse and several stories. I recorded the songs with wonderful musicians like Desi Reynolds, Noel Eccles, Fiachra Trench, James Blennerhasset, Maire Breatnach, Des Moore, Alex Donald and Susan Slott, who voiced Ethyl Blue, the personification of alcohol. Daire Winston engineered and gave great production advice. I sang – who knew? – and played ukulele, clarinet, bass clarinet, all the saxophone family and recorder. I've performed the show in theatres in Ireland, Brussels and Wales. The Arts Councils of Northern Ireland and Wales were very supportive. It remains my ultimate challenge and greatest satisfaction on stage. The show is called NewBliss and it's the short version of what you're reading, plus music. I've made an album of the songs too.

55

Looking back, I find I've had a life in years of sevens, sometimes approximate but sevens nonetheless: from 12 to 22, classics. From 19 to 28, showbands. From 28 to 35, social work. From 35 to 42, professional music including Moving Hearts. From 42 to 52, arts administration and single parenthood. From 49 to 63, musician and composer. From 63 to 72, chairman of IMRO. And the constants: from seven until now, jazz musician. From zero until now, my big brother, Dr Philip Donald, whom I love and admire. From 46 until now, sober. From 63 on, clean and sober. From 33 until now, my solid friendship with Philip Kinane. Most precious of all, from 31 until now, Alex.

Everything in me is connected: the abuse, music, my addiction and recovery. If I hadn't been abused I wouldn't have felt the necessity of escape. Abuse drove love out of little me, substituting fear, tension, feelings of inadequacy and constantly being judged, and social anxiety. My first escape was running away. My second was music. Alcohol was the third. Other drugs and sex came later. All the escapes worked until they didn't and I plummeted into a psychological abyss where I knew I needed help because I couldn't help myself.

What conquers addiction? What drives it out of one's psyche? I think the answer is love, but you have to look for it. If a New York company analyst hadn't given up his day job and dedicated his life at huge personal cost to establishing an organization that facilitates meetings with other alcoholics, I wouldn't have been able to learn from them how to survive and recover. I'm thinking Bill Wilson did that out of love for his fellow alcoholics and I'm eternally grateful to him because, without the organization he set up, I wouldn't have felt the love and respect of my fellow-sufferers. Nor would I have learned from their experience, strength and hope.

If Ivor Browne had retired at 65, I wouldn't have benefitted from his wisdom and expertise. I'm guessing he kept working because he loved helping people.

I've felt love in rooms full of recovering alcoholics. We're all strangers but we all know the most important thing there is to know about one another: that we are trying not to drink and we are helping each other to do it. If Derek hadn't said, 'If ever you need help to stop drinking, call me,' and if Carol hadn't become my unofficial guide and sponsor, my life would have been different. It would possibly have ended some decades ago. But they loved me as the imperfect, drinking alcoholic I was and they were resolved to help me. That's love.

Mostly now I feel lucky: I'm blessed with a wonderful daughter-friend, I've never been bored or lonely, I'm clean and sober, I have a few close friendships, a lovely Belfast family, a huge circle of valued friends, and I still love playing music.

I've felt love in the cancer ward in St James' hospital, in rooms full of rehearsing musicians, from audiences at gigs big and small, in rooms full of other alcoholics, from all my family, from my friend of forty-seven years, Philip Kinane, and from my darling daughter, Alex.

I feel totally at peace.

Acknowledgments

Alex Donald, my beloved daughter and friend who edited this book.

Philip Kinane, my close friend of forty-seven years.

All my Donald family, in Belfast, London and Amsterdam.

Derek, Carole and all who shared their experience, strength and hope at meetings in many countries.

Two psychotherapists, Kay and Brendan, and the late Professor Ivor Browne.

All the brilliant doctors and nurses who treated me in ten Irish hospitals.

My two dentists, David and Niall, who have ensured I can continue to play wind instruments.

My wider family of musicians and performers in several countries who unfailingly provide craic and acceptance and support.

Dee Cooley and Cormac Kinsella for helping *Music & Mayhem* reach a wider readership.

Everyone at Lilliput Press: Antony, Enejda, Stephen, Bridget and Liam for professionalism, expertise and mentoring.

Kathy Gilfillan, who championed this book from the outset.

Wonderful audiences everywhere who always inspired me to do better on the night.

My lovely neighbours whom I've lived beside for fifty-four years.

In memoriam: Eddie Campbell and Brian Bullick, Mum and Dad.

Keith Donald
Dublin February, 2025

INDEX